For the last thirty years we have made little progress in the authentic engagement of our people and the successful execution of our most vital business strategies. As leaders, we must find a better way to engage the hearts and minds of our people. Spahn's *We the Leader* puts us on the critical path to discover and act on that better way!

We are constantly focused on disrupting our industries and our businesses. How about disrupting our leadership to elevate it to unprecedented levels of breakthrough results. Spahn's *We the Leader* opens the door for game changing leadership disruption!

—JIM HAUDAN,
former CEO and cofounder Root Inc.,
author of *The Art of Engagement* and coauthor of *Leadership Blind Spots*

Winning firms are different from the norm. The difference comes from the way people and teams act out their leadership role. In this refreshing approach, Jeff Spahn asks some demanding questions and in turn turns our traditional view of the hierarchical leader upside down. This is more than just a philosophical inquiry—it is a call to action to release leadership talent at all levels to realize new value, energy, and excitement!

—STEVE MOSTYN,
Associate Fellow, Saïd Business School, University of Oxford,
Honorary Professor, Adam Smith School of Business, Glasgow University

Jeffrey Spahn's new book outlines a thoughtful approach to managing in a post-hierarchical world, where everyone is a leader and a follower at the same time, all the time. Spahn's unique combination of big-picture insights and micro-behavioral coaching tactics provides many practical examples of how we can create the mutuality that is required to meet the challenges of our time. Read it, use it, and spread the word!

—DANIEL DENISON,
Professor Emeritus, IMD Business School,
Chairman, Denison Consulting, LLC

It's exciting to read a book tracing the evolution of our understanding and practice of leadership. *We the Leader* shows us that we have a GPS guiding us forward on an emerging path toward a leadership mindset and style that finally recognizes that (1) we are the leaders of our own lives, as such, we can lead only ourselves, projects, and activities, not others, and (2) leadership is about individually and collectively following the true purpose of the team, project, or organization—what brought us together in the first place. Intrigued? Ready for this? Read on.

—TERESA DOSDOS RUELAS,
Founder and Executive Director, Cebu Farmers Market,
Communities for Alternative Food Ecosystems Initiative, Inc.

We the Leader's time is here. With millennials now the largest segment of the working population and the changing nature of work itself, legacy models of leadership no longer fit. In *We the Leader*, Jeff Spahn paints us a vivid picture of what leadership means in this new world, showing us a way forward with a practical operating model for leading and driving results. A must-read!

—JOHN FODOR,
former Executive Vice President and global distribution
leader at a renowned global financial firm

If you and your organization, company or movement genuinely value diversity, equity and inclusion then *We the Leader* is a must-read. Why? Because *We the Leader* is an operating system built upon the ideals and actual practice of diversity, equity and inclusion that mutually enhances human development, organizational results, and social justice.

—DR. SHANTA PREMAWARDHANA,
President, OMNIA Institute for Contextual Leadership

Traditional "top down" leadership models can be very challenging. Spahn's *We the Leader* emphasizes the importance of *all* people bringing value to the discussion and of the need for leaders to know how to lead and follow at the same time, or simultaneously. This model drives innovation and improved performance through inclusive leadership. This is an excellent read for any existing or new leader.

—DON SWEENEY,
Founder and CEO, Ashling Partners,
two-time cofounder and CEO of technology firms

"Diversity, Equity and Inclusion." In a world of words and phrases, but often little action, *We the Leader* is at the forefront of providing not only a blueprint, but also a proven process of leadership that results in real diversity, equity, and inclusion. *We the Leader* is a must-read for anyone interested in results, not words!

—STEVE MALBASA,
partner in a major financial firm, former top executive
at a renowned global financial company

A brilliant framework to empower people at every level of an organization to bring their gifts and talents in service of a common purpose. Many organizations are struggling to become more inclusive and to empower their organization at all levels. *We the Leader* shows how to make this happen.

—AIMEE DANIEL,
Master Chair, Vistage Worldwide Inc.

Today's leadership teams consist of individuals who are highly trained, strong-willed, and intent on making their mark. *We the Leader* provides the guidance a CEO needs to navigate in this highly charged environment. It's a force multiplier, increasing the potential for organizational success by reducing ego conflict and increasing engagement and satisfaction at all levels.

—**CHRIS DEROSE,**
former CEO, Michigan Retirement Systems,
Ohio Public Employees Retirement System,
and Municipal Employees Retirement System of Michigan

Spahn spells out the learned behaviors of traditional or hierarchical leadership: colleagues often impose boundaries that stifle their innovative thinking. I was provoked by the observation that traditional leadership results in conformity, inequality, and exclusion in contrast to the desired outcomes of diversity, equity, and inclusion (DEI) initiatives. For organizations thinking about how to design DEI initiatives that result in breakthrough outcomes, *We the Leader* is a must-read.

—**ROBERT C. SMITH,**
Partner, Ohio Market Leader, Cerity Partners, LLC

WE
THE LEADER

Build a Team of Equals
Who All Lead **AND** Follow to Drive
Creativity and Innovation

JEFFREY SPAHN

Mc
Graw
Hill

New York Chicago San Francisco Athens London Madrid
Mexico City Milan New Delhi Singapore Sydney Toronto

1 2 3 4 5 6 7 8 9   LCR   26 25 24 23 22 21

ISBN   978-1-260-47497-8
MHID   1-260-47497-6

e-ISBN   978-1-260-47498-5
e-MHID   1-260-47498-4

Library of Congress Cataloging-in-Publication Data

Names: Spahn, Jeffrey, author.
Title: We the leader : build a team of equals who all lead and follow to drive
   creativity and innovation / Jeffrey Spahn.
Description: 1 Edition. | New York : McGraw Hill, [2022] | Includes
   bibliographical references and index.
Identifiers: LCCN 2021044611 (print) | LCCN 2021044612 (ebook) |
   ISBN 9781260474978 (hardcover) | ISBN 9781260474985 (ebook)
Subjects: LCSH: Teams in the workplace. | Employee motivation. |
   Creative ability in business. | Management—Technological innovations.
Classification: LCC HD66 .S678273 2022 (print) | LCC HD66 (ebook) |
   DDC 658.4/022—dc23
LC record available at https://lccn.loc.gov/2021044611
LC ebook record available at https://lccn.loc.gov/2021044612

McGraw Hill books are available at special quantity discounts to use as premiums and sales promotions or for use in corporate training programs. To contact a representative, please visit the Contact Us pages at www.mhprofessional.com.

McGraw Hill is committed to making our products accessible to all learners. To learn more about the available support and accommodations we offer, please contact us at accessibility@mheducation.com. We also participate in the Access Text Network (www.accesstext.org), and ATN members may submit requests through ATN.

This book is dedicated to the evolution of humanity.

CONTENTS

PART I
The Foundation
We the Leader Operating System

PART II
The Diversifier
Me the Leader

Contents

ACKNOWLEDGMENTS

I could so easily acknowledge many friends and family for their support throughout my life, but here, I want to focus on the creation of *We the Leader*, the book. First, I want to mention my friend and client, Steve Malbasa. Steve had the audacity to believe that his team was a group of stars, not because they'd proven themselves as stars, though competent and capable, yes, but because that's how he saw them. Furthermore, he believed that the We the Leader operating system could help them get there. And it did.

In the summer of 2019 on the way out of attorney Marc J. Lane's office, I knew I was going to write *We the Leader*. I don't remember much of what Marc said that day, but I know exactly how I felt: enthusiastic, determined, and confident. Thank you, Marc J. Lane! Tim Brandhorst, Marc's colleague, came next, and put together an excellent book proposal, guided me to McGraw Hill, and counseled me wisely. Amy Li, my original editor at McGraw Hill, thank you for believing in *We the Leader*. I'll never forget you describing this message as "a way for people to bring their full selves to work." Donya Dickerson, who took over for Amy, thank you for your confidence and excellence in spearheading the creation of *We the Leader*. Mary Norris, thank you for your keen editorial eye. Ellen Coleman, your piercing questions and insights were invaluable. Mark Bauhs, illustrator extraordinaire, your interpretation of the We the Leader Flow Chart inspires me. Without the magic, and I mean magic, of Kelly Malone, my personal editor/writer, this book would not have been written. Thank you, Kelly.

Finally, Elke Rehbock, David Kaufman, John Kessler, Steven Mostyn, Rosalyn Taylor O'Neale, and Mike Kaufmann—what a team of leaders. Thank you for contributing your experiences and insights to the creation of *We the Leader*.

INTRODUCTION

What got you here will not get you there.
—MARSHALL GOLDSMITH
business educator, coach, and author

The current conceptual framework and practice of leadership sabotages success, especially in our post-pandemic world. In this book, I will explore why that is and present an alternative: a new flexible and responsive leadership paradigm. It's time. A recent IBM study concludes that "agility—the capability of an organization to respond quickly and pivot without losing momentum"—is a top priority for leaders "to an unprecedented degree." IBM states that more than half (56 percent) of "CEOs emphasize the need to aggressively pursue operational agility and flexibility over the next two to three years."[1] Exciting stuff! What makes it even more exciting is that concurrently society is calling for diversity, equity, and inclusion, which, if done right, provides the very agility CEOs prioritize. The key phrase is "if done right." Our present models of organizational hierarchy and their subsequent models of leadership, built on conformity, inequity, and exclusion, are the exact opposite of the diversity, equity, and inclusion needed for a culture, not a trend, of agility, responsiveness, and speed. Paradoxically, speed requires everyone to bring their full leader selves to work, which you might think would paralyze agility, and it would if done using our current leadership paradigm and practices.

The need for agility is why developing and implementing a new model is paramount, a model that converts the chaos of "too many chiefs"—CEO, COO, CFO, CIO, CTO, CMO, CPO, and more—on the executive team to consistent collective flow, exemplified in my mind as the mysterious and miraculous flocks of starlings in which hundreds, even thousands, of birds fly in a coordinated, sweeping, intricately patterned dance.[2] The flight of birds informed and inspired the Wright brothers, now it's time for birds to inspire an unprecedented experience of human collective agility. The actions of the starlings illustrate what leaders everywhere are calling for when they talk about adaptive, agile, quick-pivoting teams and when the CEO of a Global Fortune Top 50 company calls for speed.

To some this looks like chaos, yet if you stay with it, you discover it's actually the super-coordination needed to step up and create from today's perpetual chaos. In some cases, we already practice the skills required for consistent collective agility. In this book, I highlight and expand on these practices and offer an organizational and leadership paradigm to sustain them.

We live in a constantly changing world with new technologies introduced daily, perpetual connectivity, and relentless pressures to do more, faster, better. This pressure is even greater on leaders, who must personally navigate change and simultaneously guide an enterprise. With the acceleration of digital information—further accelerated by the COVID-19 pandemic—comes the need for more information sharing and processing. This necessitates everyone showing up with all they have, being the full leaders they all are, all the time. Having said that, the issue becomes how do organizations deal with the possible chaos caused when everyone is a leader alongside increased diversity. Absent a new operating system to match all of these things, there's a train wreck waiting to happen.

The same strategies and models that worked in the past will not work in the future and, even worse, risk undermining opportunities and goals. It is the reason that research at Deloitte called for a completely new way of leading.[3] Given the spiraling complexity and torrid pace of change, leaders, teams, and organizations must find ways to innovate constantly in order to thrive in this age of disruption. It isn't enough to just welcome or accept the chaos. Leaders must seek a new perspective on the very nature of leadership, acquire an evolved leadership skillset, and develop potent skills to leverage the energy of disruption into innovation and thereby success.

The rapid pace of our Digital Age, coupled with the rise of multiple generations in leadership positions, purpose-driven or socially responsible business models, and mergers and acquisitions, increasingly calls for leaders who lead other leaders. The complex problems of today's world require people with a wide variety of perspectives and expertise to gather together to realize possibilities. Innovation results from diversity, which yields both creativity and unity in execution. Diversity breeds innovation.

In many businesses, this effort manifests as eradicating silos by creating cross-functional teams, pods, or projects—all of which consist of groups of leaders. Yet our mindset and habits are rooted in a model of leading followers. It is like applying analog solutions to digital problems. Unless we are aware of the emerging context of leading leaders, we will find ourselves playing a new game with old rules (and habits) without even realizing it.

Inherent in the traditional view of leadership is that one person leads while others follow. In its most basic form, the leader goes before while the follower goes after. In going where the leader goes or thinking as the leader thinks, the follower conforms to the thoughts and actions of the leader. When we lead followers, we create cultures of conformity, the opposite of the diversity needed to create cultures of innovation. Innovation thrives on diversity and dies in conformity.

The notion and practice of leading other people has served its time. The inequity and exclusion that result are the exact opposite of the diversity, equity, and inclusion required for the creation of consistent collective flow and social justice. We can inform, instruct, and inspire each other, yet we cannot choose for or lead another. We can force people to comply, but only they can choose their own passion and commitment. Only when we adopt an operating system consistently and organically based on diversity, equity, and inclusion will we build self-perpetuating cultures of innovation. Ninety-six percent of CEOs assert that diversity, equity, and inclusion (DEI) initiatives are a personal strategic priority for them.[4]

Agility is a way of achieving innovation. For example, instead of having a Research and Development department separate from the day-to-day operations, innovation increasingly is becoming a part of everyday activity in the moment. For this reason I believe improv is both a potent metaphor and a useful practice. Basically, We the Leader is improv applied to organizational behavior. As a skilled discipline, improvisation requires exacting focus and ongoing practice, not as it is sometimes understood as an ill-prepared and undisciplined reaction to the moment.

Many organizations have evolved from traditional hierarchical leadership and adapted collaborative leadership strategies. Nevertheless, according to *Harvard Business Review* research, 75 percent of cross-functional teams are dysfunctional.[5] Collaboration, although a stark improvement from command and control, still falls woefully short in stepping up to today's innovation demands. Why? For starters, collaboration is rooted in the principle of colabor, which is an outdated Industrial Age concept and practice that assumes we are all laboring alongside each other in a factory—a far cry from our current work dynamic. At the heart of the problem is that, in practice, there is always too much, too little, or faux collaboration.

In this book, I aim to expose unconscious patterns of thought and practice and liberate leaders to embrace a new innovative leadership approach—an evolved process and exceptional practice for leading leaders that I call Simultaneity®. It is a part of the We the Leader operating system.

I created Simultaneity in response to these questions:

- How do leaders lead each other?
- How do leaders avoid the cluster mess of too many chiefs on the executive team?
- How is conflict transmuted into innovation and trust?
- How can the strengths of different leadership styles be melded?
- How can leaders make the right choice in the right time and in a way that inspires in-sync execution?
- How can we do more, faster, and better with less?
- How can we have productive meetings that end with "That was fun!"?
- How can we hold each other more and more accountable in the moment?
- How can we maximize the diversity, equity, and inclusion strengths of an egalitarian structure in the context of a hierarchy and do so in a way that simultaneously enhances individual authority and collective cocreation?

- How can teams consistently experience, "I still can't believe we did it again!"?

This book, written in five parts, addresses these questions.

Part I — The Building Blocks: The We the Leader Operating System. We'll first introduce key concepts, or kernels, including the history of leadership and then explore the idea of collective flow, which is the group experience of being lifted and guided by an energy from within each individual, between individuals and teams, and beyond traditional hierarchy into the realm of exponential potential (think a well-choreographed dance or a rowing crew pulling their oars in unison). The collective flow this produces is agility, being in the moment and highly responsive. We'll also look at consilience, the "jumping together" of seemingly opposing energies or ideas to create something new. Consilience as an innovation process is the foundation of collective flow.

Part II — The Diversifier: Me the Leader. Only you can lead you. You do this by following your own inner GPS— your internal wisdom and passion—which no one but you knows and which only you can choose to follow. Because only you can lead you, no one can lead you. Accordingly, since others can only lead themselves, you cannot lead others.

Part III — The Equalizer: Common Purpose. Inside an organization, the leaders are also followers of the organization's common purpose. This was the fundamental, yet ignored, reality of organizations before they became hierarchical. Until then, the members of an organization were not sometimes leaders and at other times followers (as in hierarchies)—all were simultaneously leaders and followers (or leader–followers) all the time. Leader–followers lead or colead teams, projects, and organizations, but not each other.

Part IV — The Unifier: We the Leader, We the Follower. We the Leader is an operating system that includes an innovative process, a mutual leadership process (Simultaneity), and a decision-making process. As I explained earlier, we built our current operating systems on the hierarchical assumptions of conformity, inequity, and exclusion. The current system of leaders and followers results in conformity and ultimately in inequity and exclusion, the opposite of the diversity, equity, and inclusion that is crucial for the innovation of consistent collective flow and social justice. Only when we adopt an operating system built by practicing of diversity, equity, and inclusion will we build self-perpetuating cultures of innovation.

Part V — We the Leader: Conversations with Real World Leaders. Through interviews, we present different points of view on We the Leader. A pair of clients discuss how they transformed a traditional hierarchical company into a hybrid hierarchy–panarchy through a permanent network of integrated teams alongside the hierarchy. A partner in the world's largest law firm asks how to lead with curiosity when she gets paid and promoted for intellectual expertise. The CEO of a company ranked thirty-fifth on the Global Fortune 500 reflects on his leading of leaders throughout his career and today's urgent prioritization of speed. An honorary professor at Adam Smith Business School, University of Glasgow, and Associate Fellow at Saïd Business School, University of Oxford, challenges a major premise of We the Leader. And a world-renowned DEI consultant and facilitator, who's spoken with audiences in fifty countries around the globe, brings unparalleled depth and breadth about the pressing need for the most fundamental practice of We the Leader. These interviews stand on their own and are referred to throughout the book for insights and points of reference.

However, before presenting the future of leadership—Simultaneity—I will begin by putting leadership in historical context.

PART I

The Foundation

*We the Leader
Operating System*

CHAPTER 1

The Disruption and Evolution of Leadership

Different work needs to get done, and
work needs to get done differently.

—GARY BURNISON
CEO Korn Ferry

O ur current models of leadership, although necessary, are becoming woefully inadequate to step up to the need for innovative cultures. A leader defined only as one who has followers yields conformity. Like an undiagnosed disease, conformity festers within our teams, organizations, and institutions, including political institutions. This epidemic blurs our vision, depletes our energy, compromises our decisions, and eradicates the diversity needed for innovation. Conformity sabotages innovation—in a world where speed and agility are the number one priority of 96 percent of CEOs.[1]

We the Leader is an operating system that is the friend of both innovation and operations, which is why I define innovation as *the creativity of the many* followed by *its execution as one.*

Elke Rehbock, a partner at the law firm Dentons US LLP, began a discussion group called Network 2025 to address the major societal issues we collectively faced at the beginning of the COVID-19 pandemic. Once the initial round of discussions ended, she "felt a responsibility" for taking the group to the next level, but wasn't sure how to go about doing that. Ultimately, she decided to share her quandary with the group—that she didn't "want the discussions to end" and needed help setting a new direction for Network 2025. Her request "really opened it up to everybody and gave space for really good suggestions" and ultimately determined the next agenda for the group.

It's almost as though Elke didn't lead. She knew she had to take the group to the next level and wanted people to follow her, but she didn't know how to get there. When she shared this story, I imagined a wheel with a hub with all the spokes pointing to her in the center. When she vacated that hub, people came forward and started to really interact. Elke had moved to a more collaborative, even mutual, form of leadership.

It is time for leadership to evolve. Our complex and uncertain times demand it. So why do we struggle to define and adopt a new, more effective approach? The root causes lie in the limits of our current definition of leadership, our understanding and practice of collaboration, and our perspective on the current context of leadership as it changes before our very eyes.

Hierarchical Leadership: The Conformity of Leading Followers

For the most part, a leader is defined as one who has followers. In the most basic form, a leader goes before and the follower goes after. The follower typically takes the path forged by the leader, takes the same position as the leader, thinks as the leader thinks, or conforms to the leader's expectations. For example, if a person steps forward and walks in a certain direction and others go after, that person is identified as a leader. If another person steps forward in that same direction and no one goes after, that person is identified as a walker, not a leader. A conductor in front of an orchestra waving her arms may be considered a leader. If the musicians do not follow her gestures, she may be considered out of her mind. A team leader who presents a strategy for execution and gains verbal commitment to execute on the strategy yet fails to see the execution through is not a leader, but rather a strategist.

This concept of leadership as defined by having followers is generally referred to as hierarchical leadership. Hierarchical leadership has been the dominant leadership form for most of human history, certainly since the birth of modern workplaces a century and a half ago. An impactful development in management and leadership theory occurred in the early part of the twentieth century with Frederick Winslow Taylor's *The Principles of Scientific Management*. In that text, he espoused that making people work hard was not as efficient as optimizing the way they worked.[2] The goal of this theory and practice was to improve efficiency within the hierarchical structure. Rather than fundamentally questioning or addressing the limits of hierarchical leadership, this evolution simply built upon the existing model of hierarchy.

When I reflect on the roots of hierarchical leadership, I'm reminded of an executive retreat for a company known for its collaborative culture that I was invited to participate in and observe. As the meeting started, the CEO and the top executives were seated at the head table—not a good start. The CEO had a bottle of Evian water sitting in front of him at arm's length. After the first break, three of the seven "leaders" at the head table also had Evian bottles in front of them and, you guessed it, at arms' length. After lunch, the room was so full of Evian bottles, you would have thought someone was on the corner selling them for ten cents! Unfortunately, this conformity didn't stop with water bottles. In the ensuing "dialogue," there was no dialogue at all. Participants listened attentively, asked questions to gain clarity, expressed support and agreement for the CEO's positions, but no one dared to challenge or disagree. Like a vicious cancer, conformity spread undetected killing innovation as participants' thinking, perspectives, and points of view mirrored that of the CEO. Of course, the evaluation forms indicated a great meeting, one of their best.

Because of their positions of authority or inherent power over followers, all leaders wear an invisible sign around their necks that goes unnoticed by most of them yet is very clear to everyone else. The sign reads, "Tell me what I want to hear." Unless leaders vigilantly and perpetually speak and act contrary to this sign inherited from hierarchical leadership, that is exactly what they'll get. Deference to authority is embedded in our culture from parents to teachers and religious leaders to bosses. It is unconsciously webbed into the human psyche, breeding cultures of conformity and tendencies toward groupthink. In fact, conformity is a necessary component of existence and evolution. Nevertheless, now is the time to more diligently build upon this common inheritance and create through our differences.

Groupthink occurs when everybody on the team or in the group thinks as the leader does. In other words, when a group behaves like followers. Many leaders seek to avoid groupthink, and for good reason, since it undermines innovation and depletes team energy. Yet in a paradigm that assumes leaders and followers, it's difficult to escape. Groupthink is innately what followers do; they go to where the leader goes, take the leader's position, and think like the leader. It's no wonder groupthink, or the epidemic of conformity, is perpetuated even among those speaking against it and intending to avoid it. An apple tree produces apples. As I said at the start of this chapter, our hierarchical leadership, based upon leading followers, becomes an epidemic of conformity when it doesn't include diversity. However, when leading followers expands to leader–followers leading each other, conformity becomes a vital ingredient for the collective flow of creativity The disease becomes a part of the solution or remedy.

The key, and for the most part undetected, obstacle to a sustained innovative culture in teams and organizations is the fundamental reality that our current cultures are built on leading followers who, by definition, follow and conform to leaders. Innovation, defined as creativity followed by in-sync execution, thrives on diversity, followed by the conformity or unity needed for in-sync execution. This unity is built *from* airing our differences, in contrast to uniformity built from avoiding our differences

Not until we repurpose leadership with an expanded definition will we cure this epidemic of cultural conformity. Avoiding groupthink requires exposing these unconscious patterns of thought and practice that contradict diverse thinking and innovation. This involves liberating followers from the limits of following by embracing a new innovative leadership technology.

A Look at Hierarchy

Hierarchy comes from the roots "archy" meaning power/authority and "hier" meaning over or above; it literally means power over or power from above. Therefore:

- A hierarchy assumes one leader or a class of leaders who exercise power over others or followers.
- This "power over" is in sharp contrast to "power with" implicit in the democratic assumptions and

values that we are equal, different, and vital pieces of the team, organization, and human puzzle.
- Some structure is necessary for collective human innovation, yet our current hierarchical structures rooted in command and control thwart human energy and ingenuity.
- The purpose of structure is to create a container for collective creativity and in-sync execution, not to exert power over with command and control.
- A hierarchical culture grows followers who by definition conform to leaders thus undermining the diversity needed for innovation.

How would hierarchies and their leadership need to change to become greenhouses of innovation growing leaders?

Collaborative Leadership

Until 1969 leadership meant traditional hierarchical leadership. But innovators such as Kenneth Blanchard and Paul Hersey with their Situational Leadership and Robert K. Greenleaf with his essay *The Servant as Leader* introduced an expanded concept of leadership, which built the foundation for what we refer to today as collaborative leadership.[3]

Collaborative leadership is shared leadership, where leadership is not relegated to one person or class but distributed based on the situation or by the leader, as servant, serving his or her followers. At the height of hierarchical leadership, both servant and situational leadership concepts were radical additions to the practice of leadership. Shared leadership, whether situational or servant style, allowed more followers to become and act as leaders by taking the lead in situations that called upon their experience and expertise or by the formal leader choosing to follow or serve the follower. This increase in mutuality expanded trust among leaders and followers, including teams. Increased trust has a cascading effect and results in more open communication, wiser choices followed by more ownership, commitment, and aligned execution. Instead of working for the boss, these evolutions in collaboration nurtured an environment of working with and for each other.

The collaboration model, however, is rooted in "co-labor," an Industrial Age concept, and still grounded in a hierarchical, command-and-control model. Conceptually, collaborative leadership was seen as an evolution of the leading/following paradigm, but in practice, there is either too much, too little, or faux collaboration.

Too Much Collaboration

Much of an industry-leading company's perpetual success was due to its collaborative culture. It had acquired the people and skills to consistently access collective intelligence that informed wise decisions. Gaining many different perspectives to inform their choices had the added benefit of activating ownership, commitment, and even passion for the execution of the decision. However, this strength began to become a weakness. Involving many people in the decisions takes time. As the company grew and the industry changed, making sure everyone's voice was included, even though the buy-in was there, the result was missed windows of opportunity. The spiraling complexity and torrid rate of change increasingly required speed and agility—both a high priority for CEOs—in decisions and execution. Not only did this elaborate decision-making process deplete energy and activate frustration, opportunities came and went unaddressed.

Too Little Collaboration

Before they reorganized and became one of the top twenty insurance companies in the US Motorists Group, Encova was a typical hierarchical company run by a boss—a smart, nice, even charismatic leader, but nevertheless the boss. With his wealth of experience in the insurance industry, the CEO was able to guide the company successfully by making timely choices. Since he made the decisions, albeit with some input from others, they were usually made in a timely fashion within that window of opportunity.

Predictably, as the company grew, one person's thinking increasingly was not enough to address the complex problems and possibilities. The result of this decision-making culture was that some decisions faltered and those that were timely and spot on lacked the necessary buy-in or commitment from those charged with executing the decisions. Doing the bidding of another, no matter how charismatic, does not compare with the passion derived from intrinsic motivation.

Faux Collaboration

Often unwittingly and with good intentions, leaders attempt to implement collaborative leadership principles but do so poorly and inadvertently undermine their desired outcome. This can manifest in various ways:

- Leaders proudly call for a dialogue, but when the outcome starts to move down an unexpected and unpreferred path, they steer the conversation to their predetermined outcome, and sometimes even discontinue the "collaboration" or "dialogue."
- Leaders withhold their points of view, which only results in deterring the communication, because everyone at the table is wondering what the leader is

thinking and feeling, and therefore is unwilling to risk contradicting the leader.
- Leaders ask leading questions that are really veiled statements. These undetected fake questions actually undermine curiosity and eventually innovation.

A Case of Too Much, Too Little, and Faux Collaboration

An industry-leading company decided to reinvent itself from a manufacturer of office furniture to an architect and designer of workspace. To accomplish this, they realized they needed to become much more creative and build a culture of innovation. They invested in creating their own university even while, for the first time in their history, they had to lay people off.

Collaboration and creativity blossomed with newly formed egalitarian cross-functional teams that saw themselves as equal, different, and vital participants. However, there were two consequences of too much collaboration: (1) Some teams were so collaborative they had difficulty making decisions in a timely fashion. They tended to massage issues and options over and over only to see the window of opportunity open then close. And (2) when things went south there was no one to hold accountable.

To ensure accountability, the company assigned formal leaders to each project team. The problem then, as George Wolfe, then vice president of their corporate university, put it, was that "leaders tend to always want to influence or take charge of decisions even though a team was brought together to problem solve the issue." The unintentional result was that "team leaders" stifled creativity in two discernable ways.

First, they asked leading questions to guide the team to their predetermined outcome. When this occurs, questions are not the expression of genuine curiosity, but rather a veiled statement to guide others to a predetermined outcome. This move is particularly troublesome when the formal leader has called for an open-ended dialogue. Although perhaps an improvement from just giving directives, team members eventually sensed this manipulation, which made them suspicious, depleting energy, engagement, and creativity.

Second, the formal team leaders, with the intention of activating interaction by creating space for others to speak and not dictating the outcome, would withhold their points of view. Initially, this move generated more immediate interaction, followed by some awkwardness, but eventually undermined team interaction. Shifting, often unconsciously, back to their hierarchical habits, the team followers attempted to guess or determine the leader's position to support it.

All three examples—(1) too much collaboration with teams stalling on making decisions, (2) too little collaboration with new team leaders "taking charge," and (3) faux collaboration, with formal leaders making veiled statements instead of asking genuine questions or withholding their in-the-moment thinking accountability—came at the cost of innovation. This raises several questions:

- How can accountability and innovation become mutually enhancing instead of mutually exclusive?
- How can leaders engage their teams authentically in the moment in a manner that invites and inspires others to do the same?
- How can leaders find the security to leverage their ignorance with genuinely curious questions that stimulate collective innovation?

- How does dysfunctional collaboration appear in the everyday functioning of teams and organizations?

The collaborative leadership model tends to lead to the same dysfunctional outcomes in organizations:

Relationships. When differences or disagreements show up people attack out of anger or avoid each other out of fear, resulting in a decrease in communication, which obviously erodes trust and then decision-making, execution, and profitability.

Decisions. Depending upon the culture, leader, or situation, decisions are made too quickly as directives from those in authority without having accessed collective intelligence and gained the buy-in of those who execute the decisions. Often, the result is poor decisions and/or mediocre to poor execution. On the other hand, decisions happen too slowly, and the result is missing the ever-increasing short window of opportunities or no decisions at all.

Team Meetings. Depending upon personality type, role, and situation, some team members tend to dominate while others tend to withhold what they think and feel. As a result, conversations stall. Those who dominate don't feel heard. Those who withdraw feel undervalued, even belittled. People leave meetings feeling frustrated. Both tend to say what they really think and feel at the "meetings after the meetings" with those who "see it their way." Triangulation strangles. Backbiting hurts. Divides deepen. Suspicion grows. Energy depletes. Opportunities flee. Problems fester.

Silos. The dysfunctions of relationships, decision-making, and meetings described above allow organization silos to continue and even further isolate. Sometimes the formal leader feeds silos, consciously or unconsciously, to maintain or increase their own power. This scarcity approach to power only diminishes the leadership development of others, forgetting the fact that the larger the pie, the bigger the pieces.

Generation Gaps. Each generation tends to have a different starting point and divergent paths for moving forward. Without a clear, compelling, and common vision and purpose, these differences become only chaotic and defeating. However, with a shared reason for being and an exciting destination, these differences, coupled with an evolved skill set for leading each other, can become highly innovative. (In Chapter 9, "The Equalizer," I champion this common purpose.) Otherwise, they only feed silos and the subsequent lack of leadership development. As is widely known, millennials highly value a meaningful work experience and opportunities to grow as people and leaders. Without such experiences, they are known to quickly gravitate to other organizations.

Leadership Development and Culture. Leading followers creates followers and a culture of conformity. Leading leaders creates leaders and a culture of innovation.

As we see from these examples, the limitations of collaborative leadership tend to stem from practical difficulties in implementation. The experience is nearly universal: it's rare that the collaborative leadership approach doesn't eventually break down. The increased sense of being overwhelmed and the disruption in today's world is compounded by the relational decision-making and dysfunctional team dynamics described above. This results in lower trust, engagement, agility, productivity, happiness, and profits.

All forms of collaborative leadership, whether situational or servant, remain constricted by the limits of "either/or" thinking and practice—as in, either lead or follow depending upon the situation or service. Although a radical development in its day, it's now time for a new radically mutual leadership built on an even more expansive approach using "both/and" thinking and practice.

As we shall see, projects today require that leaders gather in cross-functional teams to solve problems and realize possibilities, taking turns leading or following. Although this is an improvement over singular leadership, it still is very different from the mutuality derived from leaders leading each other as equals, which requires building upon communally leading and following simultaneously or in the same action.

Another way to describe this macro view of the evolution of leadership is from solo/command and control, to shared collaboration or situational leadership, to a new paradigm rooted in the idea that everyone, *at all levels*, exercises leadership. In this book, I offer an expanded definition of leadership and introduce a process where leaders don't just take turns leading or following, but actually lead *and* follow simultaneously, or in the same action. This "both/and" approach to leading and following leverages everyone as a leader, avoids the chaos of too many chefs in the kitchen, and results in teamwork evolving to team flow, perpetual creativity followed by in-sync execution.

This radical "both/and" mutuality is what attracts and retains millennials who show up expecting to lead. These emerging leaders want to be "met" by other leaders as equal partners. This is about moving from being about me, to being about you, to being about us—you and me. "How can I help or serve you?" can unintentionally be experienced as paternalistic. "How can we help each other?" invites the other to meet us as a partner, a mutual leader.

The first step for experiencing the connectedness and results of this mutual engagement is to understand the change in context and then adopt a fitting worldview, structural framework, and mindset for seeing and relating to each other as mutual leaders, especially in a hierarchy. To that we now turn.

CHAPTER 2

The Road from Anarchy to Monarchy to Hierarchy to Panarchy

*The better we understand how identities and power
work together from one context to another, the less
likely our movements for change are to fracture.*
—KIMBERLE WILLIAMS CRENSHAW
American activist

The world is changing—fast, especially given the COVID-19 pandemic. Increasingly, with the complexity of the Digital Age, even within hierarchical structures, getting work done or completing a successful project requires cross-functional teams of leaders from across the organization—IT, Marketing, Sales, HR, Legal, Design, and so on. (In Chapter 9, "The Equalizer," I discuss in detail the concept of an organization as a community of leader–followers.) Often this shift is felt, but not named or identified as a different context—a unique game with its own unique set of challenges and rules.

Today, the question has changed from "How do I lead followers?" to "How do I lead leaders?" or "How does a captain lead a ship of captains?" Without consciously being aware of this change in context and without developing new skills and processes for leading leaders, we attempt to lead leaders in the same way we led followers. This is akin to telling a cat to sit and fetch like a dog. It just doesn't work.

Perpetual disruption calls for and requires more leaders with distinctive expertise and experience to solve problems and realize possibilities collectively.

Traditional Leadership Attempts to Control and Command

In the age of turbulent change and spiraling complexity, the illusion of control is unmasked. Rarely can one leader figure out the path forward and execute with command and control. As a result, CEOs have become more dependent upon the effectiveness of their executive teams, which are collections of leaders from across the organization. Some significant companies like Salesforce and Sony have even opted for multiple CEOs.

As I've mentioned, there are now more chiefs at the executive level than ever. Many executive teams have become a collection of chiefs. To enhance responsiveness and agility, more and more companies rely on projects to find and deliver solutions. The success of these projects depends on effectively gathering leaders from across the organization into task forces, cross-functional teams, projects, or pods.

We must also consider mergers and acquisitions, where leaders from different cultures join to run a company, and the rise of millennials in the workforce, who show up ready to lead. In addition, the internet empowers more people with information and inspiration to lead their own unique lives, and when they do, they become leaders. This is a core dynamic, especially of millennials, but also to all those showing up as leaders.

Suppose we are sailing just north of the equator. Our navigation would be centered on the position of the North

Star. If we were to sail across the equator into the southern hemisphere, we no longer are guided by the North Star, but by a myriad collection of stars.

The dynamics of the Digital Age are causing a shift from the lone leader (the North Star in the northern hemisphere) to the cluster of leaders (stars in the southern hemisphere). Another way to describe this is the shift from the hierarchical (rule over) order of the northern hemisphere to the panarchical (all rule) order or disorder of the southern hemisphere.

The Rise of Panarchy

In a macro view, leadership—or the lack thereof—has evolved from anarchy (no rule) to monarchy (one rule) to hierarchy (some rule) to what is evolving today, panarchy, or *all* rule. Let's step back and take a fresh look at organizations and the individuals who participate in and lead them. Although rarely noticed, or named, today's organizations are primarily a community of equal, different, and vital leader–followers. For organizations to actualize today's priorities of speed and agility, it is imperative that they embrace this identity and employ an operating system grounded in the practice of diversity, equity, and inclusion. This concept stands in sharp contrast to traditional hierarchies and their operating systems built on conformity, inequity, and exclusion.

The Role of Hierarchy in Panarchical Leadership

Hierarchy's role is to facilitate, not control, the innovative operating system of We the Leader, which matches and leverages the emerging context of panarchy in today's

19

organizations. The notion and practice of leading followers has served its time. A key component of the We the Leader operating system is coleading. Since only you can lead you, *you lead yourself by following* your own inner GPS, or inner wisdom and passion, which only you know, and only you can choose to follow. Since only you can lead you, then no one else can lead you. Since others can only lead themselves, you cannot lead others. Leaders of their own lives may colead teams, projects, and organizations, but not each other.

Everyone is the leader of their own life. Gravity Payments' (a credit card processing service) statement "Everyone is their own CEO at Gravity" appears to recognize that everyone leads themselves.[1] Millennials—both those new to the workforce and those in leadership positions in companies—would be more open to Gravity's concept, because they, for the most part, see themselves as leaders and show up with that mindset.

Actually, neuroscience declares that everyone has the capacity to be a chief, a leader, in the full sense of the word. Our ability to rewire our brains and build new neural pathways repudiates the idea that some are meant to lead and others to follow. To avoid the dysfunction of too many chiefs on the executive team and to access the exponential power of a leadership collective, organizations need an innovative operating system that thrives on everyone leading and bringing their full selves to work—and We the Leader is that operating system.

These leaders become members of an organization. According to the *Oxford English Dictionary*, an organization is "an organized body of people with a particular purpose."[2] In other words, those in an organization have a common purpose. Everyone in an organization from the top CEO to the most recent hire at the lower levels of the hierarchy is a follower of the common purpose. This levels the playing field throughout the organization, not just on Employee Appreciation Day, but every day, all day. These followers are not only equal, they are different, and not only equal *and* different, they are vital followers of the common purpose.

Within an organization, leaders of their own lives are also followers of the common purpose. In other words, the members of an organization are not sometimes leaders and at other times followers as in hierarchies, but all are leaders and followers at the same time all the time; they are leader–followers. I call this reality panarchy.

Organizations by their very definition are communities of diversity, equity, and inclusion. Yet organizations today predominantly are communities of conformity, inequity, and exclusion. It's no wonder that in today's hierarchies, innovation falls short and the experience of diversity, equity, and inclusion is elusive.

The We the Leader operating system consists of processes for innovating, leading, and making decisions. Within this operating system, hierarchy is utilized, especially in decision-making, as a temporary tool for serving perpetual innovation, or consistent collective flow.

According to John Fodor, former executive vice president and global distribution leader at a renowned international financial firm, "Today more than ever organizations need a methodology to 'walk the talk' of their diversity, equity, and inclusion initiatives, and not only hire and train, but operate in a manner that is consistent with those initiatives. We the Leader is an innovative operating system for consistent collective flow (creativity with execution), built through the practice of diversity, equity and inclusion."

The We the Leader operating system is grounded in the evolutionary impulse of life called consilience or the "jumping together" of opposite knowledge and, according to Harvard evolutionary biologist Edward O. Wilson, energies,[3] to create something new or innovative (see Chapter 4). In the context of leadership, it's not just leading or following depending upon the situation, but communities of leader–followers coleading teams, projects, and organizations by learning to lead and follow simultaneously, or in the same act. This leading and following at the same time actualizes their identity as leader–followers. Leaders lead. Followers follow. Leader–followers don't just lead or follow, depending upon the situation; they lead and follow at the same time, in the same moment.

This We the Leader innovation and leadership method is fueled by a communication process that equips and empowers everyone to communicate with each other as equal, different, and vital individuals even within the context of a hierarchy built on conformity, inequity, and exclusion. I think of this as bringing and inviting others to bring a *curious conviction*. Upon first hearing of a curious conviction, the CFO of a renowned financial institution mused, "I know how to bring a conviction in one moment and a curiosity in another. How would I bring a conviction and curiosity at the same time?" Leader–followers colead by learning to practice a curious conviction and in the process relate to each other as diverse, equal, and valued human beings making a difference through their differences.

The We the Leader decision-making process draws upon temporary hierarchy to facilitate collective flow, satisfy the need for speed, and avoid traveling in the wrong direction, in order to make timely wise decisions.

Diversity. Equity. Inclusion.

Not until organizations' cultures align with reality and identify themselves as communities of unique, equal, and vital leader–followers will innovation and the essential DEI efforts, such as unearthing unconscious bias, really take hold. Context matters.

Hierarchies are built on *Conformity. Inequity. Exclusion.*

- **Conformity** because hierarchies maintain and thrive on leaders who have followers. To follow means to go where the leader goes, to take the position of the leader, to conform to the leader—the exact opposite of diversity.
- **Inequity** is what makes a hierarchy a hierarchy; some have a position of power over, others lack power. The exact opposite of equal power.
- **Exclusion** because in hierarchies only a few are leaders and the many are prevented from leading or being considered leaders.

Expecting DEI to succeed in a hierarchy is like putting ice in the oven and wondering why it keeps melting. The efforts of DEI and innovation will continue to be marginalized until organizations adopt an operating system that organically practices diversity, equity, and inclusion.

Networked Instead of Hierarchical

The challenges of leading leaders are exacerbated in the context of today's more collaborative or egalitarian structures for several reasons:

- The need for greater speed and agility, acceleration of digital information
- Increased digital demand

- The rise of purpose driven or social responsible businesses
- Mergers and acquisitions
- Revolving executive teams and co-CEOs
- Increased diversity and multiple generations within organizations and teams
- The perpetual need for new product and service innovation
- The rise of artificial intelligence (AI)
- The elimination of silos and the formation of cross-functional teams

All of these contribute to situations where leaders face the challenge of leading leaders.

The rise of panarchy is not a mere gradual shift. It is epochal. It is like nothing since the beginning of the Industrial Revolution in terms of scale and speed. These shifts *require and offer* a new approach to leadership, one that replaces the sometimes effective but too-often-limited approaches leaders have available now.

This epic transformation is full of peril and opportunity. The choice is ours. The opportunity is to become aware of the change of context to leading leaders and leverage this emerging environment for unprecedented innovation and consistent collective flow. What follows is a road map and vehicle for sustained success in this new and ever-changing terrain.

CHAPTER 3

Collective Flow

A good juggler improving his skills will juggle with more balls. An excellent juggler will juggle with balls of many different sizes and shapes.

—BORIS VERKHOVSKY
Director of Acrobatics and Coaching at Cirque du Soleil

One fall evening, along the banks of the Ohio River, a group of teenage boys had an experience they would never forget.

As the sun set that Friday, thousands of people, as if in a trance, headed for the heavenly stadium lights. At the sound of the BABABABA! of the Big Red band, their pulse and pace quickened. Tonight, the Big Red were being invaded by the Canton McKinley High Bulldogs, led by Rocco Rich. (Is there a better name for a football player?)

These two teams had history between them. In previous outings, the Canton McKinley High Bulldogs, one of the top teams in the nation, had dominated the Steubenville High Big Red Stallions 35–0, 42–0, and in one game, the score was 62–0 when, with seconds on the clock, the Bulldogs called a timeout to ensure a 70–0 rout. That was something the head coach of the Big Red, Abe Bryan, could not ever forget.

As expected, the game began lopsided: the Bulldogs dominated the Big Red Stallions in every way. The Big Red quarterback could hardly hand off the ball, let alone drop back to pass. Then, with seconds left in the first half, the score

14–0, the opposing quarterback dropped back to pass. As the ball spiraled through the crisp autumn air, you could hear the collective moan of the Big Red fans—even the dead ones in the adjacent cemetery—when Steubenville's star defensive back, "Rabbi," intercepted the football and returned it 80 yards into the Bulldogs end zone. Touchdown Big Red!

That end zone was the beginning of Big Red's collective flow zone.

At halftime, Coach Bryan was possessed. His words were drugs entering our blood stream. All together, we flew out of the locker room. The same linemen from the first half now opened up holes instead of being pushed into the backfield. The score was tied 14–14. Big Red had the ball on their own 40-yard line with seconds remaining in the game when Big Red's quarterback released the ball in the direction of Rabbi, who was now the wide receiver. Touchdown!!!!! Big Red won 21–14, with Rocco lying prostrate in the mud and Rabbi speaking in tongues!!

I was the Big Red quarterback. That night against the Bulldogs, our team outperformed itself, transcending into what I now call a collective zone. How did this happen? What was it that caused such a dramatic change in performance from the same personnel in a matter of a few minutes? How much of this transformation belongs to Rabbi's first-half interception, how much to Coach Bryan's halftime rant, and how much to—something else entirely? What are the dimensions of such a collective zone? Is it possible for individuals, teams, and organizations to feel that alive and to be so productive in their everyday lives? If so, how would it happen? Searching for the answers to these questions has guided most of my adult life and fueled a quest to convert collective flow from a mystical and extraordinary experience into an everyday possibility.

Typically, our experiences of collective flow are not understood; they just happen, and we are not clear why. At best we may understand them intuitively. Our goal now is to go behind what we sometimes understand implicitly and make it explicit so that we can choose to create collective flow at will. A consistent conscious choice for collective flow creates a new normal and even becomes contagious within a culture. As other leaders noticed the consistent collective flow in the executive team of one department in an industry-leading financial firm, they literally exclaimed, "I want what they're having."

Through my academic and experiential research, I came to realize that we can create consistent flow and experience the sensation *I still can't believe we did it!* at will. We don't have to hope the stars will align, that somehow we will have the luck or chemistry or a crisis to draw out our best instincts and actions. No! Together we can repeatedly create our own chemistry.

Collective Flow in Everyday Life

In "What Really Makes Teams Click Today," Gary Burnison, CEO at Korn Ferry and author of *Leadership U: Accelerating Through the Crisis Curve*, describes an instructive example of everyday collective flow:[1]

> On our last day, all seven of us scrambled to pack and get to the airport on time. In our rush, somebody knocked over a fruit smoothie and sent it flying. Standing at the door, luggage in each hand, I watched that pink lava, as if in slow motion, shoot into the air and land with a splat—right on a white rug, of course.
>
> We all sprang into action. It was orchestrated chaos, and everyone had a role. Someone grabbed

bath towels to sop up the mess. Someone else squirted shampoo (the only cleaner we had) to avoid a stain. Another person doused it with water. After a lot of rubbing and scrubbing, somebody pulled out the hairdryer—and nearly burned the rug. We felt like the Keystone Kops.

Then it was time to go. But there was our daughter Emily, giving the barely visible pink spot one last scrub with a toothbrush. When I asked Emily why she was still working, she shrugged and smiled. "We're having fun."

Collective flow is the group experience of being lifted and guided by an energy from within, between, and beyond into the realm of exponential potential. Images people use to describe collective flow include choreographed dance, the wheel that turns without friction, the crew rowing in unison, or Canada geese flying in a rotating "V" formation. What captures this "magic," and what best reflects my experience, is the image and motion of the starlings' murmurations, where hundreds or even thousands of birds fly in a coordinated, sweeping, intricately patterned dance.[2] For me, this magical image and experience is mysterious, even eerie, because it's still unfamiliar. It mirrors the mysterious, even eerie, character of collective flow—in part because it still *seems* sky bound, beyond our reach.

Basketball great Bill Russell, who won more championships than any other athlete in the twentieth century, describes collective flow as moving beyond the physical or mental realm to the magical. This description resonates for me and describes my experience on the athletic field, the experience that propelled me into a lifelong quest to understand what makes this shift happen. How do we build a bridge from collective flow being an extraordinary experience to it becoming an everyday possibility?

Through my research and experience, I've come to believe that we have the capacity to lead each other in a way that creates consistent collective flow. In other words, we don't need to wait for collective flow to happen; we can create and re-create these experiences at will, through our collective will.

Collective Flow: How It Happens

In sharing my collective flow experience on the athletic field, I've invited others to do the same. A physician, in the midst of a national crisis, was "stopped in his tracks" by a *humm* in the emergency room. It was as if a swarm of human bee-ings were being coordinated by some internal, collective GPS system. In the early days of the COVID-19 crisis, 300 engineers, medical experts, and researchers attracted by an open-source forum on the internet came together to devise a way—in a single week—to make desperately needed ventilators using 3D printing.[3]

What has *your* experience of collective flow been? If none comes to mind, recall a time while playing, conversing, meeting, or working with others that you felt alive. Or perhaps you witnessed a musical or theater performance that left you flying high. While these prompts evoke times of enjoyment and pleasure, collective flow may also occur—or maybe "must" also occur—in times of profound duress. In this vein, one of the best examples is the 2018 rescue of the boys' soccer team, the "Wild Boars."

It began as an ill-advised adventure by twelve boys and their soccer coach into a flood-prone northern Thailand cave. As the floodwater rose unexpectedly and rapidly, the escapade appeared destined to end in tragedy. Although it took ten days just to locate the team, in another eight days the entire group had been evacuated them from the cave. The rescue was the result of a composite of resources, compassion, and brainpower from around the world. In all, 10,000 people participated, including 2,000 soldiers, 200 divers, and representatives from 100 government agencies. "I still can't believe it worked," said Major General Chalongchai Chaiyakham, the deputy commander of the Third Army region. "So many things could have gone wrong, but somehow we managed to get the boys out."[4]

What makes this instance of collective flow so distinctive is that it occurred over a sustained period of time—not just the duration of a game, a performance, or smoothie cleanup, but a total of eighteen days. In addition, apart from the leadership based in Thailand, the rescue effort included a revolving group of experts, those who were recruited and those who volunteered, from around the globe. Sustained collective flow from a diverse array of experts is what it takes to solve some of our most vexing problems.

Collective Flow Demands Difference

Great leaders will lead more followers. A great leader will lead leaders with a variety of experiences, expertise, and perspectives by juggling and following. In an interview with Boris Verkhovsky, the director of Acrobatics and Coaching at Cirque du Soleil, the discussion at one point turns to "the reflexive experience of a creative leader faced with the challenges of integrating multiple areas of expertise around complex, technological, human, and poly-sensorial creative performances." The director concludes that consistent creative collaboration requires a sophisticated leadership with a complex balance of humility and authority.[5]

I prefer to call this balancing of humility and authority *harmony*, in part because balance implies separating, rather than putting together, the two dynamics. Harmony opens up the possibility that humility and authority are not only intertwining but also mutually enhancing. This mutual enhancement is exactly what I've seen with highly innovative teams. The harmony doesn't have to be complex. It requires open-learning, humble curiosity, and, at the same time, a clear certain authority, even in the same action. Harmony also reflects the consilience of two seeming opposites jumping together to create something new. This definition of harmony is reflected in the synchronization of authority/authenticity, hierarchy/panarchy, leading/following, structure/energy, and conviction/curiosity.

Upon hearing of curious conviction for the first time, the CFO of a renowned financial company responded, "I know how to be curious in one moment and to bring a conviction in another. But how do I express a conviction *and* curiosity at the same time or in the same action?" In Part IV, I will introduce the three steps of a curious conviction; here it is an example of the importance of expressing our differences for the creation of collective flow.

Collective Flow Emerges through Simultaneous Leading and Following

Reimaging leadership for collective flow begins with reimaging the very identity of a leader. We must evolve beyond the traditional leader–follower model. By "evolve," I mean to include and transcend. There remains a time and place for the leader–follower model to contribute to flow as exemplified in Coach Bryan's halftime pep talk. However, this leader–follower model is a secondary mode of leading. Its only purpose is to serve or instigate collective flow, not stifle it with command and control. (This is a very potent and important thread woven throughout the fabric of this book. As you will see in Chapter 14, it is the need, especially in crisis, for an individual leader to exercise her hierarchical authority.)

Transcending it will take recognition of three powerful potentials:

- Everyone is a leader.
- Everyone is a follower.
- Everyone is a leader–follower.

Some people dismiss these notions, immediately claiming that only some are born to be leaders. Historically, there's plenty of evidence to support this heroic individual leader model, whether in politics, religion, business, sports, or the arts. For instance, in some theatrical arts, there are the stars such as Jennifer Lawrence as the title character in *Joy* or Hugh Jackman as Jean Valjean in *Les Misérables*. These are examples in which the old leader–follower model is necessary. On the other hand, what I'm pointing to is the necessity and reality for *everyone* to be a star. How can that be? The answer is in a different context, intention, and structure. For example, in improvisational theatre there are no stars, or rather, everyone is a star, creator, and director—all at the same time.

When I first started improv classes at Second City in Chicago, the admonition to "follow the follower" struck me as strange. The traditional definition of a leader is one who *has* followers. When you think of it, when a follower is followed, that follower is also a leader, or one who is followed. In improv, then, following the follower is also leading the leader. Furthermore, since all the participants, or all the stars, follow the follower, and in doing so, lead the leader, they're followers and leaders at the same time.

There is another concept in improv that I am sure you have heard of—*Yes, and*.... What it means is you accept what a participant has said and then expand on the thought. I find the idea very helpful in life and, yes, in unpreferred circumstances when I see them as opportunities from which to create. It is important to encourage different perspectives and challenges to deepen the inquiry and creativity. Here the "Yes and ..." would be "Yes and ... are you open to a different perspective?" Genuine dialogue is not just about brainstorming and building on our thinking, it is also about being challenging and disrupting.

Remember, in improv there is no predetermined script, so there are no set roles: everyone must take a lead role for improv to work. The lead role requires everyone to be acutely present in the moment and move or lead with what comes up for them. In turn, they must invite others to take the lead role. In improv, you are the "star" when you follow another participant's line with your own line and someone follows your line with their line. You are both a leader and follower. As the improv unfolds, this participation as a leader–follower is not only true of the individual, but also true of all participants.

During an improv class, Connie and I were selected to be a suburban married couple obsessed about our lawn. As we complain about the neighbors' disrespectful kids—"How dare they walk on our lawn!"—and their unkempt yard, in my mind I was admiring the fresh grass to see if there were any blades I may have missed when cutting the lawn. Then Connie said, "My legs are tired, I'm going to sit down in the grass." I screamed, "NO!!!! You'll ruin the lawn." The entire class broke out in laughter. (There can be times for No!) Up to that point, I had rarely felt so alive. As with my teenage experience of collective flow, I want to learn to live this way—of experiencing and feeling the connection of creating something together that is fun and enriching.

In summary, in improv, everyone is a leader, follower, and a leader–follower—all three simultaneously.

How does this expanded idea of team members apply to today's organizations?

Everyone Is a Leader

Today's projects, challenges, and possibilities require doing different work and doing that different work differently. This calls for leaders from across an organization to gather in pods consisting of cross-functional, integrated teams. (See Dave Kaufman's and John Kessler's interview in Chapter 15 for a case study about creating integrated teams within a traditional hierarchy.) Millennials, who, for the most part, were raised as leaders, show up expecting to lead from day one and are prepared for this challenge; many of us need to learn how to lead the leader (neuroscience tells us everyone is a leader, even if they don't always act like it).

Everyone Is a Follower

In this view, the follower's leader is the organization's common purpose. By definition, every institution, organization, or team commits to following a common purpose. Everyone, including the board and top executives, is a follower of a common reason for being (however inadequately that purpose is defined or understood, this remains the case). Common purpose as leader levels the playing field throughout institutions, organizations, and movements. Rendering everyone as equal followers and thus equal leaders magnifies the reality of panarchy and requires a panarchical leadership approach. We need to follow the follower.

Everyone Is a Leader–Follower—All the Time

As leaders of our own lives and followers of a common purpose (whether at work or outside it), we are all leaders and followers simultaneously and perpetually. Just by following others, we are inherently also leaders.

As the art of improvisation teaches us, a community of followers who follow one another also inherently *lead* one another. There's no untangling the two; they're two sides of the same coin. To follow a follower is to lead a leader, and to lead a leader is to follow a follower. This reality, or naming of what already is, dismantles the inadequate traditional framework of a leader as one who has followers. At the same time, it calls for a new more robust model that includes leading followers in a much wider reality-based context. In other words, there's a harmonious place for hierarchical leadership within the context of panarchy.

The Foundations of Collective Flow

Since leader–followers exist in every organization, whether named or not, the question of leadership becomes not just how to lead followers or even how to lead leaders, but how to lead leaders who are followers and followers who are leaders, simultaneously and at all times. In other words, *how do leader–followers lead each other?*

The answer is through a new set of individual skills—including curious conviction—and a new set of team disciplines. To put these in context and in relation to each other, we can refer to part of the We the Leader (WTL) Flow Chart (Figure 3.1). What I've come to call Simultaneity is the process of leading and following in the same act.

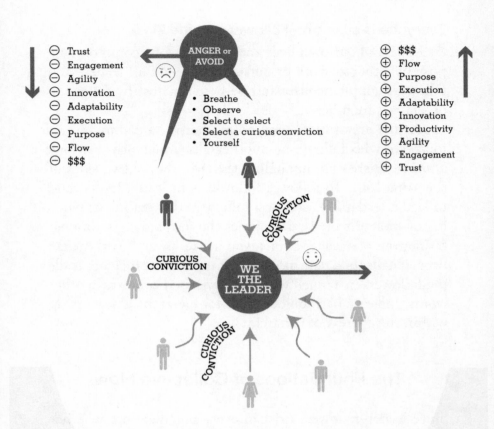

FIGURE 3.1

At the bottom of the chart, Consilience, The Innovator, represents the energy source, or foundation, for flow. This source is the creative principle of opposites, or consilience. Above it are the three pillars of flow:

- The Diversifier: Me the Leader (leading yourself)
- The Equalizer: Common Purpose
- The Unifier: We the Leader (leading each other or leading leaders)

Together this foundation and three pillars create the conduit for collective flow.

The pillar on the left, The Diversifier: Me the Leader, stands for the inner process, for everyone leading one's unique self via the BOSS Yourself process (you tell yourself what to do). The up arrow indicates the outcomes for leading one's unique self.

The second pillar, The Equalizer: The Common Purpose, represents everyone as equal leaders of their own lives and at the same time followers of a common purpose.

The third pillar (on the right), The Unifier: We the Leader, stands for the diversity of the We becoming unified as The, or One, leader.

As depicted in the flow chart, this flow state of We the Leader occurs when each unique leader BOSSes themself and chooses a curious conviction, which might be unique to them or shared by other members of the team. This BOSS-ing of self and choosing a curious conviction, depicted by the line going from each individual to the We the Leader at the center of the group, is ongoing during dialogues and decision-making. These lines represent the personal move required of everyone, that of bringing a curious conviction (curious as a learner/follower might be, while having the conviction of a teacher/leader).

We the Leader is the collective process for everyone to lead themselves and each other as well as the outcomes for doing so (indicated by the up arrow on the right side of the chart). The pillar on the left, The Diversifier, illustrates the inner process of leading oneself and the outcomes for not doing so. The pillar on the right, The Unifier, indicates the inner process for leading each other and leading leaders and the likely results for doing so.

What Keeps Us from Achieving Collective Flow?

Best depicted in Patrick Lencioni's insightful and popular *The Five Dysfunctions of a Team: A Leadership Fable,* the obstacles to collective flow are rampant. These dysfunctions include (but, I believe, are not limited to) lack of trust, fear of conflict, lack of commitment, avoidance of accountability, and inattention to results.[6] All signs that a team is *not* in collective flow, they reflect the down arrow results in the WTL Flow Chart.

To draw on our earlier example, there's an important distinction between traditional theatre, with one or two stars and a cast to support them, and improvisational theatre, with its troupe of stars. Many of the same dysfunctions persist because we are applying a traditional approach to leading/acting in a world increasingly demanding improvisation. A single moment in today's workplace demands knowledge, agility, speed, decisiveness, and execution; there is little room for memorizing lines. The framework of traditional leadership has taken us a long way. But now, as reflected in research from Deloitte, is the time for a completely new way of leading.[7]

To get beyond these dysfunctions and clear the way for collective flow, we need to activate three mindsets/behaviors:

1. Everyone needs to see themselves as—and fully become—the leader they are.
2. Everyone needs to learn that they are a follower of the common team or organizational purpose.
3. Everyone must embrace their expanded identity as a leader of their life and a follower of a common purpose, then match this evolved identity with an evolved practice of leading and following in the same action— in other words, simultaneity.

Simultaneity redefines the identity of team members from leaders or followers to leader–followers at the same time. Adopting this radical mutual identity requires developing distinct skills for practicing and living this mutuality. If we return to the WTL Flow Chart, we can compare the up-arrow outcomes of Simultaneity to the five dysfunctions, which lead to the reactive down-arrow outcomes. We can also see that those dysfunctions can be overcome with trust, engagement, mutual accountability, and human and business results. Often, the first step to move teams at odds with each other out of the dysfunction zone is to employ each one's individual skills. Once collective functioning is the norm, it becomes only natural to evolve to collective flowing—not just once in a while, but consistently, even at will.

From Dysfunction to Flow: A Case Study

Now that you're familiar with the WTL Flow Chart and its three pillars, let's examine what incorporating curious conviction and individual accountability make possible in the real world—my work with the Michigan-based Kindel Furniture.

Kindel Furniture prides itself on a long tradition of building custom furniture. The factory employs highly skilled craftspeople with artistic skills—and temperaments. These craftspeople need to work with one another because each part of a piece of the furniture they make is dependent on the part built before. Amid a dwindling market, part of the organization's strategy was to acquire other furniture companies. Of course, each of *those* companies had their own design and manufacturing processes.

Making sense of and integrating the language, designs, and processes of three different companies on a single manufacturing floor made the job of the engineering department extremely challenging, to say the least. With three sets of documents delineating how to complete a project, work gets complicated quickly. As a result, the department "silos" were more like walls, even combat zones at times. Everyone on the floor and in the engineering office would refer constantly to "the wall," as if each had the stature of the Berlin Wall. It wasn't unusual for key personnel on the floor, or in engineering, not to talk about a problem for days. Consequently, products were frequently delayed or returned, which increased costs and unraveled efficiencies. One might say that Kindel's culture was not just afflicted with the five dysfunctions, it was defined by them.

Several key players perpetuated this state of affairs, but two stand out, both for where they started and where they finished. Scott (who was on track to be the next-generation plant manager) and Darlene were both up-and-coming leaders at Kindel. Scott, who was on the factory floor, was the classic "my way or the highway" leader who regularly expressed anger by yelling or ignoring others.

On the WTL Flow Chart, this type of reaction and the energy it brings, represented by the burst at the top of the chart (anger or avoid) with the subsequent negative impact on human relations and business results, appear next to the down arrow on the left. The people surrounding the We the

Leader circle represent the crucial juncture of consistent personal flow toward We the Leader. It is important to note that avoiding this personal flow leads to the down-arrow results to personal and business well-being, whereas moving from personal flow to collective flow leads to the up-arrow results of personal well-being, human relations, and business success. I get inspired by the reality that what enhances personal well-being creates optimal business results.

Darlene, slightly more mild-mannered than Scott but no less stubborn, had recently been promoted to head of engineering. The wider context here—their different approaches, their competing priorities (speed in getting the work done on the manufacturing side; quality over expediency on the engineering side), and the inherent personal competition between two rising stars—made this situation ripe for strife, and strife there was.

Scott and Darlene clashed often, each of their own reactive bubbles spiraling into outright rage or avoidance, depending on mood and situation. When Scott came across an engineering spec that didn't make sense or was confusing, he would either scale "the wall" between manufacturing and engineering with a verbal tirade of disgust for the ignorance of engineering or knowingly follow the erroneous directions, thereby sabotaging the success of the customization and precipitating monumental delays and eventual product returns.

For Scott, my goal was to develop in him the skills necessary to move from the reactive bubble of anger or avoidance to a clear mind and centered response—to acting and responding from the heart. For Darlene, it was to stop mirroring Scott's behavior. After learning about one aspect of curious conviction—the three steps of active listening (mirroring what one hears, inviting further explanation [tell me more about x, y, z], and guessing what the other might be thinking or feeling) —Darlene consciously chose to practice them instead of slashing back at or ignoring Scott. At the same time, Scott began to practice being "a fly on the wall" and examining his own reactions instead of being controlled or led by the situation and his internal frustration. Both became aware that their former responses shrunk their whole sense of the workplace.

Employing concrete practices—active listening, fly-on-the-wall observation—took effort, and they didn't cure the dysfunction overnight. I knew they were releasing themselves from their internal prisons one day when, within an hour after scaling "the wall" and blowing up at Darlene about a faulty engineering spec, Scott paused. Soon after, he returned to the engineering department to own his reaction and apologize. Darlene received the apology openly, without recrimination, and then proceeded to ask further questions to make sure he understood. Scott, in an even tone, named and therefore tamed his frustration, a direct result of having practiced the Four Questions for Leading Yourself (discussed in depth in Chapter 8):

1. What am I observing externally then internally?
2. What emotions do I notice inside myself?
3. What thinking, assumptions, and interpretations are accompanying and feeding these emotions?
4. What do you desire?

Soon after this incident—which may sound minor but was in fact a huge and meaningful milestone for the relationship—a cross-functional task force was created, drawing from both engineering and manufacturing, to proactively address issues of conflicting designs and instructions as well as the dysfunctions that were underlying and exacerbating these issues. This task force propelled a movement toward the "green" space of collective flow. According to internal measurements by the CEO, the company achieved a more than 30 percent increase in productivity because of these efforts.

Although not a pretty story, at least at the beginning, I love what this Kindel experience represents. The complexity of so much in-the-moment customizing is where the work world already is—and it is not going back. The complexity and uncertainty inherent in customization is becoming inherent in all work. Many organizations will have to upgrade how their cross-functional, interdependent teams perform the basics of speaking and listening as equal leader–follower partners. Introducing harmony, or more precisely *consilience,* to this pressure tank is the only true way forward.

CHAPTER 4

Consilience: Innovating from Differences

Avoid the tyranny of the "or"; embrace the genius of the "and."

—JIM COLLINS and JERRY PORRAS
Built to Last

Consilience is a core dynamic and practice within We the Leader, as well as in life itself. The evolutionary biologist Edward O. Wilson highlights this concept in his book by the same name—*Consilience*—meaning the "jumping together" of seemingly opposite energies or ideas. This dynamic action of creative opposites is considered the evolutionary impulse of life. Think of procreation, where the integration of masculine and feminine energy creates human life. Alternatively, envision a battery's energy, created by a simultaneous positive and negative charge. Without both forces, there is no result.

Examples of consilience in the workplace may be found in a wide range of disciplines, including biology, physics, chemistry, aerodynamics, technology, philosophy, and leadership.

Consilience and the Biology of Leading Leaders

The most obvious and immediate example of consilience in biology is human sexual reproduction. You and I result from the jumping together of opposite sexes. The twenty-three chromosomes from each of our biological parents combine to create a unique individual.

Let's look at the words *opposite* and *unique*. Opposite is not just different. It can carry the meaning of over and against, combat, resist in such a way that leads to conflict, competition, even war. In the case of competition or war, this opposition usually results in a winner or a loser.

With procreation (for creation), difference results in a unique human being. We come into existence through a collection of chromosomes from opposite sexes to create unique, one-of-a-kind, never-before and never-again selves. Let's not forget that our biological parents, as offspring of *their* parents, are unique, one-of-a-kind, never-before, never-again human beings as well. We are created from people not just of different sexes, but also opposite sexes. Arising from opposites holds the potential for conflict. This is why managing the reactive bubble in the WTF Flow Chart is so pivotal (see Figure 3.1).

Innovating something new from a mix that includes not just differences but opposing elements is hardwired within our unique DNA. On the most fundamental level, this is the way we human beings operate. Therefore, the question arises, if we are hardwired to create something new, why do we settle for competition that creates winners and losers? Or compromise by uniting on the least common denominator, thinking that is success? Why do we act as though we are products of asexual reproduction that only reproduces clones? Why do we limit ourselves to the understanding of a leader as one who has followers that simply go where the leader goes, taking the position of the leader, conforming to the leader? Why do we balk at the idealism of creating something new when every moment is new, when we are new, when every seven years we have an entirely new set of cells in our bodies?

In this book, I offer a leadership model that aligns with who we are—unique offspring, a product of opposites, not clones of our parents. Our uniqueness is a clarion call for each of us to embrace the distinctive, one-of-a-kind human being that we are. To lead our own lives.

As unique beings, we are attracted to other unique and opposite leaders for the jumping together of something new. In contrast to hierarchies and other contexts where there are some leaders and many followers, in a collective of leaders, or a culture of leaders, we *lead* each other by *following* each other.

We know asexual reproduction breeds clones, not unique individuals. Yet we have built a leadership model that defines a leader as someone with lots of followers who go where the leader goes, take the leader's position, and conform to the leader when a leader and a follower are two sides of the coin of cocreation. When we lead, we are actually *following* and when we follow, we are actually *leading*. To become aware of this unlocks the exponential potential between us.

Consilience and the Physics of Leadership

Quantum physics has shown that light can be both wave and particle.

Light is essential for existence. Our primary source of light is the sun. This vital source of energy is composed of both a fluid wave and a concrete particle, two seemingly opposite qualities. Light is not sometimes a wave and sometimes a particle, depending upon the situation; they operate simultaneously, integrating to create light. This is an example of consilience, where two seemingly opposite elements harmonize in such a way that they create something new.

Leadership is analogous to light. It too is composed of two seemingly opposite elements interacting in the same moment, both leading and following.

Consilience and the Chemistry of Leading Together

The science of leadership doesn't end with physics; it includes chemistry as well. A rudimentary recap: Atoms, considered the building blocks of life, contain the source of nuclear energy. Atoms are composed of protons, electrons, and neutrons. Electrons are a type of subatomic particle with a negative charge; protons are a type of subatomic particle with a positive charge. They are bound together in an atom's nucleus as a result of the strong nuclear force.

Neutrons are a type of subatomic particle with *no* charge (they're neutral). Like protons, neutrons are bound into the atom's nucleus by the strong nuclear force. Thus, atoms are not composed of just the positive energy of protons, or just the negative energy of electrons, or just the neutral energy of neutrons, but of protons, electrons, and neutrons simultaneously in the same moment and action.

If the building blocks of life express the consilience of the jumping together of opposite energies for a greater whole, what implications does this have for the collection of atoms called human beings and how they lead each other and live together? Furthermore, what does it mean for them, as a species? Humans tend to prefer being with those similar to themselves, gathering in homogenous groups of like-minded people (see Chapter 16). But if atoms held only protons their energy would diffuse, if not dissipate, and there would be no atomic energy. It's easy to see how the same might be true for the collection of humans, whether gathered in political parties, institutions, organizations, teams, and partnerships. Might not our very existence depend upon our capacity to include the opposition of "yes" or "no," proton and electron, and to find a third creative way that includes both at the same time?

FIGURE 4.1 Consilience: the foundation of creative flow.

In her book *Creative Experience*, Mary Parker Follett wrote, "For integrating is the fundamental process of life, either as between organism and environment or between man and man." Some say, as Mary Parker Follett notes and Edward O. Wilson discusses in his book *Consilience*, that doing so is the evolutionary impulse of life, the cocreative work of the human species, and the very purpose of our existence. As we shall see, Mary Parker Follett insists that we make a difference through our differences, not in spite of them.

The examples of consilience in everyday life don't stop here.

Aerodynamics

We take it for granted, but when you stop to think about it, flying on an airplane is a miracle. No wonder it is considered one of the greatest achievements of humankind. To me, aerodynamics is one the most powerful examples of consilience because of the opposite energies required of the thrust forward/drag backward along with the lift up/weight down—both at the same time! Together they create a lot of turbulence that soon raises more than eighty tons high into the air at a speed greater than 500 miles an hour.

Flying on Mars verges on the impossible because there's not much air to push against. At the surface of Mars, the atmosphere is just 1/100th as dense as Earth's,[1] so to generate enough lift for NASA's four-pound *Ingenuity* Mars helicopter to rise, its two rotors, each about four feet wide, had to spin in opposite directions at more than 2,500 revolutions a minute.[2]

Just as there are two dimensions in consilient leading—the content of different perspectives, experiences, and areas of expertise along with the process of leading and following at the same time—there are two dimensions of consilience in aerodynamics: the horizontal dimension of a thrust forward and drag backward and the vertical dimension of a lift up and a weight down. Both occur at one time, lifting the passengers to new heights. In the same manner, bringing forth consilient content and practicing this consilient process consistently fuels collective flow (human murmurations) and lifts participants to new heights.

Digital Waves

Analog waves are smooth and continuous, while digital waves are discrete and discontinuous.[3] One way to remember this difference is to think of analog as an outdoor fireplace that is either burning or not burning. When it is burning, the fire and resulting smoke are smooth and continuous. When it is not burning, the air is clear, and, likewise smooth and continuous. On the other hand, digital is like a fire used to send smoke signals. There is a waft of smoke, then clear air.

Doing this repeatedly—a waft of smoke followed by clear air—communicates a signal. In this way, the digital signal is composed of discrete steps (analogous to particles) in a wave

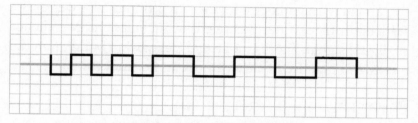

FIGURE 4.2 Digital Data Signal

while the analog signal is either a continuous wave

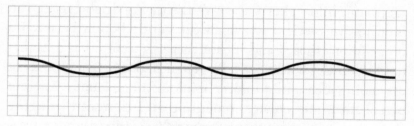

FIGURE 4.3 Analog Data Signal

or nothing.

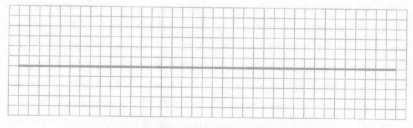

FIGURE 4.4 No Data Signal

Put another way, analog is either wave or not wave. Digital is wave and particle (seeming opposites) at the same time; it represents consilience as they jump together to send a message.

To carry the analogy further, in a digital age we need a leadership theory and practice that includes the consilience of digital signals (both smoke and clear air) to build upon the analogical practice of either smoke or no smoke.

Philosophy

We can see a strong example of consilience in dialectics, a term that describes a method of philosophical argument that involves investigating the truth of opinions and/or contradictory ideas between opposite sides. Hegelian dialectic is the method of argument employed by the nineteenth-century German philosopher Georg Wilhelm Friedrich Hegel, "an interpretive method in which the contradiction between a proposition (thesis) and its antithesis is resolved at a higher level of truth (synthesis)."[4] Hegelian dialectic is a process of discussing ideas and forming opinions that includes different perspectives and creates something greater from them. The thesis is a "yes." The antithesis is a "no." The synthesis integrates the two to devise a third way out of the opposing two ways. The Hegelian dialectic is an example of consilience in philosophy.[5]

This philosophical process of thesis–anti-thesis–synthesis sets the stage for examining the place of consilience in the theory and practice of leadership, where so much depends on thinking through how to solve problems. For example, a new product development team composed of sales executives was concerned about keeping their customers happy no matter the cost, whereas those charged with internal operations wanted a no-frills approach that would easily stay within budget. If sales digs into their priority and operations insists on theirs, without considering a synthesis or third way, a company could not launch a successful product.

The Role of Consilience in Leadership

In the book *The Prophet of Management*, leadership gurus celebrate Mary Parker Follett as the guru of them all. She espoused situational leadership and the importance of a common purpose beyond shareholder wealth far before the Business Roundtable.

Follett's management theory encompasses consilience. From her perspective, there is nothing more important to conflict resolution than embracing differences and moving through them to create something new. She had different names for this process, such as cocreation, integration, and interpenetration. All of these are built upon the same principle and practice of the jumping together of opposites for a new insight, solution, product, or service. Innovating from differences was a top priority for her. This was in the 1920s, well before the information age, the digital age, and our current norm—disruption. She understood the mandate to "innovate or die" before anyone uttered those words.

I have been deeply inspired, even awed, by her insights, particularly those around the importance of the integrating process or creating from and through our differences as the following inspired paraphrases of her thinking illustrate:[6]:

- When we reframe differences, or our uniqueness, as that which unites us, we will welcome them instead of ignoring, dreading, or diluting them.
- Disregarding or not intentionally learning and cocreating from differences is the most fatal mistake a leader can make in politics or industry or international life.

- Every difference that is respected, welcomed, and integrated with other differences evolves society by building trust that results in the riches of fresh innovative ideas, policies, and actions.
- Consilience, or the unifying of difference, is the external process of life—the creative synthesis, the highest act of creation, the at-onement.

In her book *The New State*, Follett imagined and called forth a new way of governing ourselves, one that thrived on true unity. Unity for her could only be derived from our differences. Uniformity is the union of our similarities, and the avoidance of our differences. Unity is only created from our differences. Uniformity only delays destruction and war. Unity from our differences generates innovation, economic development, and peace. What follows depicts the evolution and devolution of unity from our differences in democracy.

From Debate to Dialogue

While visiting London, I visited the House of Commons. When I entered, I was handed a pamphlet celebrating the evolution of the freedom to debate from the dictates of a king. Once inside, I was struck by how the architecture of the place supports the privilege of debate. Each side of the chamber holds a series of rising rows of seats resembling church pews directly across from another, equal set of pews. Even empty, both sides facing off each other appeared ready for a battle. After all the word debate comes from the Latin *battere,* or to fight, and in a debate someone wins and someone loses. The idea is to annihilate the differences of the opposition party and win the argument, if not by consensus then at least by the dictat (order) of the majority. The freedom to express points of view in an open forum was a significant step forward from its suppression under the rule of a king.

In the Senate and House chambers of the United States Capitol building, one is greeted by an architecture much more conducive to open dialogue or, as organizational theorist Follett puts it, integration—the collective process of creating from our differences. However, in practice, the communication in Congress more often resembles Follett's structure of uniformity, where people are united on what they agree upon, not a result derived from and through their opposing views. Instead, differences are debated and decided, at least in the House of Representatives, by the new dictatorship of majority rule. Majority rule, whether in politics, the boardroom, or teams, only delays and adds fuel to the conflict instead of creating *from* the conflict.

In 2010, as a member of the President's Council of the Chicago Council of Global Affairs, I attended an event featuring Richard Lugar, then a moderate Republican senator from Indiana. Afterward, he held an intimate dinner followed by a question-and-answer session. Having served from 1977, ultimately, until 2013, Lugar was the longest-standing senator in Congress at the time.

At an earlier time, he had shared a story about an incident in which then-President Bill Clinton, a Democrat, invited him to the White House to dialogue about the situation in Eastern Europe. Lugar made it clear that this conversation was not a debate from the Senate floor carried into the White House, but an open exploration, what Follett would call an integration or a collective creative process from our differences. During the after-dinner Q and A, I eagerly asked how often in his forty-plus years in the Senate Lugar had been invited to such a conversation with a leader from the opposition party. I was thinking at least a dozen times.

After a long pause, Lugar answered, "Two other times." As a heaviness set in, the room remained quiet. Even Lugar himself seemed shocked.

While debate is certainly an improvement over one-person rule, Follett points out that to stop there is a fatal mistake: "The ignoring of differences is the *most fatal mistake* in politics or industry or international life: every difference that is swept up into a bigger conception feeds the richest society; everyday difference which is ignored feeds on society and eventually corrupts it."[7] She points out how every difference that is avoided, not heard, judged, discredited, dismissed, fought over, or simply debated eats away at society and eventually erodes trust and corrupts society. Unfortunately, the Prophet of Management sounds a lot like a prophet of politics too.

In recent years, given the lack of substantive dialogue across party lines, it appears that Democrats and Republicans alike are stuck in each one's uniformity derived from their similarities, an inbreeding conformity. This stands in stark contrast to unity through our differences, the consilience that leads to innovation. Of course, this dynamic doesn't stop with politics. It prevails in business, nonprofits, and religious institutions as well. We human beings are homogenous. We like to be with people like ourselves. Although dismaying, inbred conformity should not be a surprise. Let's remember that by the prevailing definition, a leader is one who has followers. Followers go after the leader, go where the leader goes, take the position of the leader, and conform to the leader's expectations. Along this path, differences are annihilated, and the road to corruption is built.

Making a Difference Through Our Differences

I wrote and posted this on LinkedIn just after the 2020 United States presidential election.

To citizens of the United States of America,

We have voted in historic numbers. Our emotions are boiling, our differences razor sharp.

We are not apathetic and ignoring our differences.

We are expressing our differences with conviction and energy.

There is creative opportunity here!

Unity only comes through our differences. Uniformity avoids differences. We are the United States of America, not the Uniformed States of America. Our unity comes through our diversity of race, gender, economic status, and political affiliations.

We have debated or listened to debates, expressed our approval by voting and our disapproval in protests.

Let's not stop there.

Now is the time to turn our differences into opportunities to create a new way, unique for our time. Our differences are expressions of our unique DNA, geography, family, education, faith, life experiences, etc. Human life is created by the coming together of different or opposite sexes to create a unique human being. According to evolutionary biologists, life continues through the jumping together of different energies to create something new. Our differences are not just something to ignore or to fight over, they are constant opportunities to create something new.

Let's channel the palpable energy of our emotions and create from our unique experiences, different perspectives, and opposite votes.

Where would we start?

With what we have in common.

"At a polling station in the New Church of Faith, just outside Orlando, Florida, a woman named Veronica, 35, said she had voted for Mr. Trump because she feared for her freedoms. Moments later, a woman named Dorothy, 45, emerged to say she had voted for Mr. Biden because she feared for her freedoms."[8]

Let's start by gathering together as Republicans and Democrats to explore what we have in common—our fear and the value of freedom.

Deep down we long for a new faith in each other, otherwise we wouldn't be so enraged.

It's time to elect each other.

"We the people . . . to form a more perfect Union."

The Blind Men and the Elephant: Exploring Difference

This reminds me of the classic story of the Blind Men and the Elephant, a tale that originated in India, probably in Hindu lore. In the parable, six blind men visit an elephant for the first time. They learn what this unknown creature is like by feel. Each man touches a different part of the elephant (the side, tusk, trunk, leg, ear, tail), then describes that part as the whole (it's like a wall, spear, snake, tree, fan, rope). The punch line: *Each was partly in the right, yet together they were all in the wrong!*[9] I have told this familiar story, or a version of it, countless times to enlighten, equip, and inspire leaders to reframe the different viewpoints within their organizations as opportunities to innovate. Rather than barriers to teamwork and unity, these alternate outlooks can become doorways to innovation and collective flow. The story of the blind men and the elephant points out how easy it is to make "the most fatal mistake . . . that if left unchecked . . . eventually results in corruption,"[10] not to mention the suspension, miscommunication, poor decisions, and declining business results or the down-arrow results in the WTL Flow Chart.

Of course, it's not enough to just acknowledge and express our differences. Neither is fighting about them. The challenge is to allow these differences to "interpenetrate" each other and forge a new, often third way forward. This cocreative process requires a particular mindset, a set of personal skills, and group or team disciplines. This consilient cocreative process of creating from our differences thrives on diversity, equity, and inclusion, and thus provides an ongoing organic, innovative process that creates a diverse, equitable, and inclusive culture.

The tricky part of the blind men's experience is each *was* right. Their individual perspectives were accurate. Yet from each perspective, the elephant was quite different. Each man's certainty in his individual perspective led to their dismissal of other points of view. The blind men succumbed to another fatal mistake, assuming their particular point of view was universal, that their piece was the whole.

This mindset feeds the silo mentality that keeps teams, units, and departments limited to uniformity around what they have in common, instead of joining the different pieces of the puzzle. As we shall see, a key mindset for creating from our differences is to remain aware that, although our perspective is valued and perhaps accurate, it is also only one portion of the whole picture. The blind men rightly valued their individual point of view and expressed it with justifiable conviction, yet each failed to be curious about the other interpretations of the elephant.

To address this dilemma, we need to bring a curious conviction (discussed in detail in Chapter 13). This occurs when curiosity kicks in about the whole picture *and* the other pieces that comprise the whole. Seeking knowledge of both the part and the whole simultaneously is another example of the jumping together of two seemingly opposite, conflicting or competing notions or energies. This comes into play, for example, when the department manager focuses on their department, their work, their success—and unwittingly disregards the importance of the whole. What use is a "leg like a pillar" that is cut off from the elephant?

One president of an international consulting firm envisioned an executive team of presidents (all with the title of senior vice president) who simultaneously attended to their own success *and* the success of the departments they managed as well as the entire company. In her wisdom, she was inviting the senior vice presidents to see the entire elephant even as they focused on one part. What's a tail without the body? How can an ear say I have no need of the rest? She was saying that as a senior vice president, each of you has a responsibility for the whole company as well as your part. She understood this integration as more than balancing separate equals but also harmonizing seemingly opposite interests in a mutually enhancing way.

Bringing, and inviting others to bring, a curious conviction leads to being able to name and recognize the implicit subtleties by which we can consistently create collective flow at will.

Great minds think differently. And, as illustrated by the story of the blind men and the elephant, each may be partly in the right, but together they are all in the wrong.

Reframing Differences

The following two examples tell of how we might reframe our differences creatively.

What If There Were a Third Way?

While writing this book, I interviewed a former president and CEO of a top-tier medical school. During our call, he expressed his concern about the rising interests of today's medical students to build social responsibility into their school curriculum. Dr. T worried that overloading the curriculum with social responsibility would dilute the foundation of medicine in science in an already demanding education experience. He recalled the days when, in addition to science, medical students were required to discover new patient relationship skills such as listening and empathy. He believed adding social responsibility to the curriculum would be too burdensome, and jeopardize equipping a physician for their already daunting task.

After reflecting back his perspective and concerns, I posed the question, "What if, from your differences with the students, it wasn't either your way or their way, but that a third way could be created?" After what seemed like a long pause his agitated tone shifted to a *hmmmm* . . . Then he said, "Learning to be more empathic with patients made me a better physician, so maybe becoming more socially responsible could do that too." Just suggesting a possible third way shifted his judgment and certainty to curiosity. Hmmm . . . what might that look like. Here begins the fundamental cocreative process of life.

Inviting Conversation

As another example, in 2016 the start of a football game became the focus of a debate ignited by the decision of Colin

Kaepernick, quarterback for the San Francisco 49ers, to kneel during the national anthem as a protest against social injustice following the death of another black person at the hands of a police officer. In response, another quarterback, Drew Brees of the New Orleans Saints, said that he "will never agree with anybody disrespecting the flag of the United States of America." In a huge backlash, many major professional athletes denounced Brees's statement. A more nuanced reply came from Tony Dungy, a black NFL Hall of Fame coach, who said he didn't "downgrade Drew for that" because "he may not totally understand."

Dungy went on, "It may have been not exactly the way he wanted to express it, but he can't be afraid to say that, and we can't be afraid to say, 'OK Drew, I don't agree with you, but let's sit down and talk about it.'" He held out the possibility of misunderstanding and called for a conversation. By evoking Brees's right to express himself and for others to have a different point of view, Dungy pointed out that we can't be afraid of our differences. He didn't downplay or outright dismiss them, but acknowledged the importance of each party to express themselves before inviting others to welcome those differences as an opportunity to have a conversation. Bringing one's perspective and conviction, without the need to convince the other or "win" the conversation, coupled with sincerely listening to understand and not judge, builds trust, if not agreement. Doing so always holds the promise of finding a third way, which might be as simple as everyone understanding and respecting players kneeling with their heads down and standing with hands on their hearts as diverse, yet valid, expressions of the shared value of freedom.

That's our path forward: making a difference through our differences.

Structure and Flow

Leadership is about harmonizing structure and energy for ourselves, our teams, and our organizations. Imagine, if you would, a helicopter view of a flowing river. If the banks of the river disappeared, there would be a flood. If the water suddenly dried up, we would have a ditch. The flow of the river requires both the water and the banks simultaneously. As with a river, collective human flow requires both the structure of the banks and the energetic flow of the water. Today's traditional leader–followers organizational hierarchy with an emphasis on a fixed structure can easily become dried-up ditches. At the same time, the emerging leading–leaders nonhierarchical or egalitarian organizational structures—such as agile organizations, holocracies (organizations with no assigned roles where employees move between teams and tasks), and networked organizations with cross-functional teams—can fall prey to a lack of structure. This can result in the flood damage of no accountability or the sheer chaos of too many chefs in the kitchen.

For example, an industry-leading company recognized the need to reinvent itself with more innovation. To spark creativity, they created egalitarian project teams, teams of equals with no formal leader. Many of these teams were highly successful, but several floundered. Although the egalitarian approach ignited creativity, it lacked the disciplined structure for accountability when projects went south. To remedy this problem, individual leaders were appointed for each team. However, it became obvious that the accountable leaders tended to steer the conversations to their own predetermined outcome, thereby squelching the generative creativity of the groups. The egalitarian approach resulted in a flood with no accountability and the new single-leader structure resulted in a ditch of dried-up creativity.

To ensure continual and contagious group flow requires a leadership process based upon leading and following and doing both at the same time or in the same action. Simultaneously leading and following harmonizes structure and energy. Harmonizing goes beyond the neutrality of balance to a mutual enhancing dynamic where energy strengthens structure and structure expands energy. In other words, harmonizing is not only about a relationship of equal weight, but a balance that intermingles in a way that is mutually enhancing. We accomplish this because the radical mutuality of everyone leading and following in the same action creates a perpetual energy of trust that is harmonized with a structured decision-making model.

In coming chapters, we will see that this decision-making model accesses collective intelligence and commitment in a manner that mutually enhances the individual authority of any formal or designated leader. Harmonizing structure and energy creates conditions for consistent collective flow, constructively channeling an abundance of energy and creativity via a structured decision-making process. In our analogy, the abundance of energy provides the water and the structured decision-making model the banks, so that the team and organizational river can perpetually flow.

As evolutionary biologist Edward O. Wilson once said, "A consilient conversation is the fastest way across the communal mind." Two significant examples of the positive results of consilient conversations are Unilever and Salesforce:

In 2018, under former CEO Paul Polman's tutelage, Unilever's 28 Sustainable Living Brands grew 69% faster than the rest of the business and delivered 75% of the company's growth. Meanwhile, the company reduced waste 96%, CO_2 emissions 65%, and water extraction 47% per metric of production since 2008.

Salesforce has achieved great returns for shareholders *and* stakeholders. It is a net-zero company because Salesforce views the planet as a stakeholder. It adopted 170 public schools, pays men and women equally for equal work, and has given away $300 million as part of its stakeholder return. And the company married all of that with having returned 4,000% to its shareholders since 2004.[11]

Here are two examples of companies overcoming the tyranny of people or profit and planet or profit by embracing the genius of each. Business thrives when it aligns with the creative impulse of life itself by marrying the differences, or seemingly opposite interests. We the Leader applies this both/and genius to leading. Without a "me" there would be no we, which leads to our next part, "Me the Leader."

PART II

The Diversifier

Me the Leader

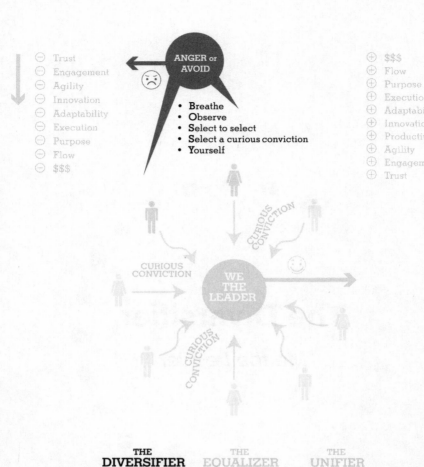

ANGER or AVOID

- Breathe
- Observe
- Select to select
- Select a curious conviction
- Yourself

⊖ Trust	⊕ $$$
⊖ Engagement	⊕ Flow
⊖ Agility	⊕ Purpose
⊖ Innovation	⊕ Execution
⊖ Adaptability	⊕ Adaptability
⊖ Execution	⊕ Innovation
⊖ Purpose	⊕ Productivity
⊖ Flow	⊕ Agility
⊖ $$$	⊕ Engagement
	⊕ Trust

CURIOUS CONVICTION

WE THE LEADER

THE **DIVERSIFIER** ME THE LEADER

THE EQUALIZER COMMON PURPOSE

THE UNIFIER WE THE LEADER

3 Pillars for Innovation Flow

+ The Innovator **Consilience** −

CHAPTER 5

Only You Can Lead You

Traveler, there is no path, the path is made by walking . . .
—ANTONIO MACHADO
"Traveler, There Is No Path," *Border of a Dream: Selected Poems*

Gravity Payments is a credit card processing and financial services company based in Seattle, Washington. In 2014, Haley Vogt, marketing coordinator, fought to promote the company and its cofounder and CEO Dan Cox by nominating him for *Entrepreneur* magazine's Entrepreneur of the Year Award. A week later, she received notice that Dan had been selected as one of the top ten finalists. She was then asked to submit an essay about why Dan deserved the award. Hayley dashed it off. Dan made the cut, one of five. Next step was to submit a video—in fewer than five business days! At this point, Haley approached her boss, who then approached Dan. Both told her to end her efforts, feeling it would take too much of her time and focus. But Haley persisted. They could create the video in-house, she told them, at little cost. That video received nearly ten times the views than those of the other finalists, Dan won, and the buzz from that win provided Gravity with a level of exposure they never imagined.

About a year later, Haley's boss shared with her why he eventually okayed the video. "He thought it'd teach me a lesson about failure and prioritizing my time," she said. "He ended with, 'I'm glad you didn't listen to me.'"

When I heard this story, my first thought was *Who is leading whom?*

When we lead our own lives—and meet, interact, work, and live with other people who are leading their own lives—the paradigm of leadership shifts from the idea of leaders leading *followers* to that of leaders leading *leaders.*

Given the discoveries of neuroscience and concurrent skill building, we no longer have to live as victims of our own hardwiring. Instead, we can lead our own lives by developing skills and practices that create the space and will for fresh and conscious choices, moment by moment. These new ways of thinking and being in turn carve new neural pathways, breaking through our brain's resistance to veering off the safe, proven way we've always done things. By changing our thoughts and actions, we create a new way of doing and being. We're leading our own lives.

As an increasing number of people assume leadership of their lives, we as a species contribute to the further evolution of the human brain. This occurs in part by further developing the corpus callosum, the band of nerve fibers connecting the brain's left and right hemispheres, which aids information processing, among other functions. At the same time, thinking and acting in a new way contributes to the evolution of panarchy, where increasing numbers of people more consistently show up as leaders.

In general, the complexity and speed of today's workplace requires leaders to collaborate across an organization. Companies like Capital Group call these groups "pods." Others call them "cross-functional teams." Encova, as we see in Chapter 15, structured integrated teams—or teams of leaders—alongside or parallel to the hierarchy. In this way, formal leaders have the traditional responsibility to lead followers in the hierarchy *and* the responsibility to lead leaders in their ongoing designated integrated teams. Some pinpoint the beginning of this movement to Elon Musk's and Steve Jobs's calls for the elimination of silos. No matter whose idea, these are examples of leaders leading each other.

Leadership and the Brain

Let's step back for a moment to get a wider view of the evolution of leadership from monarchy to hierarchy, and, finally, to what I am setting forth, panarchy (the rule of all). The assumption informing monarchy (one ruler) is that only one person can lead, historically because of divine right. With the increasingly complex world and the resulting evolution of society, it became obvious that more than one person or family can lead, which led to the rise of hierarchies (some rule over others). Today, an avalanche of neuroscientific information reveals that everyone can develop their executive function and capacity to respond instead of react, which leads to the conclusion that "everyone can learn to lead."[1] It follows that if everyone can learn to be a leader, then by identifying oneself as a leader, if not acting like one, everyone has leadership potential.

Much of our lives are lived from the autopilot of the brain depicted in the WTL Flow Chart (a version of which appears at the beginning of Part II) by the reactionary bubble (Anger or Avoid), which has resulted in unproductive, and eventually destructive, behavior depicted by the down arrow. As Tara Swart, the author of *The Source: The Secrets of the Universe, the Science of the Brain*, writes, "We don't question where these underlying entrenched habits come from and whether they serve us any longer; we switch off and let life happen to us, assuming that much of it is out of our control. But every single thing that we do reinforces a pattern or pathway and consolidates our autopilot behaviors. In doing so, the underlying concept that things are just the way they are convinces us more than ever that life happens to us and we are to a large extent powerless to control it. However, neuroscience shows us that we can take back control of our minds by rewiring our brain's pathways to make lasting, positive changes to our lives."[2]

These scientific conclusions and assumptions show how the question isn't *if* someone is a leader but what *kind* of leader that person will become. Every leader has the option to allow their lives to be led from reactive energy (the down arrow in Figure 3.1) or responsive proactive energy (the up arrow). According to neuroscience, each of us has the capacity to choose between reactive and proactive leadership and their subsequent results. Research published in the *Harvard Business Review* revealed the average CEO spends 36 percent of their time leading reactively or in response to external circumstances, including others' behavior.[3] As author Carol Dweck points out, traditional organizations are designed to run on the reactive, or fear, since they are structured so that leaders lead with power over others and the subsequent fear that follows. To build and lead agile organizations, however, leaders must make a personal shift to run primarily "in the creative."[4]

A long time ago, our brains consisted largely of the limbic brain—the primordial, emotional, deeply intuitive part of the brain—surrounded by a thin sliver of outer cortex. As the brain evolved, humans developed the prefrontal cortex, which has since grown larger. The prefrontal cortex rules logic and creativity. It helps us analyze and interpret our experiences, take risks, and work toward a goal, all of which involve higher-level thinking, or executive function. As Tara Swart writes, "Being able to consider opposing views in our mind and come up with new solutions and responses is one of the highest functions of an optimized brain. We can all learn to do this. . . ."[5]

In Chapter 4, I introduced the idea of how leaders considering opposite views discover something new with *consilience*, "the jumping together" of seemingly opposite energies. Here, we expand the application of opposing energies for innovation, moving from differing perspectives to include two seemingly different actions: (1) leading, or going before, and (2) following, or going after. Here, we apply consilience with the jumping together of opposing perspectives and the jumping together of seemingly opposing energies of leading and following. As we saw in our discussion of aerodynamics, flight takes two dimensions of opposition; in the case of consilience, it is opposing perspectives and opposing actions occurring at the same time to create and sustain collective flow. By practicing this level of consilience, we can carve new neural pathways, which can optimize our brain.

Tara Swart goes on to say, "We can forge fresh ways of thinking, strengthen our higher-level 'executive' brain functions (complex decision-making, problem-solving, planning, self-reflection), and learn to master our fright–fight–flight primal brain responses."[6] When we react with fright–fight–flight reactions, we are not leading our own lives, but rather allowing ourselves to be led by external circumstances, including the behaviors of others. (In Chapter 8, I introduce proven exercises for shifting our reactive, destructive, down-arrow energy to proactive, creative, up-arrow energy. This activates our ability to respond, or response ability, to lead our own lives and contribute our part in creating consistent collective flow, of which consilience is the foundation.)

We're All Wired to Lead

We used to believe that our brain stopped growing when we did—no new neurons, our character hard coded, our potential set in stone. However, modern neuroscience and the advent of brain scanners proved this idea false. Before the invention of the computerized axial tomography (CT) scan in 1972,[7] brain scientists were only able to study and learn about the brain from autopsies.[8] While learning from a dysfunctional system or body part can provide some knowledge, it has its limits. For example, it was believed that the brain of adults over twenty-five years old didn't change or grow.[9]

Theoretically, then, all of us over the age of twenty-five would have had an excuse to be stuck in our old ways— insisting, "We have always done it this way," and "That's just the way I'm wired"—to resist change or justify habits. Today, neuroscientific studies show that our brains are far more malleable than we thought. This neuroplasticity means that we can change how we think and how we behave. In other words, we can rewire our brains to re-create and lead our lives.

When I first presented the idea of leading leaders and assuming that everyone is a leader during conversations with prospective clients, teams with whom I worked, and HR executives, the objections flew. I remember a presentation to a renowned company in the financial industry in the early 2000s, which someone from HR Leadership and Development came to observe. "But not everybody is a leader," he said. "Some people just want to follow, and we need that. Everyone can't be a leader." Interestingly, that objection never came up within the teams themselves. They all saw themselves as leaders, in part because their former leader saw them not just as leaders, but as stars who went on to be the team everyone wanted to work with or emulate and that redefined the industry. This is rare. Typically, formal leaders are threatened by at least one member of their team, especially when teams are as talented as this one.

At Encova, during the transformation to integrated teams, they emphasized the idea that everyone is a leader. During this time, a woman approached the CEO in the lunchroom and told him straight up, "I don't want to be a leader here. I just want to do my job and go home." Dave, the CEO, could have responded, "Well, I appreciate your telling me, and I just want to note that you're leading your own life by telling me what you think and desire, and I hope you continue to lead in this way." Instead, he said, "We value your role here and invite you to see yourself more as a leader as it works for you."

However, with the rise of neuroscience and the capacity to measure change in the brain, it has been repeatedly shown that—with particular techniques and persistence—adults *can* really change their minds and subsequently lead their lives. We just have to work at it. "Our brains actively grow and change during childhood," notes Swart. "In contrast, as adults, we have to *consciously* direct ourselves to grow and develop as people. Quite how much we can use the inherent flexibility of the brain to enhance our experience of life is actually mind-blowing."[10]

An example: A senior vice president of a company respected in their industry got to where he was because of his success in sales and ability to translate his undying belief in the company's service and industry stature into a compelling and convincing narrative. This skill to persuade was his sweet spot. Now, in the context of a diverse team of leaders across the organization, he was being asked to build upon his expertise by practicing consilience, bringing his knowing convictions and his unknowing curiosity to the group at the same time.

When I received his (unscheduled) call at 2 p.m. one afternoon, he was frustrated by his inability to communicate with his teammates in operations. They told him to stop trying to "sell" them. This was particularly challenging since his prior success was predicated on convincing people. He was exasperated and really struggling. This was a crucial learning moment. As we talked about the different contexts from sales to peer leaders, I could sense neurons carving new pathways in his brain as he had the *aha* moment: "Oh, okay, I can bring my convincing conviction *and* let it go. I don't have to give up my convincing energy, belief, and passion, but I just need to let go of the result or any predetermined outcome." A silence followed and I could almost feel his sigh of relief as he said, "I can do that." His team went on to introduce a new service that increased sales tremendously and redefined the entire industry to this day.

Being on a team or in an organization where there is a shared process and language for leading oneself and each other as leader–followers goes a long way to more quickly developing and then sustaining the creation of new habits that open new neural pathways. It's very exciting to see people who are less developed in these areas jump forward as this senior vice president did.

We Are All Leaders

In making our case for the need for panarchical leadership, we have established that, for better or worse, everyone is a leader of their own life. In addition, increasingly, more leaders are showing up in organizations. This is the case for multiple reasons, including that millennials arrive ready to lead.[11] In addition, the complexity of today's work requires expert leaders in various fields (such as legal, marketing, IT, human resources, operations, etc.) to gather and lead each other in cross-functional teams or pods. Add to this the knowledge that neuroscience has proven that we can lead our own lives by developing new neural pathways in our brain by directing the way we think and feel in a manner that changes our behavior and builds new habits. All of us are designed to lead our own lives, to learn and activate the executive functions of a leader, and to lead each other. Panarchy is here!

In her book *The Neuroscience of Leadership*, Tara Swart writes, "What we know now about the brain's ability to change itself is that, within limits, you can change yourself; that is, you can learn to be a leader—at all levels, as a self-authoring person, through focused attention and practice. This is good news for both organizations and leaders, because it means that leadership qualities and capabilities can be learned and improved though experience together with training and development."[12]

Being able to consider opposing views in our mind and come up with new solutions and responses is one of the highest functions of an optimized brain. This evolved capacity to make a difference through our differences mirrors consilience and serves as the energetic foundation of our WTL Flow Chart.

For me, the capacity to quantify new neural pathways in the brain, those that strongly influence how we respond in the moment and create our future, is exhilarating! No wonder the book *Neuroscience of Leadership* declares that everyone can learn leadership. Not only are we all CEOs of our own lives, but according to neuroscience, we all have the capacity to be CEOs in the fullest sense of the word by developing our own innate capacity to do so. This assertion means that everyone is at least a leader in waiting. As illustrated in Figure 3.1, the quantifiable research showing that everyone has the potential to lead themselves from the reactive results of the down arrow into the creative results of the up arrow is so very hopeful and exciting. It stands in contrast to being relegated as followers of a few leaders in the hierarchy of most organizations and institutions of today.

You can create and evolve your brain, so you can create *your* world. That's because you always have the choice to reframe your world as an opportunity to grow and contribute to the experiment of being human instead of a victim. Wow! The bad news is I, like most people, sometimes create what I do not prefer about my life. The good news is if I created it, I can *re*-create it.

From the perspective of neuroscience, everyone at least has the potential to learn to be a leader—every human being has the capacity to lead. Organizations can be regarded as gardens, planted in the belief that if given the right environment the seeds (people) will naturally blossom into their full selves. While on one level the seeds are already who they are, they still need to be seen, nurtured, and harvested. You know where I am going with this. The same is true for leaders. As gardeners, leaders first need to believe that the members of their team or organization are leaders, capable of leading their own lives with the ability to respond and not just react to life's circumstances. They also need to believe that these potent leaders can lead each other. This requires believing in oneself as well as others, so that nurturing and growing leaders does not end up in the clash of egos or the proverbial too many chefs in the kitchen.

If these chefs work together—one on each course, for example—their collaboration could result in collective flow and the field of exponential potential. This involves a belief that panarchy (all leaders) doesn't need to result in anarchy (the experience of no rule and sheer chaos). As mentioned earlier, one of my first clients, Steve, set the stage for our work together by believing, feeling, and seeing his team not just as potential leaders, but as stars. His vision was to create an environment for these stars to interact as a constellation of stars that impacted the galaxy and, while becoming one, each star shone brighter than it ever could have on its own. Being a huge Mohammed Ali fan, Steve was delighted to hear of his poem "ME / WE." That's the poem in its entirety, not just the title. If you look at it "upside down" the ME becomes WE, and the WE becomes ME, illustrating the harmony and unity of the individual and collective interests. That's the magic of the WEME.

In summary, it is clear that, as proved by neuroscience, we all have at least the capacity to lead—and to not just lead, but to lead at the highest level. Having this capacity doesn't mean that we will exercise it or exercise it in an optimal way. In our next chapter, I look at the dynamic of leading our own lives through conscious choice. Each one of us is unique. As we shall see, leading ourselves as unique leaders has broad implications for the traditional practice of leading followers.

CHAPTER 6

Leading the Leader that Is You

Your time is limited. Don't waste it living someone else's life. Don't be trapped by dogma, which is living the result of other people's thinking. Don't let the noise of another's opinion drown your inner voice.

—STEVE JOBS
cofounder, Apple Inc.

We lead our lives through conscious or unconscious choices. By choosing to remain unconscious to our inner states—how we think, feel, perceive, react, our buttons, biases, what drives us, what shuts us down—we choose to allow ourselves to become unduly influenced by external controls from the media, authorities, institutions, and leaders, leading to diluted, if not toxic, thinking and subsequent lame, if not destructive, decisions.

Why is being self-aware so important? Our inner states inform our decisions. If I'm unaware of my inner state—that I might be tired and stressed and need to back away from the keyboard for a few minutes—the next thing I know I'm responding to what feels urgent rather than what is actually important. Leading is not about a position but a state of mind. When we are unaware of the impact of internal storms on our inner state of feeling and thinking, we become unmoored from our true unique selves.

You: The Never-Before-Never-Again Leader

Tara Swart distills the functions of the four lobes of the cerebral cortex this way: "Broadly, there are visual, auditory, and even language centers and more in the brain but all functions rely on complex networks to fire simultaneously and, like a fingerprint, the maps in each of our brains for all functions will be unique and dynamic."[1] She concludes with this: "No wonder human beings are difficult to manage!"[2]

Let's extract the concept of unique. Obviously, our brains are similar in many ways. At the same time, each brain originated from the unique genetic makeup of each human being. So, although brains look and are similar on many levels, in its DNA each brain is different. Furthermore, we shape our brains through our own set of unique experiences and relationships with people in our families, community, and network.

These unique sets of people with their own individual and collective experiences—like my collective flow experience on the athletic field—ignite a varied, complex, and, yes, unique set of functions that create distinctive neural pathways. Ultimately, these pathways create unique maps within our brains, each map containing a variety ways to get to the same or different place. What's more, even when we use a common language or a common word, it's open to a variety of meanings depending upon which definition of the word is in play and the varied contexts in which the same word is used. And let's not forget that the context itself is unique. Why? Because, unlike in the movie *Groundhog Day*, every moment is new and different on multiple levels. Are you, like me, getting a sense of the fascinating and intriguing value of the uniqueness of everyone's perspective, experience, thinking, feelings, and desires in every moment? WOW!

If we use the prevailing definition of a leader (one who has followers who go where the leader goes, takes the position of the leader, or conforms to the leader), it is easy to unwittingly forget or overlook the value of the utter uniqueness of each human being in every moment. Instead of engaging in the exhilaration of the evolutionary impulse of life, which is to be creative with others or to create together, it is easy to succumb to following our reactivity with anger or avoidance or the (sometimes subtle) addiction of leading with power over others as in faux collaboration.

What if instead we had an explicit and prevailing definition of leading that named everyone as the unique, never-before-never-again leader that they are? If we engaged not in the repetitive grind of work in a typical hierarchy, but in seeing the new, full-of-potential leader in every now moment? What would that be like? Would Monday become the favorite day of the week? Would company after company be able to innovate on the scale of huge discoveries every month? Instead of musing, "No wonder human beings are difficult to manage!" we could be exclaiming with the greatest champion of the twentieth century, Bill Russell, how the physical and mental becomes the magical of collective flow.

Neuroscience has proven that this is not a pipe dream. We can all become the leaders we are. By living in accordance with what neuroscience tells us, that each one of us has a unique brain that defines each of us as capable of being a leader in the fullest sense of the word, we can learn—and consistently choose to experience—the magic of collective flow. Just as our brain comingles the activities of the right brain and left brain, we can all become leader–followers. As I have documented, collective flow already happens; our task is to make explicit what sometimes happens implicitly. Thus, collective flow can become the norm rather than the exception, and then the constant rather than the norm. This is all very doable, *if* we develop new neuropathways by expanding our definition and vision of leadership and then expand these roadways with new skills that, repeated, become habits ingrained within our individual lives and organizational cultures.

Only You Can Lead You

Since you are totally unique there is no set path to leadership. You create your own journey by leading yourself, by listening and following your inner voice. No one else can feel your feelings, possess your distinctive passion, make choices for you, know—and then act on—your purpose.

Others can guide and inspire you by leading their unique selves, but only you can lead you.

Just as only we can lead our own lives, we cannot lead another person's life. Only they can do that. It then follows that leaders cannot lead others, only others can lead themselves. This reality contradicts leadership in the strict or literal sense of the word—going before to create a path for others to follow.

Put another way, everyone is a leader of their own lives. Leaders can lead teams, projects, or organizations, but not other people: only they can lead themselves. As Jack Welch said, "If you don't lead your life someone else will." You are a leader. You have the power to lead your own life. This is an inspiring affirmation and a scientific principle. The question isn't *are* we leaders, but *how* are we going to lead? As discussed, we create or lead our own lives either by choosing, however unconsciously, to live from our reactivity or to exercise our response ability to express our authentic true selves. We lead ourselves to the downward spiral of fear or the upward spiral of freedom. In each moment we have a choice. Do we lead from our reactivity or do we lead from our ability to respond and create?

The foundation of leading is not a role or set of particular traits, but a choice, one we can select over and over to create our own reality. (See "My Hardest Truth" in Chapter 7, "BOSS Yourself.") This perspective lies in sharp contrast to being victims of our fate, unable to choose a new path. When holding a victim identity it is easy to look externally for someone else to lead, heal, or save us rather than to develop the practice of leading ourselves. Looking outside for someone to follow is different from clearing our own unique and unknown path forward, being pioneers of our own lives, and leading ourselves.

The Act of Following

To lead more of our own lives requires that we become increasingly aware of what we perceive, feel, think, and desire and then to choose to express ourselves. No one else can really tell you what you think, feel, see, and desire. No one else can lead your life but you. Others might guess, or dictate, but only you are truly capable of knowing and leading the authentic you. In the traditional hierarchy, a follower typically prioritizes knowing what the leader observes, feels, thinks, and desires so that they can follow the leader by acquiring those very same characteristics. This, as we now know, isn't necessary.

Certainly, we can learn a lot from, and be influenced by, others, and we may even feel we totally agree with them. Doing so *consciously* can enhance our self-leadership. This is not the same as following or conforming to another and abdicating our own responsibility to become ourselves. What's the difference? The role of following.

Whether we are leading or following, we are leaders. Let me explain. One way we lead our lives is to, often unconsciously, choose to react to external stimuli such as circumstances and other people's actions (indicated by the down-arrow in the WTL Flow Chart, see Figure 3.1.

In the last chapter, we discussed how neuroscience makes victimhood obsolete because we can all learn to become leaders. Neuroscience also makes leadership founded on leading followers obsolete. Not because no one follows, but because, as leaders of our own lives, we follow our own inner guidance and dreams, and, as leaders of an organization, we are all followers of a common purpose.

The militaristic organization model of fighting a war—whether in the battlefield, in the marketplace, or an internal war of words—is no longer adequate. What's emerging are organizations full of leaders forging a future together. Systems scientist Peter Senge defines these "learning organizations" as "organizations where people continually expand their capacity to create the results they truly desire, where new and expansive patterns of thinking are nurtured, where collective aspiration is set free, and where people are continually learning to see the whole together."[3]

In such organizations, there is a place for formal authority, but only as the exercise of this authority provides the needed structure for collective flow. Here, the purpose of the formal authority is not to control but to facilitate collective flow. For example, there are times, if timely decisions aren't made, the creative flow of the group can be disrupted because the group remains stuck or misses a window of opportunity.

I realize that the dangers and constraints of victimhood are not new to many of you. What I am saying is that the tentacles of victimhood still stretch into our most basic understanding of a leader as one who has or possesses followers; just look at the language used on some social media platforms, such as Instagram, Twitter, and Facebook, and contrast it with LinkedIn, which uses "connections." As we have seen, a follower goes where the leader goes, takes the position of a leader, conforms to the leader without checking in internally. To take such a follower position is to abdicate our own responsibility to lead our lives, to forgo our unique being and doing as a partner in the human enterprise. For example, if all we do is sit and wait to be told what to do and how to do it, how can we partner in new concepts and ideas? It's one thing to learn from others. It's another to follow others. Learning from others expands us, while conforming constrains us from recognizing and actualizing our individual and collective freedom and creativity. As I've heard from women clients, after being encouraged to be less passive by offering their perspectives and "speaking their minds," they receive 360° feedback about being too "aggressive." Damned if you do. Damned if you don't.

In contrast, in the partnership model of a learning organization we have a community of leaders learning as they teach and teaching as they learn, leading as they follow, and following as they lead.

What do I mean? Our model and definition of a leader as one who has followers is still rooted in the antiquated science that our brains don't change after twenty-five years of age. This belief has been the justification of the idea that smarter people must lead. This makes some sense on one level, but the so-called smarter people that lead are usually white males, often confined by a logical intelligence and similar educational experiences in MBA programs. This builds a homogenous pool of leaders that infringes upon the diversity and equity needed for today's innovation, not to mention the dignity, uniqueness, and respect of each human being.

We lead ourselves into our future reality (down or up arrows in Figure 3.1) by the way we choose to think and feel, often unconsciously. However, we always have the power to choose our way or to lead ourselves. We can exercise our choice in learning environments, attempting to be a catalyst for change within the organization. Serving as a catalyst can take the form of making changes within your own team. One of my early clients did just that. Soon other teams wanted what they were having. As a result, top talent wanted to be on her teams. If you don't have your own team, look for learning teams that you might be part of. If no such teams exist, do as many millennials do: find a new work environment where you can experience diversity, equity, and inclusion. In so doing we create new neuropathways and actually change our brains and the thinking and feeling that creates our future.

Now is the time to extract victimhood from our current understanding and practice of leadership. Let's replace it with an evolved vision and practice founded on leading ourselves then leading each other—by leading and following in the same action.

Earlier, I described panarchical leadership by pointing out the rise of leaders in today's organizations. Whether its millennials showing up as leaders or, given the spiraling complexity of today's world, leaders gathering from across the organization, leaders are on the rise. However, just because one is a leader doesn't mean she or he acts like it. Acting like a leader begins with leading one's own life. This opportunity is available to everyone, and as humanity evolves more and more of us are courageously deciding to lead our own lives. This movement is often expressed as living one's passion or being authentic. Bringing one's full humanity to work also increases the presence of leaders in today's organizations.

Steve was overwhelmingly successful in retirement sales and caught the attention of the powers that be. Eventually, they invited him to head up the retirement plan sector for a renowned financial company. From the get-go, in our very first conversation about his team, he described them as leaders and stars. This wasn't because the members of his team had proven themselves to be stars—competent and capable yes, but not proven stars. Steve's wide eyes and impassioned tone revealed his belief in his teammates.

Today's environment increasingly requires leaders with different expertise convening to form a cross-functional team or pod. According to research documented in the *Harvard Business Review*, 75 percent of these teams are dysfunctional.[4] Unlike Steve, many of those at the top of these leaderful teams fail to see them as a group of leaders, let alone stars in their own right. They fail to understand the changing context from hierarchy to panarchy. As we shall see, in this emerging context, in order to avoid the "too many chefs in the kitchen" mess, leaders also need to be followers, simultaneously.

In the emerging age of panarchy, where increasingly more people step up to lead, it is imperative for leaders of leaders to learn an explicit and repeatable process for leading their own lives. The practice of leading your own life is foundational to leading leaders and the experience of collective flow.

As leaders lead from their own center to the center of the team or group (depicted by the straight and squiggly lines on the We the Leader Flow Chart), they access the flow of energy between and beyond the collective. This results in leading not just from the bottom up or the top down, but collectively leading from the center out. The practice of leading your own life is to BOSS Yourself:

B-reathe

O-bserve

S-elect to select (make a conscious choice to choose)

S-elect (choose)

BOSSing Yourself becomes even more crucial in the context of collective flow.

It requires everyone, or at least a strong critical mass of leaders, to simultaneously lead their own lives and access that experience in order to be lifted and guided by an energy beyond the sum of their individual parts. Previously, I highlighted the pitfalls of following. Now I will introduce the practice for leading your own life, which is a crucial pillar for consistently accessing the collective flow of We the Leader.

CHAPTER 7

BOSS Yourself

*There is no such thing as destiny. We
ourselves shape our lives.*
—GIACOMO CASANOVA

This new way of leading yourself, or BOSSing yourself, is
grounded in becoming the leaders that we are. Becoming this leader, and expressing the qualities of self-leadership, contributes to the evolution of panarchy. The components of self-leadership are the same as those found in the qualities of emotional intelligence, also known as emotional quotient (EQ). Studies show that while few corporate leaders possess a strong EQ, this form of intelligence in leaders contributes to the job satisfaction of everyone in the organization, boosts productivity, and positively impacts the bottom line. Those with high EQs know themselves, their teams, and their customers much better than those who don't have it.

I see EQ as the capacity to know oneself and others and to transmute one's e-motions (energy in motion) to energy that moves conversations, meetings, teams, projects, and organizations forward. For example, you might experience frustration or anger when the team flat out rejects your proposal. You have the choice to transmute those emotions into positive action or curiosity. In every moment, we can choose how to react to our emotions. At times, because we're trapped or controlled by our emotions, we unwittingly, or unconsciously, react with anger or avoidance.

Bossing yourself begins with coaching yourself by raising your self-awareness. You do this by consistently asking and journaling your responses.

Four Questions for Leading Yourself

Studies show that self-awareness increases confidence and creativity,[1] contributes to better decision-making,[2] relationship building,[3] effective communication, and employee satisfaction.[4] And, according to a Korn Ferry study, companies that have employees with high levels of self-awareness do better financially.[5]

Yet despite all the benefits of being self-aware, few truly understand what it means. A recent large-scale scientific study that included ten separate investigations with nearly 5,000 participants indicated that 85 to 90 percent of professional participants are *not* self-aware, although most believed themselves to be.[6]

So how do we increase self-awareness? Periodically, particularly when facing a challenging situation, ask yourself and respond to the follow questions to increase your awareness or the capacity for being the leader of your own life. The most effective way to practice this exercise is to journal your responses and process them with a colleague or coach familiar with this methodology.

1. What am I observing externally then internally?
2. What emotions do I notice inside myself?
3. What thinking, assumptions, and interpretations accompany and feed these emotions?
4. What do you desire? What choices are you ready to make?

Often when asking yourself these questions, the temperature of your reaction lowers significantly and you can avoid flight, fight, or freeze reactions and respond efficiently and effectively. I will discuss these four questions in greater detail in the next chapter.

Observe Rather than Obey Your Emotions

I am writing this chapter as we just began year two of the COVID-19 pandemic, and I have noticed that in this time of upheaval I'm feeling more fear than I have for a long time. For example, I recently bought a new car and decided to take it for a drive the next morning, at around 9:30 a.m. Usually at that time, the traffic is crazy. But the streets were empty. The air damp, chilly. As I drove down Chicago's Magnificent Mile, I saw store after store—for some reason the Gucci store is the only one I can remember—all closed, new sheets of plywood nailed over their picture windows. I gasped, felt a shortness of breath, fear rising, and a pressing down or depression all at once. When I returned home, I turned on the news. Riots had broken out across the city. "We've never seen anything like this," the newscaster reported, referring to the riots, the ghost stores, the absence of life, and then the camera panned across boarded-up shops along the Magnificent Mile, exactly where I'd just been—no cars, no people, just silence. And in that silence, a lone coyote trod down the middle of the deserted street. Shocked, I felt the fear swelling up; my chest was burning. It felt like the coyote was taking over. A sense of hopelessness settled in. Would we ever get out of this? I've never felt like that before.

My natural reaction is to judge this external experience of fear—which isn't necessarily mine but latches onto me—as negative. However, now I'm beginning to understand the gift of experiencing fear. There are two expressions of fear. The fear we feel and experience and the fear we bury without ever explicitly experiencing it. This unconscious fear is stored as pain bodies, or fear bodies, that we are not aware of. Eckhart Tolle, who coined the term "pain bodies," describes them as "the human tendency to perpetuate old emotion," which is accumulated in our "energy field."[7] These unrecognized fear storage units draw energy from our bodies, without our realizing it, like unrecognized apps on our phone. As a result, we start to dim rather than shine. If these are unaddressed, we end up checking out. When we feel and experience fear, we unwittingly tap into one of these pain bodies, or storage units, and often experience a fear beyond what the circumstances call for.

You can transmute fear the same way you transmute negative emotions by closing the energy-draining fear app by naming, feeling, and breathing into the fear. Releasing fear stops the energy-draining fear app and opens up space for more observation and less judgment, much of it fed by fear. We can then authentically welcome and be thankful for the feeling and experience of fear, or as Rumi says in his poem "The Guesthouse," when referring to feelings, "welcome and entertain them all for they clear me out for a new delight."[8] One of my mantras is "Fear is fuel for firing me forward."

The Hardest Truth: Recognizing Your Own Complicity

When I was at an emotional all time low—my marriage was breaking apart, I couldn't see my daughters as often as I would have liked—someone said, "You created your situation." Internally I screamed, *No, I did NOT! I did not create this situation. No f**king way.* My inner rage illustrates author Neville Goddard's statement: "Man's chief delusion is his belief that there are causes other than his own state of consciousness,"[9] which I sometimes believe and sometimes don't. Consciousness means our own inner awareness of our observations, feelings (e-motions), thoughts (including assumptions), and desires.

Here's an example. Recently, in a CEO coaching session, the ongoing mediocre performance of a sales executive came up. It had been mentioned before.

"What are you observing?" I asked the CEO.

"Well," he said, "Bill equates playing golf and building a relationship with getting the job done, even when missing his numbers. That's not getting the job done."

"Have you had a direct conversation with him about this?" I asked.

"No."

"Why not?"

"Hmm . . . the chair of the board wants to keep him."

With just a few questions to help build his awareness of himself and the situation, the problem became the CEO's. Certainly, that in itself doesn't fix the problem, but it shifts it to being *his* problem, something he has control over. Without becoming aware of owning his ability to respond or his responsibility, he could never solve the problem.

As I look back, I see how I contributed to my situation. It wasn't only the other people. I can see that I chose this situation on a subconscious level to let go of things—thinking, emotions, worldviews, and assumptions—that were holding me back. In letting go, I experienced more of the person I really am, and was able to lead myself more effectively. If I hadn't created the situation I was in, or felt it, or willed it on some level, all I could do was blame others and play the victim. However, by recognizing that I chose and willed this on myself on some level, I was able to become aware of why I did so, and what I needed to change or let go of, and by doing so able to transmute my emotions from frustration, anger, even rage to peaceful centeredness, and make new choices from that place. By doing so, I could become the boss of my life instead of being bossed and tossed around by circumstances and other people.

Leading our own lives requires "response-ability," the ability to respond by way of a conscious choice, rather than the opposite, automatically reacting, completely unaware of how or why we're doing what we're doing. When that happens, our thoughts and feelings begin to dictate and take over our lives, taking us along unpreferred paths, such as the direction my life had taken when my marriage ended. To influence our own reality involves becoming aware of these current and stored-up reactive energies, thereby developing our ability to consciously respond, as to the four questions.

We have the option to accept that we have created this reality for ourselves, consciously or unconsciously. Some thoughts and feelings we consciously choose; other thoughts and feelings occur below our level of awareness, in our subconscious. Just because these thoughts and feelings are subconscious doesn't mean they stop sending energy and messages that create our reality, whether we are aware of them or not. Therefore, if there is something I don't like about my reality, and I want to change it, that change begins with becoming aware of the thoughts and feelings that created it.

When we consciously choose how to respond as individuals, teams, or organizations, we experience the up-arrow results of the WTL Flow Chart (see Figure 3.1). As we learn to transmute our reactive energy—as depicted in the reactive bubble in the Flow Chart—into an individual heart-centered presence, we become aware of our power, in whatever circumstance, to choose how we want to show up. This ability to respond results in the up-arrow benefits shown in Figure 3.1.

Self-help books are filled with ideas and ways to help develop self-awareness, regulate emotions, and make new choices that result in leading more of oneself. The We the Leader approach has liberated hundreds of leaders and their teams from the prison and destruction of reactive anger or avoidance. This downward spiraling vortex is passed down from generation to generation within a family, an organization, or a society, and is accumulated in our own lives through perpetual reactivity until we step in and take control by assuming *full* responsibility for our state of being and our lives. And I meant it when I said We the Leader liberated hundreds of leaders and their teams because acquiring an ability to respond creatively to all that life puts forth liberates us to bring our full unique and authentic self into every situation, including "work." By learning these skills, we can clear the way for the unique leader within each of us to create together from our differences, rather than deal with the differences our uniqueness brings by separating through avoidance, dominating with abuse (emotional, verbal, physical), or homogenizing through seeking and gathering only with people like us.

The painful truth about the painful situation I found myself in was that I was leading my own life, unconsciously, and the direction wasn't what I wanted. The good news is that if we create our reality, we can change it. We can lead our lives in the present moment, and we can lead our lives into the future we desire.

Mastering Emotions:
The Key to Changing Our Lives

To fully maximize our energy and wisdom as the leader of our own life, it's crucial for us to harness "the more primal and intuitive parts of the brain where our unconscious habits and behavior patterns are stored."[10] To manifest our full, uniquely human intelligence we need to learn how to stop being at the mercy of our feelings and learn how to sensitively and accurately read and respond to other people's emotions—at work, in families, and in relationships. The balance of logic and emotion is important, as is everything in between, but the traditional or black-and-white idea that logic is good and emotions are bad is shifting toward the new scientific truth that mastering our emotions holds the key to changing our lives.[11]

Yet many of us so often want to keep the emotion out of it. Sometimes we say this in reference to a successful conversation or meeting, as in "We had a successful conversation. We kept the emotion out of it," meaning, we didn't *express* overt emotion. That doesn't mean emotions were avoided, consciously or unconsciously. Emotion is a source of creative energy, so keeping that creative energy out of the conversation is hardly successful in a world where innovation is queen. The key is to bring the e-motions into the conversation in a constructive fashion.

As Tara Swart writes, "if we want to thrive in our lives—especially given the rise of artificial intelligence and machine learning—it would be wise to focus most of our energy on trusting our gut, mastering our emotions, and feeling in control of creating our own future."[12] A word of warning though, if we attempt to trust our gut or access its intelligence while in a down-arrow reactive mode, where we're controlled by our emotions, our gut sense will be used to support fear-based decision-making and leadership, resulting in a reign of internal and external terror as exemplified by more leaders, particularly political leaders, today.

The same is true for logical thinking. If we engage or think we're engaging in logical thinking, yet we're controlled, if only in that moment, by our emotions, our perspective can be significantly limited and even flawed. Remember the blind men and the elephant? Think about how many regretful decisions you may have made when in a state of reactivity rather than response-ability, and you are not alone; consider the times you noticed these same decisions made by loved ones and friends.

So how do we take more responsibility for our lives and avoid these costly decisions and consequences? As with the CEO, often our inability to lead others effectively begins with leading ourselves. How do you at this point in your life lead yourself? No one else can lead you but you. You can only participate in leading with others to the extent you lead yourself. I offer some simple practices and exercises for becoming a better leader in the next chapter.

CHAPTER 8

How to BOSS Yourself

In that space is our power to choose our response.
In our response lies our growth and our freedom.
—AUTHOR UNKNOWN
quoted in Stephen Covey's *7 Habits of Highly Effective People*

The foundation for We the Leader's concept of collective flow is that every leader within the WE actually leads their own life and is not led by external circumstances or other people. Instead of prioritizing or focusing on leading others, We the Leader prioritizes and focuses on being your own boss. As I've discussed, only you can lead you; only others can lead themselves. As each member of a team, project, or organization leads themselves, then and only then do they colead, or We Lead, it. As members lead with their own curious conviction, they experience the creativity, unity, and ease of "The Leader" (see The WTL Flow Chart at the beginning of Part II). In this chapter, we will confirm that indeed you are the leader of your own life and introduce immediately applicable and proven processes for leading your own life.

Be Your Own BOSS

Before we continue, let's review the basics of being your own BOSS. Being your own boss often refers to running your own business. I've expanded the meaning to encompass running your own life. The acronym **BOSS** stands for:

1. **B**reathe consciously.
2. **O**bserve or notice and then suspend judgment on your internal state of being.
3. **S**elect to select—consciously deciding to decide and not just react. It's one thing to just select *or* decide, it's another to select *and* decide *and* observe yourself doing so—to be aware of deciding, which is an expression of Step 2. Becoming increasingly aware that you are making a decision, that you have the power to choose in this now moment, helps reinforce the belief that you always have that power, even though sometimes reactivity clouds your awareness of it.
4. **S**elect. Consciously decide what to choose.

You breathe intentionally to clear your mind so you can see clearly or observe what's happening around you and inside you. Then, as an observer of your life in real time, you exercise your power to not only watch this live play, but to decide how to act in this play and create the movie of your life.

When you are your own BOSS, you are focusing. You are choosing to take those deep breaths. You are choosing to step back and observe yourself and the situation and to let go of criticism. You are selecting to select responsibility for your life by repeatedly making conscious choices. You're being the **BOSS** of what you can control—your emotions, thoughts, and actions—instead of bossing others, whom you can invite and perhaps inspire, but really can't change.

Take a minute to practice the BOSS process.

1. **B**reathe consciously by relaxing into your exhales. If your mind wanders, bring it back to the exhale.
2. **O**bserve yourself from the perspective of a fly on the wall, or a compassionate grandmother sitting in a nearby chair. You are observing yourself in a live play. Notice

and let go of all judgment about yourself and others. When in a dialogue, perhaps one needing an eventual decision, suspending judgment just as you'd hang a coat on a hanger and put it in the closet. If decision time comes, put on the cloak of judgment and discern what direction to take. Here, judgment is not so much about people being "good" or "bad," "right or "wrong"; it is about accessing wisdom from our differences.

3. Continue to relax into your exhales.
4. Select to select. In the space between stimulus and response, take a moment to look at what's going on in the live play you're observing as an audience member, knowing you can choose how to respond by making a conscious choice instead of an unconscious reaction. Consciously deciding to decide reinforces the idea that, indeed, we always have the power to choose. Our decisions are not simply a result of our unconscious reactions.
5. Select or choose to choose. In this step, you consciously decide what to choose. Examples might include choosing gratitude, or to suspend judgment, or to let go of certainty by asking a genuine question and actively listening to the response.

Now let's break down the process into smaller steps.

Breathe Consciously, Find Your E-motions

Being your own BOSS focuses on what you and you alone can control, and really the only thing you can control is your inner state of being. Breathing consciously helps you relax so you are more likely to step back and observe. In addition, when you are in a relaxed state, you're more likely to notice and locate your negative or positive e-motions.

Let's try a simple breathing exercise:

1. Sit comfortably in as quiet a place as possible.
2. Pay attention to your natural breathing rhythm, notice the pace of your inhale, and exhale without attempting to change it.
3. Move into a deeper and deeper breath and relax into the exhale, perhaps include a sigh or ahhhhh!
4. Continue for one minute, then over time, build to five to seven minutes, depending on your experience with breathing exercises.

Inevitably your mind will wander. When it does, merely return your attention to relaxing into the exhale releasing any self-judgment, irritation, or distractions that may arise. Choose to be patient with yourself. If you notice any unpreferred inner feelings such as anxiety, fear, or stress, locate the feeling in your body. For example, you may feel tightness across your shoulders or in your neck, a twisting in your stomach, a rapid heartbeat, a headache, and so on. As you notice this feeling, gently breathe into that area repeatedly, welcoming the energy, embracing it, and allowing it to come and go. If practiced regularly, this exercise will help you become centered and grounded, enabling you to become present in this now moment. This centered presence transmutes any negative energy or e-motions into a quiet receptive stillness. If the unpreferred energy persists, simply continue the exercise, and on the exhale, purse your lips to make the sound of the wind.

On the other hand, as you experience positive feelings such as peace, lightness, joy, or a warm heart, locate that feeling in your body, then amplify this e-motion by breathing into it with gratitude and imagining the feeling expanding into your body and beyond.

Remember that our feelings are energy, e-motions, for moving conversations, relationships, projects, teams, organizations, and lives forward. An assertion that I find empowering when I notice fear is "Fear is fuel that fires me forward." As I breathe into the fear and exhale it, I imagine my breath blowing on the fire in my belly and fueling me forward and upward. Another is "Every moment, no matter the circumstance, I always have the option to choose and experience a peaceful centered presence."

As everyone on a team or participating in a project becomes centered, they are then poised to be present, listen, and speak from their own center to the center of the team or group, which activates team flow. This is illustrated in the WTL Flow Chart (shown at the beginning of Part II), where the straight and squiggly lines connect the members of the group (through curious conviction) to the center, to We the Leader. For flow to happen, everyone in the group needs to be a conduit for this energy. In other words, everyone must be leading their own lives.

During a meeting or project, natural pauses or moments of silence allow participants to re-center, or the leaders or facilitators can initiate a pause for twenty seconds so attendees may breathe consciously and become centered. Fifteen seconds of relaxing into the exhale can shift the reactive down-arrow energy into innovative up-arrow energy. Breathing into the positive feelings of peace, lightness, joy, clarity, and so on amplifies the flow energy. See the part in Figure 3.1 where the bold arrow points from We the Leader (in the center of the chart) to the up-arrow results.

Centering allows you to move from a reactive state to a state of logic and calm. "When we are in a highly stressed state, our prefrontal cortex—the part of our brain responsible for rational thinking—is impaired, so logic seldom helps to regain control. This can make it hard to think straight or be emotionally intelligent with your team. But with breathing techniques, it is possible to gain some mastery over your mind."[1]

Gaining mastery over your mind not only affects your emotion and logic, it affects your entire body. "Self-induced positive emotions are reflected in the pattern of one's heart's rhythm, which in turn increases the coherence in bodily processes. This shift in the heart rhythm plays an important role in facilitating higher cognitive functions, creating emotional flexibility, and facilitating social connectedness. Over time, this establishes a new inner-baseline reference, resulting in improvements in attention, behaviour, and measures of health and wellness."[2]

The impact doesn't stop there; for example, Rob Burch, CEO of Kindel Furniture, increased their production by 30 percent. Rob credits the increase in productivity largely to following the WTL Flow Chart, which began with everyone on his executive team learning to BOSS their own lives instead of trying to boss each other. This BOSSing of oneself itself begins with stepping back and breathing to relax, center, and become poised to lead oneself. This breathing is a personal practice as well as a team practice during meetings. Companies all over the globe advocate breathing in their mindfulness training. Those who follow the philosophy of mindfulness researcher/practitioner Jon Kabat-Zinn employ breathing as an important aspect of mindfulness, including at the start of all meditations. Perhaps Chade Meng Tan, who founded the Search Inside Yourself program at Google and the Search Inside Yourself Leadership Institute (SIYLI) can be credited for the popularity of mindfulness programs in the corporate world.

This practice of breathing and leading oneself is pivotal, and results in up-arrow results when practiced consistently or down-arrow outcomes when not. Everyone showing up as the leader they are hinges on being fully present. The BOSS practice makes that happen.

Another scientifically espoused way of breathing consciously is diaphragmatic breathing:

1. Sit comfortably in as quiet a place as possible.
2. Take a deep breath through your nose, down the back of your throat, and into your abdomen, filling it as though it's a big balloon. Hold the breath for three seconds, or longer if desired.
3. Breathe out through your nose, letting your abdomen fully deflate as you exhale.
4. Continue breathing in and out, as you become more relaxed; focus on the rise and fall of your abdomen, rather than your chest.

When unpreferred feelings arise, breathe into that feeling, receiving it, allowing it to clear. Continue breathing in and out until the feeling dissipates. If you're feeling a preferred emotion, breath into it, allowing it to expand, expand, expand.

There are multiple techniques for breathing consciously. The key is finding and adapting those that work for you. By "work for you," I mean those that help you get to that still, centered place, where you have the awareness to step back and observe what's going on within and around you. As you develop your own conscious breathing practice, whether upon waking in the morning, going to bed at night, during breaks, or as you move to a meeting, you can carry this practice with you throughout the day. Teams practicing Simultaneity regularly begin each meeting with a minute to clear their minds or "empty their cups" by practicing breathing consciously. This practice helps amplify the power of those deep breaths we all need throughout our day. Eventually, as you might have gathered, this practice becomes embedded within your team's or organization's culture, helping to build the foundation for consistent collective flow and all the personal and business benefits illustrated in the innovative aspects (up-arrow) in the WTL Flow Chart.

Observing Oneself, Empowering Oneself

In her book *The Source,* Tara Swart describes the role metacognition—or "thinking about thinking" and becoming "aware of one's awareness," rather than "functioning on autopilot"—plays in becoming your own boss. Developing this skill is key to becoming your own BOSS. Metacognition, she writes, is a "function of the prefrontal cortex (PFC), the term comes from the root word *meta,* meaning 'beyond.' The PFC monitors sensory signals from other regions and uses feedback loops to direct our thinking by constantly updating our brain depending on what is playing out in the outside world."[3]

Awareness or the capacity to observe ourselves—and observe ourselves observing ourselves—is crucial because by doing this, we become cognizant of the space between our observer self and our physical self. This experience reminds us that we are *not* our reactive feelings and thinking, and, therefore, we're free and empowered to make fresh conscious choices moment by moment. Herein lies freedom and growth.

Observing the space between stimulus and response is different from judging. Judgment can occupy and even consume our minds, blurring and eventually blinding us to this space of possibilities, making us feel trapped and helpless, further judging ourselves, blaming others, and often making decisions we regret.

A foundational exercise for building one's self-awareness or capacity to observe is the Four Questions for Leading Yourself.

The Four Questions for Leading Yourself

I introduced the Four Questions for Leading Yourself in the previous chapter. Now, we can go through these steps in more detail.

1. What am I observing externally then internally? For example, externally you might be noticing that your colleague continues to interrupt you in front of peers and superiors. Internally, you notice some raw thoughts and feelings like "Who does he think he is interrupting me like that. God Damnit! I don't interrupt him! I'm so tired of being demeaned in this way. He doesn't interrupt our male colleagues!" Notice that the question is *What are you observing?* not *What are you judging?* Of course, internally you may be observing your judgment which may in turn result in judging yourself for judging. The key is to observe all of this as the proverbial "fly on the wall." This present detachment, as simple as it sounds, is powerful, even magical.

2. What emotions do I notice inside myself? E-motions, whether so-called positive or negative, are energy for moving forward conversations, relationships, projects, and so on. Observing the energy of rage, peace, fear, anger, disgust, and so on, is different from judging yourself. Welcome these e-motions as the free and infinite energies they are. Just as we refine raw crude oil to move us forward in vehicles, this four-step process, if practice consistently, will empower you to refine and channel your raw crude emotions to enrich conversations, relationships, teams and projects, and so on.

3. What thinking, assumptions, and interpretations are accompanying and feeding these emotions? For instance, in in the example provided in question 1, she might be assuming *He doesn't respect woman, including me!*

4. What do I desire? What choices are you ready to make? Hmmm . . . as she sits with this, she may conclude that the next time this happens *I'm going to compose or center myself and simply make the observation,* "You just interrupted me. Are you aware of that?" Or, "My assumption is that you just interrupted me. Is that your understanding?"

Often when asking yourself these questions, the reactionary temperature lowers significantly and we can avoid flight, fight, or freeze reactions and respond efficiently and effectively.

Live Play Exercise

Sometimes when you feel particularly stuck, you might need to take another approach to activate your observing and creating capacities. An exercise to increase your capacity to observe is to pause and view your scenario as if it's a scene in a live play.

Let's look, for example, at the colleague who interrupts you. You, your colleague, peers, and superiors are in a meeting. You speak, and sure enough, your colleague interrupts you. Take a breath. Imagine yourself in the audience watching yourself live out your situation—your colleague, peers, and superiors are all on the stage. Since this is an improv play where the script isn't predetermined, the *you* in the audience has the power to go up on stage and create the next scene. This is agility. Increasingly, it seems that life, business, and work offer us more and more, if not constant, opportunities that require agility or leading one's own life. Practice this exercise in your next meeting. In the space between stage (stimulus) and audience (response), can you choose to observe, suspend your judgment, and decide how you want to lead? While there are many variations of the Live Play exercise, the Living Out of Body Experience is one of my favorites and one that always helps provide distance and perspective.

Living Out of Body Experience

You don't have to die to have an out-of-body experience. In fact, a consciously chosen out-of-body experience can help you be more alive.

Here's an example. Just this morning as I sat down to write this chapter, I had some serious performance anxiety. My mind was rattling: *Is this book going to be worth reading? Will I make the deadline? When will this writer's block pass? I just want to finish this chapter. I don't want to write from this emotional state.* I felt the agitation and heat of anxiety in the middle of my sternum and chest. I was anxious about being anxious. How could I shift this down-arrow reactive fear-based energy resulting in the down-arrow of personal and business results? How could I transmute this destructive down-arrow energy into the creative up-arrow energy with all its positive personal and business results?

I weighed my options. I could choose to have an out of body experience to align myself with my core/heart center by consciously choosing to observe myself. This mental exercise and experience guided me to access the space to exercise my power to choose how I show up. In other words, to lead the leader (to lead myself) instead of being led by external circumstances and the subsequent internal reactivity of fear.

I took a breath and imagined I was sitting in the audience of a live play. The scene before us was me sitting anxiously in front of my computer wringing my hands and then pacing back and forth, even pulling my hair.

As I perceived my live self from my reflective self in the audience, I begin to realize, *Hey, I'm not confined to my physical self and the experience of mental slavery. Rather, there's a part of me that is free from this reactive prison.*

In the space experienced from my observation, I chose to experience my freedom by going up on stage, inviting my reactive self to sit down as I pulled up a chair. Now we began to take deep breaths together, relaxing into the exhale, deeply relaxing into the exhales over and over.

Next, we breathed deeply into the anxiety and fear within the center of my chest and held the inhale for a count of three, then slowly relaxed into the exhale, repeating and deeply relaxing until the energy shifted from the torment of fear to that centered peacefulness.

While doing this, I call forth a third dimension of myself depicted by the usher in the theatre—an observer of the observer, a compassionate Grandmother Witness. She, as a dimension of me, observes without any judgment, full of compassion for all in every moment. After the breathing and observing without judgment, I feel relaxed and centered, quiet and ready to make new choices. I decide to listen for my inner guidance. In doing, so I was inspired to write the piece you just read.

Yes, it can take some time upfront to practice this self-leading exercise, yet the benefits include showing up fully engaged, more immediate and direct communication, and the subsequent snowballing trust, all of which accelerate accessing collective wisdom and making decisions followed by aligned execution. On the other hand, the consequences of not doing so when necessary can be devastating, resulting in broken relationships and poor decisions that result in the failures of the down arrow. This is a classic example of slowing down to speed up, which Dave Kaufman discusses in Chapter 15. I've seen executives not exercise these self-leading skills and get caught in conflict with colleagues, make poor decisions, and change companies only to repeat the cycle, prematurely end their careers, or spend lots of time and money in individual therapy, which certainly helps, but is typically really slow. There's something about practicing these exercises for leading yourself in the context of a team and organization of others leading themselves that builds new habits much quicker. With the support and mutual accountability, it becomes contagious! And leads to collective flow.

Select to Select, Be the BOSS

Now that you have breathed consciously by taking that deep breath, relaxed into the exhale, and/or practiced diaphragmatic breathing, you can recognize and step into the space between stimulus and response. In this space, you're free to observe your own current life as a member of the audience to your own unique live play of your life. As the creator, producer, and star of your own life, no matter the scene, you can decide how you will think, feel, and act in this now moment and every moment. You always have the power to choose, but sometimes the uncertainty, complexity, and downright pain and fear that arises clouds our memory of who we really are.

We are not followers of other people. We are not followers of our life circumstances, imprisoned to our own mental slavery. No! In *every* moment, we are leaders of our own lives, equipped with the belief that only we can lead our own unique lives. Only we are responsible for what we think, feel, say, and do. In this place of awareness, we're united with our transcendent invisible observing self and our physical being, full of breath, feelings, thoughts, and desires. We exercise this unity, this wholeness, this oneness by becoming aware that we *always* have choices, and then in full awareness continuously choosing to be the BOSS of our own lives. Choosing to suspend our judgment that, like lightning, strikes so quickly, choosing to be curious, choosing to speak out, especially when no one else will state the obvious because it might be unpopular, choosing to listen to others even when what they say abhors you, choosing and inviting others to constantly choose a curious conviction.

Select Gratitude First, then Curiosity

Choose gratitude and curiosity. Given all the positive research on the benefits of appreciation and gratitude, I suggest prioritizing gratitude. Select gratitude, not just because it fosters health, happiness, and creativity, but it's also a very efficient way to actualize your intentions, goals, plans, and dreams.

It works like this: the fulfillment of what we desire stems not out of thin air but from the reception and enhancement of what we already desire. The seeds for the fulfillment of future goals are embedded in our current fulfillment. We nurture and grow these seeds through our gratitude for our current successes no matter how seemingly small or large. This active appreciation of our current fulfillment activates new desires. Any experience of dissatisfaction of the gap between our current reality and ideal reality, and the subsequent complaining, strained positivity, apathy, or dormant gratitude only serves to infect or cut off our deeply held desires. Active gratitude involves feeling our current gratitude and seeing, feeling, and imagining it expanding abundantly. Passive gratitude is a *ho-hum-yeah-I'm-grateful* proposition, void of any heartfelt emotion.

Typically, we name the real then the ideal followed by a plan to bridge the gap. If we only focus on the distance between the real and ideal or the absence of abundance then that's what we get—the absence of abundance in our lives and projects. As a result, we perpetuate the distance from the ideal in our lives and projects. Beginning the planning process with gratitude for the real, even if it only clarifies what you don't desire—balances the problem with opportunity. Allow the gratitude to become like a snowball rolling down a steep hill, picking up steam as it takes everything in its path into its lofty white sphere, growing larger and more powerful with each single flake of snow, speck of dirt, and blade of frozen grass. Every future manifestation has its basis in who and what you are right now.

Select curiosity. Suspend judgment by noticing how it arises, but don't judge the judging. Breathe into it and let it go. Repeat several times if necessary.

We suspend judgment and certainty by realizing our certainty is only a piece of the truth not the entire truth. Remember the puzzle analogy? Selecting curiosity allows us to become curious about other people's pieces, especially when they're different from ours. Suspending judgment and certainty is the foundation of bringing a curious conviction. Suspend doesn't mean not having conviction or certainty, but setting it aside temporarily to allow for a thorough investigation. It is like hanging your favorite jacket in the closet until you choose to wear it again.

We also nurture our curiosity by asking questions. In times of stress, tensions resulting from differences or downright conflict, we may choose to ask, "Am I really understanding what she is saying?" "How did he come to such a conclusion?" "What might be emerging from our differences that we haven't thought of before?" "What's being created from this void of silence?"

What if you find yourself in a staunch hierarchy or reporting to a boss who definitely sees themself as leading you, a follower? Remember you can always select to select. In these circumstances, you can choose to lead yourself more deeply by asking and journaling your response to the Four Questions for Leading Yourself. Next, process these responses with a trusted friend, colleague, or coach while continually practicing the BOSS process, asking yourself what, if any, of the responses to the four questions are you ready to communicate to your boss. One place to start, if possible and you're not already doing so, is to observe what your boss does well and genuinely communicate that observation to your boss. For instance, "I really appreciate the way you speak so clearly and directly about what you want." I call this "catching people doing it right." Then ask your boss if they're open to your thoughts about improving your working relationship. If the response is "yes," then use the content in the four questions to simplify your thoughts or to make requests such as, "I would like you to ask my input as part of your decision-making concerning marketing issues," assuming marketing is your area of expertise.

If anything close to this approach seems unrealistic given the situation and your relationship to your boss, then look within your organization for bosses and teams that offer a learning and shared leadership approach. If none of these teams exist or hold the potential for a more shared learning and leading opportunity, find another organization that does.

Let's step back now and take a look at the WTL Flow Chart. Our purpose is to understand the dynamics of collective flow so that we can consciously and repeatedly choose these conditions, and thereby experience the agility, speed, and adaptability of collective flow at will. The energy for this flow comes through the innovative process of consilience. The three pillars provide a channel for that energy to be purposeful and creative instead of random and destructive. The first pillar starts with you the unique leader of yourself whom only you can lead. This is in contrast to starting with leading other people. In fact, since only you can lead you and only others can lead themselves, you can't lead others, which makes leading you all the more important. What happens when a collection of leaders of their own lives gather to accomplish a common purpose? What is this collection of leaders? A community of equals.

PART III

The Equalizer

Common Purpose

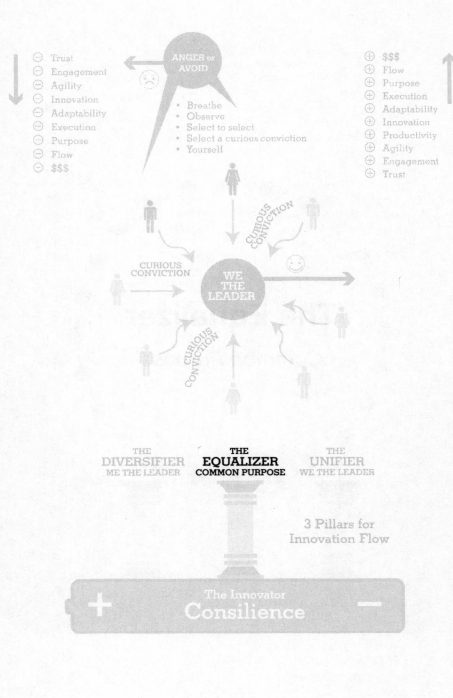

CHAPTER 9

We the Leader: Separate and Equal

Leader and followers are both following the invisible leader—the common purpose.

—MARY PARKER FOLLETT
management consultant and author

I wrote this book hoping to contribute the We the Leader operating system as an equal, different, and vital piece of the evolving practice of leadership. In my view, Part III: The Equalizer is the most important part of We the Leader.

Let's dive in by exploring these questions:

- What if instead of a hierarchical system with some leading many, organizations were actually communities of equals?
- Suppose this equality meant that everyone is an equal leader and equal follower at the same time, what would that be like?
- What if this seeming path to anarchy was actually the portal to consistent collective flow?
- Imagine that learning to colead one another as equal leader–followers was the new way of leading, and that this egalitarian approach could solve our seemingly unsolvable problems, such as:
  - Finding a sustainable and renewable source of energy that actually purifies rather than pollutes our atmosphere

- Discovering a supply chain for timely distribution of our abundance of food so that no one ever goes hungry
- Getting ahead of disease and pandemics by anticipating them and developing safe and proven preventions
- Experiencing an organization that brings forth and expands our uniqueness in ways we never imagined possible, while creating a consistent and expanding culture in which to engage with other diverse leaders to make a difference through our differences, and doing it with the speed and agility necessary for organizations today

How would that feel?

Now that we know the questions, we can start by looking at what constitutes an organization. An organization is a group of people gathered together for a common purpose. As we saw in Chapter 2, everyone in an organization is by definition a follower of the common purpose.

This has at least three implications:

1. It reinforces the idea that people lead organizations, projects, and teams, but not each other. Only you can lead your own life and only others can lead their own lives. Leading another person isn't truly possible. When we try to do it, we breed conformity, the exact opposite of innovation (not to mention personality cults, whether in politics, business, or religion).
2. Everyone—including the top executives and formal leaders in the hierarchy—functioning as followers of the common purpose makes everyone in the organization an equal. Everyone is a follower; therefore, leading and

following become two mutual aspects of cocreating/
coactualizing the purpose into action.

3. Equalizing everyone as a follower of the common
   purpose coupled with everyone as a leader—at least
   of their own lives and increasingly in organizations—
   creates an egalitarian organization of leader–followers,
   leading and following at the same time, all the time.

If everyone in a purpose-driven organization is a follower
and the organization has an increasing number of leaders, by
which I mean self-leaders—millennials especially, but also
experts and cross-functional teams—and needs everyone to
lead, then this emerging reality threatens the prominence of
hierarchy.

Recalibrating Hierarchy for Consistent Collective Flow

The purpose-driven organization calls for a reimagining
going from what is primarily a hierarchy, where some rule
over or lead others, to a panarchy, where everyone is a leader–
follower. This organizational structure, in which everyone is
leading and following a common purpose, sharply contrasts
with the experience of today's hierarchical structures, where
few are leaders and many are followers, which goes against
our innate identity as leader–followers and contributes to our
stagnation. That said it is important to recognize that hierarchy continues to play a vital role by serving the creativity and
in-sync execution that an organization needs.

Panarchy doesn't eradicate the need for hierarchy, but hierarchy is no longer the primary or dominant structure. Instead,
it's a necessary and vital secondary option. For example, in

times of crisis it is paramount for the hierarchical leader to make a timely and authoritative decision. However, if that leader only or primarily makes authoritative decisions—not just in times of crisis—they won't have developed the necessary trust for aligned execution of that decision. (We'll discuss this idea further in Chapter 14, which melds the benefits of directives and dialogue in a mutually enhancing manner.)

While hierarchy is sometimes needed, the danger of following an authoritarian leader is that personality, religious, or political cults can arise, leaving us vulnerable to the tyranny of one person leading many followers rather than an organization, institution, or country. Not only is leading or following one person ill advised, it's also an illusion because the follower becomes a puppet of the leader and thus a shell of their authentic self. Remember, only you can lead you.

Couple this revelation with the understanding that everyone is the leader, or CEO, of their own life, and we not only level the working field but also raise it so that everyone in the organization is on the high-level ground of a community of equal, unique, and vital leader–followers. As leaders of our own lives, we can choose to be a member of an organization, team, or project, and, therefore, no matter what our rank in any hierarchy—from CEO to frontline worker—we choose to lead our lives by becoming followers of the collective's or organization's common purpose. Therefore, *everyone* in an organization is a follower. This levels the playing or working field. Because all members are leaders of their own lives and followers of a common purpose, then everyone in an organization, on a team, or on a project is always both a leader and a follower, or a leader–follower, at the same time, all the time.

Raising the equal ground of followers to a high level of leader–follower releases yet another level of energy and liberation, but we're not done yet. Identifying everyone as not just a follower or a leader but a leader *and* a follower at the same time all the time taps into the very source of life energy and innovation, or consilience—in this case, the jumping together of leading (going before) and following (going after)—to bring about new leadership of leader–followers.

With the recognition and following of the equalizer, or common purpose, we tap into a higher level of energy in three ways:

1. Raising everyone to the high level of leader–follower empowers energy.
2. The unity of the seeming opposites of leader and follower amps up the source of innovative energy, or consilience, which is the foundation of collective flow. (See the WTL Flow Chart at the beginning of Part III, where both the positive and negative charge on the Innovator: Consilience are necessary to create the charge, or energy, of the battery).
3. This harmony of opposites—created by the amplified energy fueled by the consilience of the positive and negative charge triggered simultaneously—provides the necessary structure of the Diversifier, Equalizer, and Unifier (depicted by the three pillars) to channel the energy.

You'll remember that in Chapter 4 we compared a collective flow to the flow of a river, where much water (flow energy) can stream over the banks (structure) creating a flood but, if the banks are too prominent or dominant, the riverbed runs dry and becomes a ditch. When it comes to energy voltage, when energy increases, the structure needs to be adjusted to avoid the flood of out-of-control energy when it isn't creatively channeled through the traditional hierarchies. For example, when Steelcase, in an effort to reignite innovation, created project teams without a formal leader, some teams thrived because they organically held the structure to channel the new energy that resulted from equalizing the teams. Many teams, however, floundered because they were not able to naturally structure themselves to make timely decisions and hold each other accountable (more on this in Chapter 14).

When we increase the voltage, we need to revisit the appropriate structure to maximize the flow of this resurgent energy. By doing so, we call for a shift in organizational structure. In many ways, this new structure is already unfolding, shifting from the traditional, staid hierarchy of one or few leaders to a flexible panarchical structure of leader–followers. This new structure includes a measured and adaptable hierarchy, which provides the flexibility needed so that the resurgence of energy can be channeled into collective flow. For instance, when Dave Kaufman created equal integrated teams (see Chapter 15), he did not dismantle the traditional hierarchy but created a hybrid by establishing a panarchical structure of equal integrated teams alongside the established hierarchy. In addition, within the integrated equal teams of leader–followers, they applied the We the Leader decision-making model, allowing a designated leader to ensure timely decisions and accountability when needed.

This egalitarian harmony of structure and flow actualizes consilience in at least two ways:

1. It creates a lighter structure that allows for increased flow. This more flexible structure results from declaring everyone equal leaders, followers, and leader–followers, thus avoiding the overbearing hierarchy that disrupts collective flow with its attempts to control.
2. It provides the context for the organic living of diversity, equity, and inclusion (think about how the world came

together to rescue the Wild Boars soccer team), instead of obligatory training, which has been proven to be unsuccessful.

This movement toward egalitarian structure is already afoot in today's organizations. Just look at the rise of networks, flattened organizational structures, agile projects, and cross-functional teams.

This is what I mean when I say it's time to recalibrate hierarchy. By *recalibrating*, I refer to neither its domination nor its elimination. I mean changing hierarchies' purpose of command and control, or power over, to intending to facilitate collective flow with appropriate authority.

To illustrate my point, in a conversation with Ken Vandermark, a jazz composer, performer, 1999 MacArthur Foundation "genius" award winner, and subject of a 2007 documentary, I asked him about the role of composition within improvisation. I was intrigued because on one level, the two—composition (a predetermined score or act of power over) and improvisation (an in-the-moment collective creation)—contradict each other.

"Oh yeah," he said, "good question." Then he lit up. "The last piece you heard, I composed to start the improvisation with the instruments and skills of each musician in our group in mind."

So here we have it. How the seeming opposites of hierarchy and panarchy jump together to create a new in-the-moment sound. This integration of authority and freedom is not only the cutting edge of collective creativity as asserted and practiced by jazz musicians but also exactly the breakthrough dynamic needed in today's organizations.

The purpose of the We the Leader operating system is to provide this very dynamic. One of the key ways it does this is by artfully integrating the role of authoritative decision-making in the context of panarchical teams in a way that sparks creativity *and* personal power! (For more about and how to do this, see Chapter 14.)

Diversity, Equity, and Inclusion

Now is the time to step back and call an organization what it is, an egalitarian community of leader–followers, in order to unleash another level of energy and intelligence to solve our seemingly unsolvable problems. When people jointly surrender to such a common purpose, they discover a way to innovate by including everyone as equals with different vital parts to play to actualize that common purpose. For example, Dave Kaufman (Chapter 15) discusses how changing the purpose—from selling insurance or making a return on an asset to being there for people during their time of deepest need—raised the level of motivation for his senior leadership team. He accompanied this renewed sense of purpose with the egalitarian structure of integrated teams.

Other than following a common purpose, being part of an organization means showing up fully as the leader of your own life, welcoming others who show up fully as the leaders of their own lives. By leading each other as leader–followers, we can coactualize the common purpose by creating wildly creative and fun solutions to the most pressing problems of the company and the world. When this takes place, a fascinating dynamic, at least to me, occurs. When we lead our own lives, we follow our own inner beliefs, passions, and wisdom. At the same time, when we lead organizations or teams, we follow the common purpose. In both cases, our leading (ourselves, teams, projects) is following (the common purpose) and our following (the common purpose) is leading (ourselves, teams, and projects).

Without this refreshed identity of today's organizations, today's DEI efforts are hamstrung, destined for mediocre results at best, and dynamite energies of resentment at worst. In contrast, leading by following, or leading and following at the same time, taps into another level of energy entirely because this egalitarian model is a manifestation of consilience, which provides the energy source or foundation for the We the Leader Flow Chart. Therefore, everyone being a leader–follower isn't a stagnant identity; it is an energizing equalizer that propels an organization into exponential potential. It also fosters creativity because everyone brings the diversity of their unique selves and then creates and executes on the strategy for actualizing the common purpose.

This observation of *what is* (that we are all equal leader–followers of the same purpose) has ramifications that reverberate throughout the organization into the core identity of its individual members and the collective, the very nature and practice of leadership, the prioritizing of structure, and the experience of collective flow. It liberates and compels us to reimagine every aspect of our organizations' culture. Establishing everyone as the single leader of their own life fosters universal uniqueness *and* the thorough diversity of the collective organization. Since innovation thrives on diversity and the subsequent creative energy of opposites, rampant diversity is a launchpad for a quantum leap of innovation.

The Equalizer of the common purpose redefines leadership as fundamentally mutual, not singular or for a few. The focus of leadership shifts from a leader leading followers, or even leaders, to leader–followers leading projects, teams, and the organization together. Subsequently, this shift in leadership actualizes a foundational network structure of diversity, equity, and inclusion instead of the prevailing hierarchical structure of conformity, inequity, and exclusion.

A structure built upon the real diversity, equity, and inclusion and the subsequent identity and mutual leadership around a common purpose is a vital pillar for the collective flow (see the Equalizer in the WTL Flow Chart). We've explored consilience as the evolutionary impulse of life and innovation, the jumping together of diverse or opposite perspectives, interests, and energies into something new just as the opposite sexes jump together to create a new and unique human being. Without the vibrancy that equality and diversity bring to innovation and to would-be innovators, organizations, teams, or projects remain imprisoned to the confines of a conforming, inequitable, and exclusive hierarchy. With the energy of the evolutionary impulse of life derived from the uniqueness and equality of leader–followers, collective flow becomes the contagious norm, not the exception, of organizational experience and execution.

Since we've established that only you can lead you, the question becomes "How do these follower–leaders of their own lives, the organization, team, or project—and leader–followers of the common purpose lead each other?" When it comes to leading each other, we need an explicit way of leading that jibes with this leading and following dynamic. Purpose as leader creates a company of people who simultaneously are leaders and followers. Unless purpose-driven organizations realize and activate this new reality, they will not optimize their organizations. Actualizing our common purpose requires that we need not only reimagine who we are as individuals, teams, organizations, and the appropriate panarchical structures, but we also need to release our outdated habits for leading followers and adapt new skills and habits for leading each other as leader–followers.

We need a significant upgrade of skills for conversations, decision-making, and accountability to execute on this purpose. I'll outline these skills and processes in Part IV.

PART IV

The Unifier

*We the Leader,
We the Follower*

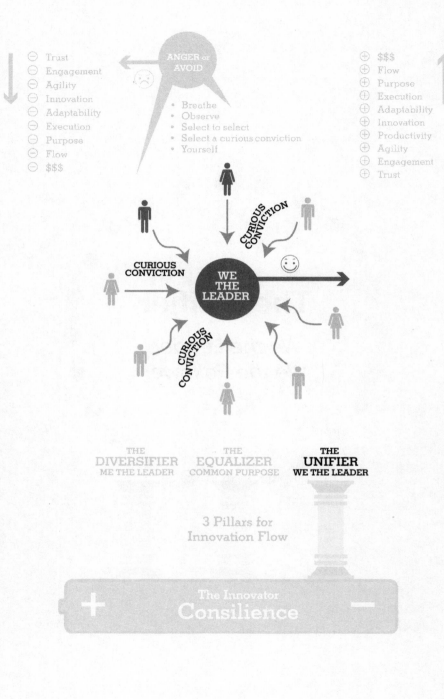

⊖ Trust
⊖ Engagement
⊖ Agility
⊖ Innovation
⊖ Adaptability
⊖ Execution
⊖ Purpose
⊖ Flow
⊖ $$$

ANGER or AVOID

• Breathe
• Observe
• Select to select
• Select a curious conviction
• Yourself

⊕ $$$
⊕ Flow
⊕ Purpose
⊕ Execution
⊕ Adaptability
⊕ Innovation
⊕ Productivity
⊕ Agility
⊕ Engagement
⊕ Trust

CURIOUS CONVICTION

CURIOUS CONVICTION

CURIOUS CONVICTION

WE THE LEADER

THE
DIVERSIFIER
ME THE LEADER

THE
EQUALIZER
COMMON PURPOSE

THE
UNIFIER
WE THE LEADER

3 Pillars for
Innovation Flow

The Innovator
Consilience

+   −

CHAPTER 10

We the Leader:
Separate and Simultaneous

Leadership is plural . . .

—MIKE KRZYZEWSKI
men's basketball head coach, Duke University

I defined We the Leader as an operating system that includes an innovation process, a leadership process, and decision-making process. I called this part of the book "The Unifier: Me the Leader" because it brings together the unique and diverse leaders who are simultaneously followers of the common purpose as "The" Leader.

As we've discussed, the innovation process is founded upon the principle and practice of consilience and the leadership process, leading and following simultaneously, is called Simultaneity. (I will introduce the decision-making process, which grows out of and supports the practice of Simultaneity in traditional hierarchies, in Chapter 14.)

Perhaps it was unconscious, but the concept and practice of We the Leader started with, or was advanced by, Steve Jobs's and Elon Musk's mandate for "no silos." With this injunction, departments or parts of an organization were no longer primarily independent segments tangentially connected, but rather equal, different, and vital pieces of the organizational puzzle. This shift required the leaders of these departments to gather together more frequently and intensely to solve problems and realize possibilities. In other words, to follow the common purpose of the organization.

The world was and is changing so quickly and becoming so increasingly complex that to fulfill the common purpose more and more leaders must lead each other. This plural leadership has been taking place, for the most part, without naming the change of context occurring in our midst. The call for no silos required leaders to not just lead followers, but to change their mindset and habits to also lead leaders.

For example, a client came to me with the typical silo problem: the isolation of different departments. There was the investment department. Wow! That silo was not only separate, it was also huge and wielded its power with bravado and arrogance, clearly seeing itself above the operations, HR, and legal departments. It was almost as though one farm (the investment department) was competing with the neighboring farm (the organization). The CEO saw this problem and called for no silos, but when the silo leaders got together, they had no idea how to talk, or interest in talking, to each other, let alone acting like partners with interdependent operations that needed each other. However, the industry was changing rapidly. The organization needed to change. The change, they soon found out, was not just structural—that is, setting up joint meetings—but actually talking and leading the company together. Of course, they were skilled in leading the followers in their own segments, but they didn't have a clue or much desire to lead the company together.

There is a success side to this story. As the team began using the We the Leader operation system, in particular the coleading process of Simultaneity, it exposed toxic behavior by a key leader who was hindering the progress getting key leaders to cooperate. This person resigned, which opened a fresh opportunity to reset and learn to lead the company together. The We the Leader operating system didn't stop there; they cascaded the process into the senior and middle management levels.

As we saw earlier, leading leaders as if they're followers is like telling a cat to fetch and sit. It doesn't work. No wonder 75 percent of the cross-functional teams created because of the "no silos" mandate are dysfunctional.[1] That's a lot, but it makes sense, given the lack of awareness of the change in context of leadership from leaders leading followers to leaders leading followers *and* leaders, and the subsequent skill deficiency. As in the pension organization example, most top-level executives aren't consciously aware that the context has changed or needs to change, so when the change occurs, they resist, often unaware of their resistance. The result is leaders reverting to their habit of leading followers when the context has changed to leading leaders.

However, some leaders instinctively know how to lead leaders; Abraham Lincoln comes to mind (see sidebar). However, rarely are these leaders aware of how they do it. Therefore, it's nearly impossible for these rare leaders who *do* know how to do it to teach or allow their methodologies to become contagious. The practice of Simultaneity is about making these implicit leadership mindsets, skills, and habits explicit so all the leaders throughout an organization can lead each other as leaders.[2]

Lincoln's Curious Conviction

Lincoln led the United States through one of the most disruptive times in its history. In our current age of disruption, perhaps it is time to not only emulate his leadership style, but build entire teams of Lincolns.

This would first require identifying some of Lincoln's key leadership practices. Then, by practicing those in your leadership role, you could inspire and teach other team members to do the same.

One foundational practice of Lincoln that you and your team can replicate is the mutually enhancing integration of two seemingly opposite qualities—humility and confidence. In his book *The Courage to Create,* Rollo May notes that Lincoln was a leader "who openly admitted his doubts and as openly preserved his commitments."[3] He then observes that "the person with the courage to believe and at the same time to admit his doubts is flexible and open to new learning."[4] Yet he also acknowledges the paradox of this courage: "It is the seeming contradiction that we must be fully committed, but we must also be aware at the same time that we might possibly be wrong."[5]

You and your team can emulate Lincoln's courageous and uncanny way of enhancing his confidence with humility and his humility with confidence through the practice of *curious conviction*, which we'll explore in depth in Chapter 13.

This democratization of leadership is not about to stop and is only advancing further with the arrival of artificial intelligence. "We're seeing the democratization of software—the consumers can now be the creators," Ravi Kumar, the president of the Indian tech services company Infosys, explained in an article in the *New York Times.*[6] It shows you how AI will take away jobs of the past, while it creates jobs of the future." Today's silos are being eradicated, not only in organizations, but across sectors with everyone having access to information, innovative tools, inexpensive computing, even money.

The author of the article, Thomas L. Friedman, writes:

The reason the post-pandemic era will be so destructive and creative is that never have more people had access to so many cheap tools of innovation, never have more people had access to high-powered, inexpensive computing, never have more people had access to such cheap credit—virtually free money—to invent new products and services, all as so many big health, social, environmental and economic problems need solving.

Put all of that together and KABOOM![7]

If Friedman's observations and predictions are accurate, we concurrently have a world where the rich are getting richer than ever before *and* where everyone has more access to the tools needed to address the huge problems we face and become financially successful. In other words, to become the leaders they are.

As a result, the world is increasingly becoming a community of leaders. The breadth and complexity of today's challenges not only require leaders from across an organization to lead together, but global pandemics, global climate change, and a faltering global economy require leaders from across the globe. And just as this need arises, it becomes apparent, even vital, that what it means to lead is to adapt, to learn how to lead together. Otherwise, the complexity of everyone trying to lead without knowing what they are doing will only turn on itself and us as we stumble into the vortex of chaotic destruction.

Friedman's article continues:

It starts with the fact, explained Kumar, that the Industrial Revolution produced a world in which there were sharp distinctions between employers and employees, between educators and employers and between governments and employers and educators, "but now you're going to see a blurring of all these lines."[8]

The blurring of sharp distinctions between leaders and followers ("no silos") continues within leadership itself to the point that, as we have seen, today's organizations are increasingly becoming communities of leaders.

Parallel to that, explained Kumar, accelerations in digitization and globalization are steadily making more work "modular," broken up into small packets that are farmed out by companies. Companies, he argues, will increasingly become platforms that synthesize and orchestrate these modular packets to make products and services.[9]

These modular packets, or work groups, mirror the necessary inner organizational gathering of leaders into cross-functional teams, projects, or pods that resulted from "no silos." However, they will be increasingly externally focused, and companies, Kumar says, "will increasingly become platforms that synthesize and orchestrate these modular packets (of leaders farmed out by companies) to make products and services."[10]

I've talked about a leader as one who has followers. Leaders go before and followers go after. Transferring the context from leading another to leading yourself, you are both the leader and follower at the same time. We lead ourselves by listening to our thoughts, emotions, and intuitions. We continue leading ourselves by making choices and then following ourselves by going after or acting on our choices. When we place a magnifying glass over this concept, we find it involves an internal blending of following and leading so that leading looks like following and following looks like leading, as if they are one and the same.

When we lead each other, we're internally leading and following and externally practicing a curious conviction, which, as we shall see, is the simultaneous process of following with curiosity and leading with conviction. When we examine what is actually happening, we realize we are simultaneously leading and following internally and with each other.

This description and example remind me of Dr. Swart's observation that "we need to understand the brain as a series of systems rather than a set of locations or a story of two halves."[11] She's referring to what she calls the myth of left-brain, right-brain. Continuing, she writes, "The advent of fMRIs of healthy brains (instead of diseased) has proven that the brain is a dynamic collection of systems and networks, cross-brain connections and complex lateral firing."[12]

Think about how the left and right hemispheres of our brain are constantly intermingling. Similarly, instead of the role of leader *or* follower, our leading is following and our following is leading. Just as the separation of the brain is now outdated, so is the separation of leading and following. This free intermingling and simultaneity of leading and following, learning and teaching, receiving and giving is the sweet spot of individual and collective flow. In his book *I and Thou*, Martin Buber refers to all living as meeting a moment of radical mutuality where giving is receiving and receiving is giving.[13] Oh, that all meetings were like that! Perhaps they actually are except that we just don't recognize it.

I like to think of this dynamic as the harmony of seeming opposites referred to in our exploration of consilience. Beyond balancing or intermingling, seemingly opposite energies and activities are mutually enhancing. By this I mean when we learn as we teach, or lead as we follow, we simultaneously enhance our following and leading; we do not just hold them as equals in balance or comingle them, but do so in such a way that the following enhances the leading and the leading enhances the following. Here, the energy and effectiveness of each is not impeded; it is just neutral, or improved somewhat, but, in tandem, goes beyond what leading or following could ever be by itself. The energy and effectiveness of leading as we follow and following as we lead creates consistent collective flow. The idea is not just about what the two opposites create together, but it is also about their simultaneous evolution. By cocreating, by leading and following in the same action, you become more your unique self and I become more my unique self. When the game for the great Bill Russel moved from the physical and mental to the magical (see Chapter 3), he said, "I could feel my play rise to a new level."

We are all leaders and we are all followers, or leader–followers, at the same time, all the time. These three points support this identity of leader–followers:

1. We are all leaders.
2. As members of an organization or team with a common purpose, we are all followers of the common purpose.
3. We are leaders and followers at the same time.

We are all leaders. That starts with leading ourselves *and* following ourselves in the same action. In doing so, we create collective flow. This concept supports Dr. Swart's observations about the brain intermingling leading and following. Similarly, when we lead organizations, teams, or projects, we lead as we follow and follow as we lead. The question now is how to do this. For that, we turn to Simultaneity.

CHAPTER 11

Simultaneity Innovates Innovation

Simultaneity creates an environment that will allow your team or company to operate at unimagined heights. Our decision-making processes became exponentially more effective and efficient; and as a result, we increased profitability significantly.

—STEVE MALBASA
partner at a major financial firm

S imultaneity begins with reidentifying each person in the organization as one who is a leader–follower at the same time, all the time. In this chapter, I will introduce this truly innovative approach to leadership, one that opens a new realm of leading-edge thinking that my clients describe as "exponential potential."

Our current models of leadership are inadequate for the needs of today's world, where uncertainty is the norm. What we need is a new leadership model that innovates innovation. The process of *radical mutuality*, in which everyone is a leader and follower at the same time, calls forth the fullness of everyone's simultaneous humanity, genius, and leadership. To do this requires learning to explicitly lead and follow in the same action.

Simultaneity is a unique innovative leadership that innovates innovation. As explained in Chapter 3 and depicted in Figure 3.1, consilience is the jumping together of seemingly opposite energies. Simultaneity, as a leadership process, is likewise a jumping together of two seemingly opposite energies—leading *and* following. This is not just shared leading and following over the course of a day, but leading and following in the same moment, in the same action, and by not just one leader, but by every leader leading and following in the same action.

While this is happening, the conformity embedded in the leader–follower model is eradicated, and the uniqueness and fullness of each leader–follower's genius blossoms to enhance the diversity that fuels the innovative dynamic. The combination of more diverse perspectives with a consilient process amplifies innovation to unprecedented levels, yielding a unique and innovative leadership process that innovates innovation.

Our definition of "innovation" is creativity followed by in-sync execution, or collective flow. The creativity comes from the consilient nature of Simultaneity and the in-sync execution comes from the radical mutuality of Simultaneity. This mutuality of everyone being equal, different, and vital—even in the context of necessary hierarchy—breeds ever-expanding perpetual trust that fuels in-sync execution, not to mention an organic experience of diversity, equity, and inclusion.

The Future Is Now: The Impact of Simultaneity

While implementing the methodology of mutual leadership with Rob Burch, formerly of Steelcase and currently CEO of Kindel Furniture, he said, "Jeff, you're underestimating the value of this program."

"What do you mean?" I asked.

He then reached for the closest napkin and began to draw the figures that follow. Referring to the Figure 11.1, he said, "This represents the communication of one person, the leader, or expert, to many, the team or organization. Let's say as an expert, he brings a value of 10 to the conversation."

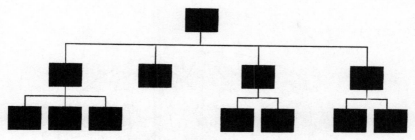

FIGURE 11.1 Value of one: 10

Then, referring to Figure 11.2: "This is how the communication was when you first started working with us. There was more interaction than in [the first figure], yet most of it was channeled through me as the designated leader. I remember when you pointed that out. Let's say that has a value added of 55, a significant increase.

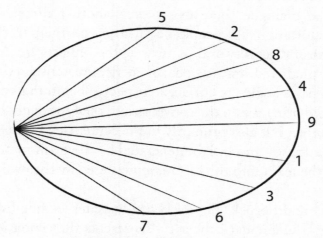

FIGURE 11.2 Value Added: 55

"Now we are beginning to communicate more like this," he continued, referring to Figure 11.3. "As this begins to progress it goes beyond a value added to a value multiplied. The results can be exponential."

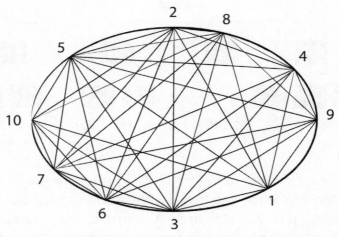

FIGURE 11.3 Value Multiplied: 3,507,800

As I reflected on this conversation, I realized that within genuine dialogue there exists even another dimension of communication. As people begin to speak their truth in a context of discovery and inquiry, as the philosopher Martin Buber predicted, a word, idea, or energy greater than the sum of the parts begins to surface.[1] As people begin to name this idea and bring it into the conversation, they speak not only to each other, but also primarily to the center (see Figure 11.4). As the energy and insight generated by the team matures, it leads the team into the future, represented by the oval in the center.

The shuttlecock (Figure 11.5) illustrates leading from the center. The circular rubber tip represents the center leading the team or organization forward. Here we have leadership,

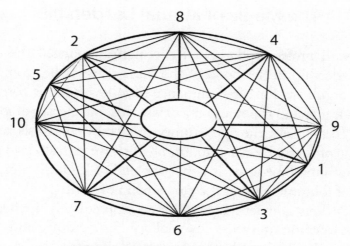

FIGURE 11.4 Value Potential is . . .

not from the top down or even the bottom up, but from the center out. When this happens, decisions appear. This dynamic was well described by Ralph Larsen, former CEO of Johnson & Johnson: "We don't really make decisions, we extrude them."[2] Collective learning activates the collective will, which yields synergy and opens the possibility of the team entering the zone of optimal performance.

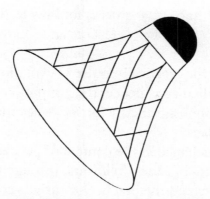

FIGURE 11.5 Infinite Value: $3,507,800^{10}\cdots$

The Magic of Mutual Leadership

Harvard professor Barbara Kellerman announced the end of leadership in her book of the same title.[3] If her compelling argument for the dominance of followership is correct, then leadership is not just at a crossroads, but a crisis of identity. In my view, the opportunity created by this crisis is the magic of mutual leadership, from which we learn to lead and follow simultaneously. It is not the end of leadership or the rise of followership but the partnership of both.

Curious conviction provides an immediately applicable human communication technology for leading and following simultaneously that generates the magic of mutual leadership, which breeds radical trust. The priceless power of trust leverages the one true source of sustainable competitive advantage of any company, their leaders and followers.

Simultaneity is innovative leadership that innovates innovation because it:

- Reflects the latest findings of neuroscience.
- Reveals the hidden context of organizations as communities of people all of whom are leader–followers all the time.
- Introduces an innovative process for how leader–followers lead each other as leaders and followers (at the same time).
- Comes out of the creative impulse of evolution and innovation, called consilience, the jumping together of seemingly opposite energy for the conception of something new.
- Expresses consilience in the context of people who are in the same action leader–followers, through the process of Simultaneity and the practice of curious conviction. (Consilience shows up in the seemingly opposing

energy of leading, or going before, and following, or going after, at the same time, and in the practice of curious conviction when making a statement and asking a question, or advocating and inquiring, in the same action.)

- Sets forth that leading is following and our following is leading because in these states of radical mutuality the subject becomes the object and the object the subject, (for example, when the teacher is learning while she teaches).

What Neuroscience Teaches Us about Simultaneity

We have seen from observation of brain activity how neuroscience reflects Simultaneity. The ability to consider opposing views and come up with new solutions and responses is one of the highest functions of an optimized brain. Happily, this is something we can all learn to do.[4] By using our evolved capacity to make a difference through our differences, our brain mirrors consilience, jumping together opposites to conceive something new. This is the energetic foundation of the WTL Flow Chart (see the chart at the beginning of Part IV).

The way the activity of the brain is reflected in the Simultaneity process also supports the concepts of self-leadership, traditional executive function leadership, and the evolving movement toward panarchical leadership (leading and following at the same time). Learning to lead each other without succumbing to the train wreck of "too many chefs" requires learning to lead as we follow and follow as we lead just as our optimized brain considers opposing points of view and seemingly different activities at the same time. Just as the brain creates new neural pathways to accommodate opposites, so we can train ourselves to see ourselves and others as leaders and followers simultaneously to seeing differences or opposition as opportunities to innovate.

The possibilities do not stop with leading or taking back control of our individual lives. As leaders of our own lives, we can join forces with other leaders, and collectively create new neural pathways for leading each other into consistent collective flow or in-the-moment innovation followed by in-sync execution. Up until now, the collective force of teams and organizations of leaders has been the exception and not the rule. Now, with an explicit plan, we can use our advanced science-based skills for leading ourselves and leading each other to solve heretofore unsolvable problems and to realize possibilities beyond our imagination (depicted in the WTL Flowchart at the beginning of Part III). We can climb out of our autopilot ruts and take flight together.

In his book *Why Humans Like to Cry: Tragedy, Evolution, and the Brain*, Michael Trimble simplifies our concept of the brain, writing, "The left side of the brain is for doing things that are pointing and propositional, while the right side is concerned with urging and yearning. Or the left brain stores and uses what is known, and the right brain is always on the lookout for what is new and engaging."[5] The role of the corpus callosum is to communicate between these two opposites, the known and the unknown, which is one of the highest of the executive functions found in the prefrontal cortex.

This integration of seeming opposites shows up in Simultaneity with different, even opposing, perspectives and interests and the seemingly contradictory process of leading (going before) and following (going after) at the same time. We integrate these polarities (leading and following in the same action) by introducing a curious conviction. Here again is the juxtaposition of seeming opposites in that apparent oxymoron. On the surface it appears contradictory, yet as we activate our higher brain functions by considering these two actions together then go further and create new neural pathways for bringing a curiosity and conviction in the same action . . . wow! We've created the missing ingredient to conscious and consistent collective flow. We now have the adeptness to lead our own lives along with the high brain function of consilience, all the while innovating innovation.

As conviction expresses the known of the right brain and curiosity the unknown of the left brain, doing both together at the same time mirrors the communication of the two hemispheres of the brain. Practicing a curious conviction activates new neural pathways and exercises and develops one of the highest of executive brain functions—namely, simultaneously embracing opposites, in this case, what is known and unknown. It makes you, your team, and your organization smarter and more innovative, and all the while your brain is evolving.

The brain has evolved from the limbic system (emotion, relating, bonding) to the cortex, including prefrontal cortex (logic and language). In a sense, it is the opposite of the most recent evolution of leadership, from one person exercising command and control through raw intellect and logic to the shared-servant situational leadership requiring greater emotional intelligence.

Our new evolution of leadership is the rational intelligence of the solo leader and the emotional intelligence of shared leadership jumping together to form a collective intelligence of thinking and feeling, speaking and listening, as one. As Iain McGilchrist suggests in *The Divided Brain and the Making of the Western World*, "The two halves of the brain . . . deal with information differently. The left half likes to deal with pieces of information in isolation; the right half with things as a whole."[6] As we shall see, when bringing a curious conviction it is paramount for everyone participating in collective flow to bring their convictions as a *piece* of the *whole* conversation, meeting, or project puzzle. Everyone seeing and presenting their own perspective, assumptions, and beliefs as pieces of the emerging whole puzzle is the portal to consistent collective flow and the magic of the Simultaneity process. Obviously, this also calls upon the activation and development of the corpus callosum to bridge communication between the right and left hemispheres of the brain. Embracing the differences within the various pieces of the puzzle and between the pieces and whole engages the optimal brain.

The corpus callosum—as connector of limbic and cortex and as bridge between the right hemisphere, or emotional region of the cortex, and the left hemisphere, or logical region of the cortex—serves a vital role in developing *both/ and* thinking, the opposite of *either/or* thinking. Both/and thinking relates, for example, simultaneously to both feminine and masculine, yin and yang, particular and universal, individual and collective, knowing and not knowing, pieces and the whole, and leading and following in the same action. As Dr. Swart puts it, "In true brain agility, the source (brain) is optimized to fire on all cylinders. This leads to well-rounded decisions. From the point of view of neuroscience, this makes absolute sense to me: it is most strongly about balancing logic and emotion."[7]

Given the evolutionary impulse of consilience and the role of the corpus callosum in integrating the limbic emotion and verbal logic, perhaps the next evolution of the brain will be the further development of the corpus callosum. Perhaps we'd see greater agility when it comes to Simultaneity and faster or more spontaneous consilience, which would result in greater and swifter innovation. Here, Swart is speaking from the perspective of neuroscience about the principle of evolutionary biology and the practice of consilience, the foundational base and source of energy at the base of the WTL Flow Chart, which represents the concept. I prefer the terminology of *harmonizing* emotion and logic to balancing different, yet neutral, elements of equal weight. With harmony I see the intermingling of opposite energies into a mysterious and beautiful symphony of sound, dance, and collective creativity.

Swart sees "the balance of logic and emotion as a key objective" for optimizing brain function and making wiser decisions. What often appear to be opposites, emotion and logic, are actually constantly jumping together, and this dynamic is yet another example of the evolutionary impulse of consilience.

The way Dr. Swart describes the activity of the brain reflects the activity of leading and following in the same action or the dynamic of leading as we follow and following as we lead. I apply this same connective logic to leadership by understanding leadership as a series of interactions between leader–followers rather than just the positions or roles of the two halves of leading and following. Like the brain intermingling emotion and logic, Simultaneity leadership interweaves leading as following and following as leading in a mutually harmonious way.

Neuroscience intersects, supports, and calls forth Simultaneity on at least three fronts:

1. Separating the functions of the right brain (emotion) and the left brain (logic), although with some basis, fails to accurately describe the reality that emotion permeates throughout the brain and integrates with logic as two sides of the same coin or two dimensions of the same activity. In other words, the right brain and left brain

comingle. This reflects the overall view of leading and following in Simultaneity. The jumping together of emotion and logic for optimal brain function mirrors our integration of the activity of leadership, which is about leading and following at the same time, all the time.

2. This dynamic plays out with the past assumption that the right brain is about exploring the unknown while the left is about storing the known, which mirrors the separation in traditional leadership that one leads because they know and one follows because they don't know. However, neuroscience now shows that although the right brain starts with the unknown and the left brain with the known, given the integration of the two hemispheres, the known becomes the unknown and the unknown the known. Simultaneity mirrors neuroscience's intermingling of the knowing leader and the unknowing follower by combining leading and following or knowing and not knowing with leading and following at the same time. This becomes tangible by utilizing a curious conviction, or knowing and not knowing, simultaneously.

3. According to neuroscience, the right brain tends to see the whole and the left brain the pieces. Simultaneity reflects both at the same time by introducing the distinctive step of a curious conviction—bringing one's conviction as a piece while at the same time being curious about what's emerging in the whole dialogue or project puzzle.

In the next chapter, we will further explore leading and following in the same action through the three steps of a curious conviction.

CHAPTER 12

Simultaneity Practice: The Art of Curious Conviction

Suppose we were able to share "meanings"
freely without a compulsive urge to impose our
view or to conform to those of others and without
distortion and self-deception. . . . Would this
not constitute a real revolution in culture?

—DAVID BOHM
Changing Consciousness

"It was like walking into a beehive. Everyone was quickly, but efficiently, buzzing around—each movement precise, knowing exactly what to do, where to go, and who they needed to speak with to get the job done. I couldn't quite put my finger on it, but there was an excitement and energy in the air; a true buzz around the place."[1]

Someone wrote this description after their first day working at Gravity Payments, a credit card intermediary. There was an arresting, captivating buzzing around one common purpose. Yet this wasn't in response to a crisis, but rather just another day at work. The author goes on to say: "Everyone was on a mission. But why? And who was in charge here? I came to find out that we all were."[2]

We've established that everyone is the CEO of their own lives, yet another example of the rise of panarchy (all are leaders), and that 75 percent of cross-functional teams—themselves teams of leaders—are dysfunctional.[3] Think of your own experience with a group of leaders in an executive team, board, or project. The question is, How can everyone be a leader and, at the same time, work as a team?

That's what this chapter is about. Not only is everyone the CEO of their own life, but everyone also has the capacity to be a CEO of an organization or a leader in the full sense of the word. Of course, everyone in an organization is also a follower, or equalizer, of the common purpose. This is how the potential conflict of a group of leaders is avoided, and how it can create conditions for collective flow. If there are only leaders then you risk chaos. If there's only one follower or few followers, you risk malaise and lack of direction, and miss out on collective intelligence and innovation. But if you can harmonize leading and following, you can create conditions for consistent collective flow. This happens when everyone is a leader and a follower (or a leader–follower) all the time, and at the same time.

The Third Way: Act as a Team

Harmonizing leading and following aligns with how our brains work. Just as our right and left brain do not function as two separate parts but always interact in an integrated way, so, too, do leader–followers act as two parts of the whole. Similarly, the act of leading includes both conviction and curiosity, the known and unknown, the pieces and whole, and leading and following at the same time. The right brain gravitates to the unknown with curiosity, while the left brain seeks out the known for convictions. We need both simultaneously to put our perplexing puzzles together. Creating a culture of leader–followers aligns our organizational collective brain with our individual human brain, resulting in getting everyone in sync for consistent collective flow.

Still, even a special place like Gravity Payments is not without its own challenges.[4]

The year 2020 was rocky. With the COVID-19 pandemic shutting doors, millions of people were laid off or furloughed. Companies faced this hard choice: eliminate a great team that will be difficult to rebuild, or somehow absorb massive financial losses.

In an interview with *Entrepreneur* magazine, Gravity Payments CEO Dan Price spoke of a third way: to act as a team. "Your team is so much smarter than you," Price said. "Mine is. Give power to your people, be honest and democratic. They will find solutions that you can't see."[5]

Price, who made headlines in 2015 when he took a million-dollar pay cut to institute a $70,000 minimum annual salary for his employees, wasn't looking to lay people off, but he was feeling pressure. "Businesses love to talk about caring for people, but the conventional wisdom is, what really matters in these situations is your balance sheet," Price states. "Leaders will do layoffs deeper and quicker than needed so they can start rehiring sooner and manufacture a comeback story." Gravity Payments processes credit card payments for more than 20,000 small businesses, and as their clients' revenue disappeared at the onset of the pandemic, so did Price's. "We were losing $1.5 million a month . . . We had three months before we'd be out of business."[6]

Price found himself between the rock of firing people and the hard spot of absorbing multimillion-dollar losses and jeopardizing the life of his business. A real gap. I imagine Price thinking this through over and over in his mind trying to solve the problem, feeling like a failure. After all he's the CEO, he should have the answers! What do you do? One day, perhaps while walking his dog, a thought popped to mind: *What about posing this dilemma to my team and seeing what they come up with?* After some collective deliberation his team came up with the idea that instead of laying people off, let everyone anonymously volunteer for pay cuts. His team volunteered nearly half a million dollars a month. Some offered their total pay. Others offered 50 percent. Some offered 5. (Price capped all contributions at 50 percent.) "It extended our runway to somewhere between six and twelve months," he says.[7] By late summer, he was confident enough in Gravity Payments' future that he paid back all employees.

When in Doubt, Ask for Help

What made it work? Price leveraged his ignorance. He let go of the outcome. He couldn't figure out an answer and, instead of pretending he knew what to do and forcing an answer—or inviting outside experts in to provide one—he went, albeit in apparent desperation, to his team.

We could say he did this and that. But when it comes down to it, he asked his team for help.

This is no small point. What made the team believe that Dan really wanted and valued their input? Would he really listen? Or was he just trying to gain buy-in for a decision he had already made or would make on his own? After all, he was the CEO and owner of the company.

There's a story I tell CEOs and their teams. Wearing my sport coat, I approach one of the team's members and say, "My mom bought me this jacket for my birthday. What do you think of it?" Typically, the team member tilts her head and says something like, "Well, I think it looks great on you." Then we look at what just happened. I asked for input while I had the coat on, so she's unlikely to say something negative like, "It looks a little tight around the waist," as I could easily take offense. We talk about how she might have said, "I don't like the brass buttons," and how that could cause me to think, *But my mom picked those out*, and get defensive, especially if my mother had recently died.

I next take a different approach. Taking my coat off and laying it on the back of the chair so she and everybody else can get a full view, I say, "I'm in the process of designing a men's jacket and would welcome and very much value your feedback about this one. What's coming up for you?" Now the same person leans back, takes a strong look at the coat, and responds, "The brass buttons really don't work with the black color. I would shade the black into a light grey and add purple buttons for some pizzazz." Now in my mind I may be thinking, *No way am I going to put purple buttons on this coat.* But, noticing this internal response, I can instead reply, "Hmmm . . . a light grey color with purple buttons. Would you tell me more about the purple buttons?" We then can continue with this line of reflective listening and curiosity, especially about what triggers my judgment. I learn much more than in the first encounter.

Typically, in most organizations today, when a CEO or formal leader walks into a room, people internally are on guard, physically adjusting their posture as they literally reset their body as well as their minds. Generally, this happens unconsciously and within seconds.

I tell CEOs and formal leaders that when they walk into the room they are essentially wearing the coats their mother gave them. If they want to access genuine feedback and generate collective flow, they need to take those coats off. They need to intentionally or consciously choose to hear the genuine thoughts and feelings of everyone present. They then need to find the language that communicates that intention to their particular audience.

In one way or another, Dan Price took his coat off. He left his organizational authority at the door and the members of his team believed that he not only welcomed and valued their candor but also insisted on it. The army uses the expression *Leave your stripes at the door.* "The most senior leaders in the room set the tone. When they make themselves vulnerable and admit to errors, it gives everyone else permission to do so too."[8]

A Piece of the Puzzle

Productive and meaningful dialogues among diverse groups of people are like assembling a puzzle. Everyone brings their pieces (points of view) to the table and commits to honestly sharing their opinions and convictions about an issue. At the same time, they express interest in hearing perspectives from other participants to enrich the dialogue. As everyone shares what they think and feel in the moment as a piece of the conversational puzzle, each participant leads with the assertion of their conviction and follows by surrendering to the curiosity of what others bring to the table, particularly when their pieces reveal differences, challenges, or opposition. Asserting and letting go in the same action is how participants lead and follow at the same time. They affirm the tension of opposites by being curious about what is emerging in the conversation and through differences the conversation starts to have a life of its own. It begins to lead the group forward. This dynamic is illustrated in Rob Burch's diagrams in Chapter 11 as the wisdom and energy from the center, or the conversational puzzle, activates the collective will, which yields synergy and opens the possibility of the team entering the zone of optimal performance.

Formal leaders, meaning designated leaders in a hierarchy, can play a pivotal role in framing and advancing these conversations. The leader might begin by saying, "I'd like to frame our conversation about this issue as a puzzle. All points of view are encouraged and welcomed, and sharing them provides our team with an opportunity to gain input, build understanding, create from our differences, and develop a shared perspective about the issue, which can help us create a common foundation for addressing it."

The Three Waits Technique

Sometimes the formal leader or boss is inclined to withhold his perspective to "make room for others to speak." This can be a helpful temporary move for leaders who tend to dominate conversations. One way to address this tendency is for the dominant leader or team member to practice the Three Waits—waiting three times before speaking. It works like this: Let's say that the dominant leader or team member feels strongly that it's not only okay but imperative to compete with the company's customers on certain levels. As a dominant participant, instead of stating this position upfront, he (and I use "he" here, because in my experience, usually the dominant leader or team member is a man) practices reflective listening by mirroring what others say, especially if those speaking hold an opposite view—in this case, not competing with customers. Each time he feels the urge to speak, the dominant leader waits, practices reflective listening, and mirrors what others are saying or what he hears emerging from the conversation. After waiting three times, the dominant speaker then sets forth his conviction as a piece of the emerging conversational puzzle.

I don't have research on this practice, but 90 percent of the numerous times I've experienced dominant leaders practice the Three Waits, someone else expressed the dominant leader's point of view. Although a bit of an ego deflator at first, and perhaps necessarily so, this move not only allows the space for others to express themselves, it also allows for the dominant leader to step back and listen to see the issue through a wider lens than just his own. Gaining this broader perspective accesses more of the team's collective intelligence and assists in deepening, clarifying, and strengthening the dominant leader's thinking as he presents his pieces of the puzzle.

Once the Three Waits has been practiced several times, the network of communication becomes much more interactive, as in Burch's third diagram in Chapter 11 (reproduced here as Figure 12.1), and causes the group energy to flow more.

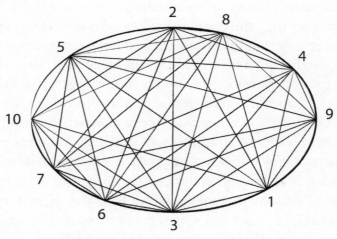

FIGURE 12.1 Value Multiplied: 3,507,800

Now, when the former dominant leader shares his convictions as a piece of the conversational puzzle, other members of the team trust that the leader is no longer attempting to dominate, but realize that the formerly dominant member is assuming an equal, different, and vital role along as part of the entire team.

The goal is to get everyone's views on the table, especially those that differ, by suspending judgment and certainty. Being inspired by curious conviction (speaking plainly and passionately with a sincere interest in considering different points of view) can yield meaning and satisfaction for participants. At best, when practiced by everyone simultaneously, all participants can access collective wisdom and tap into collective flow.

The Paradox of Humility and Confidence

In Chapter 10, I suggested that this might be the time to not only mirror Lincoln's leadership style, but to build a team of Lincolns. To take that concept a step further, this team would embody the paradox of humility and confidence, of being "fully committed" and at the same time aware "that I may possibly be wrong."

Humility is rooted in the Latin *humilis*, meaning low or lowly. It's often defined as having a moderate or low view of oneself. It also has deep roots in Christianity and other Western religions. Sometimes I find myself suspicious when I hear leaders of organizations and religious institutions touting humility without, at the same time, harmonizing it with confidence. Here's why.

Leaders tend to be confident and followers humble. Emphasizing humility can become, perhaps unconsciously, a way for leaders to maintain their position and power over followers. What I'm calling for, and it seems what Lincoln emulated, is for leaders to be both confident and humble at the same time. Humble followers are not what the world needs, and that's not who we are.

We are confident and humble leader–followers!

Each and every one of us has a part to play in the enterprise of humanity, an equal, different, and vital part. Our participation, our perspective, our expertise is of infinite value. We are all unique pieces of the puzzle of humanity. This means that, as valuable as our part is, it's limited. We cannot complete the puzzle or solve our problems without our partners' pieces. Here's where humility comes in. It's not that I believe my perspective is moderate or lowly, but that I need others to receive my part, and I need others to bring forth their parts, so that together, we can solve our organization's most intricate puzzles. We should all be confident that we have a unique and vital part of the "answer," and the humility to know that we cannot find it without inviting and inspiring others to bring forth their unique and vital parts.

Confidence and humility are another example of the jumping together of seemingly opposite energies as in the creative impulse of life, consilience. With curious conviction, confidence shows up, articulating what you currently observe, feel, think, and intend with the clarity that you are a unique human being with a distinctive and vital perspective. Humility comes forth by offering your convictions as a piece of the human puzzle. Being curious about others' unique and vital pieces makes you a follower. Bringing a curious conviction fully aligns with being the leader–follower that you are.

CHAPTER 13

Leading with a Curious Conviction

*It is the seeming contradiction that we must be
fully committed, but we must also be aware at the
same time that we might possibly be wrong.*

—ROLLO MAY
The Courage to Create

Sitting outside in the corporate campus of a renowned industry leader, the practice of a curious conviction came up. The then CFO remarked, "I know how to be curious in one moment and bring a conviction in another moment, but how do I bring a curious conviction in the same moment or in the same action?"

What a pivotal question! As we look at the WTL Flow Chart, this is the point at which you must make a choice. Will you select the route of the down arrow—representing judgment, negative emotions, and an either/or mentality—and allow yourself to be controlled by your external circumstances? Or will you choose to take a deep breath, step back, and observe your inner reactivity and select the up arrow and choose to create from our differences over judgment and adopt a centered self-expression of avoiding or fighting anger? In a heated moment, or when triggered, this choice can seem impossible or nonexistent.

Dr. Swart reminds us how challenging this can be. "Being able to consider opposing views in our mind and come up with new solutions and responses is one of the highest functions of an optimized brain." She then reminds us of the benefits of exercising the mental practice of consilience: "Creative thought is free to flourish, rather than being shut down by a brain that is stuck on auto pilot."[1] The down arrow in the WTL Flow Chart depicts a brain that is stuck on autopilot or reactivity. A brain that can practice consilience and embrace the friction of opposites as an opportunity for innovation is the foundation of an innovative culture (also depicted in the WTL Flow Chart, which further flourishes with the leadership practice of Simultaneity.

By leading and following in the same action, Simultaneity is itself an innovative practice of consilience. Simultaneity is expressed in everyday life by practicing the coming together of the seeming opposites, knowing and not knowing, as we do in a curious conviction. When everyone in the organization, on the team, and on a project practices a curious conviction, it activates and sustains trust, collective insight, and rapid responsiveness.

There are three steps of a curious conviction:

1. Believe in consilience or the innovative process of creating from opposites.
2. Bring a conviction as a piece of the conversation or project puzzle.
3. Be constantly curious.

Believe in Consilience

The best way to illustrate the power of the belief in consilience is with the story of a man with a wheelbarrow standing at the edge of the Grand Canyon, having stretched a tightrope across the chasm. As the crowd gathered, he asked,

"How many of you believe I can walk this wheelbarrow across the canyon on this tightrope?" Many responded, "Yes, we believe. We believe! " Then he asked, "Who then will get into the wheelbarrow as I go across?" No one responded and the crowd quickly dissipated. It's one thing to give intellectual consent, quite another to exercise active belief. It's one thing to believe in the opportunity of opposites and another to act upon it with a curious conviction.

Believing in consilience requires embracing it in our identity and relationships, and in the way we innovate. All three are rooted in the notion of consilience: identifying as a leader and a follower, relating to others with a constant mutual influence, and innovating from our differences.

- **Consilience in identity.** We the Leader is founded on three key identity observations: First, each of us as a member of an organization, team, or project are followers of a common purpose. Second, we are all leaders of our own lives and have the full potential to be leaders in the full sense of the word. Third, we are all leader–followers, at the same time all the time.
- **Consilience in relationships.** As leader–followers, we are equal, different, and vital human beings, mutual partners who constantly influence each other. Whether we realize it or not, there is a constant interplay between us. Mary Parker Follett calls this a circular response. It's how leader–followers relate to one another. We are constantly giving and receiving at the same time, which sets up the parallel idea that as constant givers and receivers, we are constant leaders and followers at the same time all the time. This description of circular response caused Mary Parker Follett to conclude, "We are creating each other all the time."[2] Leaders give direction. Followers receive direction.

- **Consilience in Innovation.** We identity as leader–
  followers in a mutual relationship with each other in
  order to innovate from our differences. Remember
  the Hegelian Dialectic (see Chapter 4), where
  we have the thesis (yes), the antithesis (no), and
  the synthesis, or consilience. Similarly, we have
  a fundamental choice, whether or not to line up
  with the energy of the evolutionary impulse of
  life by deciding that in our opposites we have the
  opportunity to create.

Believing in consilience means identifying yourself and
others as leader–followers, relating to others as equals, different but innovating with and through our differences, and
vital leader–followers or partners.

Bring Conviction as a Piece

Think about the process of Simultaneity and in particular
bringing and inviting others to bring a curious conviction
to putting a project/puzzle together. Seeking a new way to
solve a problem as a team asks all participants to enter into
a dialogue by playing the roles of both leader and follower
in the same moment. Many leaders are comfortable playing
these roles at different times during an extended exchange
or discussion, but doing so simultaneously requires learning
and practicing the art of curious conviction.

Accomplishing leading and following as a single action
by bringing a curious conviction is similar to putting together
a puzzle where the outcome is not yet clear,[3] as if there were
no picture on the box. In the same way, the outcome of the
dialogue puzzle is unknown.

1. Imagine a group of five of us or twenty of us in a circle putting a puzzle together. We each have five to six pieces turned upside down. When we look at the puzzle box, there's no image. It's a blank box, so we don't know what it is a puzzle of, as we typically do. Now we start the puzzle.

2. All pieces appear face down (in conversation this would be keeping your thoughts to yourself) and in front of the various people putting the puzzle of thinking and feeling together. Everyone turns their pieces right side up, noticing the shape and color of their pieces, then we start to look at our neighbors' pieces (in conversation, this would be sharing your thoughts).

3. Now we start to push the pieces out into the center between us, realizing that all the pieces have different shapes and colors. All these different shapes and colors may stir some anxiety for some and excitement for others. Plus, we don't even know what the puzzle is.

4. Moving on, we begin looking for connections between our pieces. Some satisfaction kicks in as we create clusters of pieces, yet frustration, as well, because we still have no idea what this is! "Look at the color and shape of this piece. It doesn't belong here! There must be more than one puzzle." "Is this some kind of a trick? Is it a rhino, spaceship?" Now some frustration is setting in.

5. Taking a deep breath everyone stays with it and keeps making connections, and by inviting those pieces that are different, eventually some connections are made. There's a cluster here and a cluster there and then a couple clusters come together. "It's a jet," someone exclaims. "No, I don't think so," another says. Suddenly, all the pieces and clusters come together. With a slight sense of awe everyone is just staring at the assembled puzzle.

Please note that no one took one or all their pieces and hid them in their pocket. Otherwise, the puzzle would never be completed. Each piece is equal, different, and vital. All the pieces are needed to complete the puzzle. One piece missing and the puzzle is not complete. Also notice that no one said, "My piece is the whole puzzle," and tried to convince everyone else that that was the case. And no one put their puzzle piece forward only to pull it back. In others words, no one brought their pieces forward only to pull them back and therefore not let go of them.

Now let's take what was learned from that example to the practice of Simultaneity and, more specifically, a curious conviction to a conversation or project puzzle in which there is no known or predetermined outcome (similar to the challenge Dan Price, the CEO of Gravity Payments, and his employees faced when they feared the business would not survive the pandemic). In solving puzzles, feelings are an important piece. As we saw in Chapter 5, emotions are energy that moves a conversation, relationship, or project along—e-motions. If ignored and not transmuted, feelings can cloud one's ability to put the puzzle together. Other pieces may include a variety of perspectives, or points of view; remember The Blind Men and the Elephant. Of course, mixed together with these diverse feelings and perspectives are different ways of thinking because, although on some level everyone's brain is similar, everyone's brain is unique just as they are. Note as well that all of these pieces and their components occur in the now moment, not the participants' best pre-thought-out ideas designed to impress, but their raw, not-yet-refined thoughts and feelings at that time. Clearly, navigating this requires practicing the disciplines of improvisational technique (see Chapter 3).

The responses to the four Me the Leader questions are another way to identify the pieces of a project puzzle. These questions reveal the current pieces of the puzzle:

1. **What are you observing?** Observing involves suspending judgment and certainty and noticing what is, which requires as objective as possible a view of the facts about what is known and identifying the questions to be asked about what remains unknown. In the case of Gravity Payments, the knowns were the financial figures and the projected endpoint (three months) for the business if no changes were made. The unknowns included how long the pandemic would last, how Gravity's business and the way we do business in general would change as a result of the pandemic, whether their business could survive—and wave after wave of further unknowns no one could predict.

2. **What feelings are you observing?** The previous question focused on external facts and projections. This question focuses on your emotional response to the external situation. Please note that observing your emotional reaction is different from identifying with your emotional reaction. The first is illustrated by saying "I'm afraid" or "You're making me angry." Here, the approach is "I'm noticing that I'm feeling afraid or frustrated."

3. **What are you thinking or assuming in this now moment?** What assumptions are you making? How are you interpreting the data? What questions are coming up?

4. **What do you desire?** Your desires may be related to the outcome or the current process. For example, you may desire or hold the intention that we will find a creative way, a third way, beyond these seemingly opposing forces. Alternatively, you may desire that people listen to divergent points of view rather than ignoring, judging, or attempting to dismiss diverse perspectives.

These four questions all at once in the moment may well feel overwhelming. However, if the four questions become personal habits for leading your life, they increasingly become second nature. If your teammates apply them as well, it is very re-enforcing. Finally, the Simultaneity process allows and encourages intentional and unintentional moments of silence, in which participants may reflect and gather themselves by asking themselves and then each other these same questions.

In creative conversations and moments of real innovation as seen in the Gravity example, everyone asserts and surrenders their pieces of the puzzle. No one withholds their piece in fear of being shut down. No one, not even the formal leader or experts, attempts to convince others that his or her point of view will solve the puzzle. In other words, no one withholds what they currently think and feel, and no one imposes what they currently think and feel. No, everyone asserts what they think and feel, and then surrenders it or lets it go to the space between one another's thoughts and feelings. That is the key—the magical moment—when everyone asserts what they think and feel and lets it go in the same action. They lead with the pieces of their convictions and simultaneously follow with their curiosity about the pieces of others. This is the moment when their leading is following and their following is leading. It is like that moment when the tennis ball hits the racket and in the same moment and in the same action the tennis ball is both received and responded to, given to the other player. (This is the moment, often unrecognized, when our leading/giving is our following/receiving. The moment of Simultaneity.)

There is a moment when putting a puzzle together that we put our piece down and let it go. There is a parallel moment in a conversational puzzle when we put our pieces out there, when we lead with our convictions, and let them go. In that moment of asserting our convictions and letting them go like pieces of a puzzle, we are practicing a curious conviction. This is not a convincing conviction, but a curious conviction that, at the same time in the same moment in the same action, is curious about the other pieces. In this action, we are leading with our convictions and following with our curiosity.

When everybody simultaneously practices a curious conviction, they listen as they speak, follow as they lead; they are leading and following simultaneously. This jumping together of opposites is a manifestation of consilience, the evolutionary impulse of life, the core practice of collective innovation. Sometimes we practice a curious conviction unwittingly. We feel and see the magic of something new emerging from our differences. Here are a few examples: the idea to save Gravity, or a new product that not only produces massive income and redefines the industry but increases revenue by 45 percent in the midst of a pandemic, or a new strategy of tech and touch that propels a regional company into the top 20 nationally, or an enlivened culture that builds the foundation for a bold and successful merger. (See the sidebar for how the Wright brothers practiced a curious conviction.)

Anyone, including the formal leader and dominant participants, who holds back, withholds their pieces, or dominates the conversation nullifies the ability to put the puzzle together. In the context of putting a puzzle together, a conviction, even one that's strongly held, isn't convincing. This is particularly so because innovation is forged through our differences. We make a difference through our differences. Within the context of puzzling, a conversation (conviction) should be an act of self-expression intended to contribute an equal, different, and vital piece to the conversational puzzle, not an attempt to convince or conquer other people or their perspectives.

171

Of course, there is a time and place for convincing, as we shall see in Chapter 14.

Jack Dorsey, the CEO of Twitter, and his team were facing an extremely challenging and significant task for their company, the United States of America, and the freedom of human beings. How to regulate and monitor the speech of those who use its platform—in particular, at that time, the most powerful person in the world, the then president of the United States. The implications for the future of speech on social media are huge.

Here's what we know about the debate and discussions that endured over months according to the *New York Times* investigation drawn from nine interviews with nine current and former company employees and others who worked with Mr. Dorsey outside of Twitter:

> Some executives repeatedly urged Mr. Dorsey to take action on the inflammatory posts while others insisted he hold back, staying hands-off as the company had done for years.
>
> That set off internal debates. Mr. Dorsey observed the discussions, sometimes raising questions about who could be harmed by posts on Twitter or its moderation decisions, executives said. . . . Mr. Dorsey had expressed interest in finding a middle ground. . . . He often delegated policy decisions, watching the debate from the sidelines so he would not dominate with his own views. And he frequently did not weigh in until the last minute.[4]

As in Dorsey's case, CEOs often withhold their live-in-the-moment puzzle pieces from important conversations so as not to dominate. However, in my experience, it's clear that everyone is wondering what the formal leader, or in this case, the CEO, is thinking. Theirs is an equal, different, and vital piece of the puzzle just like everyone else's. It seems to me that in these instances the CEO has not "taken his coat off" and, therefore, the team believes he's still wearing it. As formal leaders persistently take their coats off by clarifying their intentions and using language to match those intentions, and then welcoming and reflecting points of view that oppose theirs, they can act like the equals they are and move the conversation along much quicker.

The unspoken message in withholding like this is "If I speak my truth in the moment like the rest of you, everyone will acquiesce to my point of view and we will not have a robust conversation." How condescending is that?!

In Dorsey, we have an example of a formal leader being curious yet withholding their convictions in the name of not dominating. Later in this chapter, we will discuss an opposite example, Steve Jobs bringing a conviction yet without a curiosity.

Extraordinary Innovation

The Wright brothers didn't just invent flight. They utilized a unique communication technology. They combined conviction with curiosity and achieved extraordinary results.

In his book *The Wright Brothers*, David McCullough illuminates the communication strategy that made their inventions possible—they regularly engaged in heated exchanges for days on end, each brother passionately advocating for his own ideas. They argued so much, in fact, that their sister threatened to leave home if they didn't stop.

Arguing was just the first phase of their communication technique. The second phase—the innovative phase—didn't kick in until they became curious about the other's point of view. So genuinely curious, in fact, that they often adopted each other's viewpoints.

The Wright brothers combined conviction with curiosity. The result was extraordinary innovation.

Given the relentless pressure to adapt to changing conditions, today's leaders don't have the luxury of arguing for days on end as the Wright brothers did. To fuel extraordinary and responsive innovation, we need a game-changer. The speed and agility required for success in the current reality requires skillfully combining conviction with curiosity in real time.

Of course, this communication technology only worked for the Wright brothers because both of them did it. The pivotal element that leads to success is developing your team's capacity to utilize this approach together.

In a world of "innovate or become obsolete," gaining every advantage in the marketplace is essential. Combining conviction with curiosity has changed the world before, and it can galvanize your team.

What would be possible if your team were fluent in the communication technology the Wright brothers employed?

How might innovation take off in a culture that values the ability to intelligently hold the tension of opposing viewpoints while simultaneously looking for the emerging genius in differences?

What would it feel like to have the freedom to express your ideas with conviction and authenticity, allowing others to do the same, and innovating together with curiosity?

One way to think about this is a movement from convincing, which means to conquer, to conversing, which means to turn toward each other, as in doing a puzzle.

Be Constantly Curious

Curiosity, rooted in not knowing, is what creates convictions. Practicing a curious conviction as an expression of leading and following simultaneously or in the same action is consilience, or the jumping together of opposites, the very foundation of collective innovation.

Our context for curiosity certainly includes the wider context of general inquiry, but our focus is on one another's opposing opinions in the belief that our differences are nothing but opportunities to cocreate. This cocreation is arguably the very purpose of life and, consequently, the foundational purpose of all institutions, organizations, projects, and teams. For this reason, our collective cultures at their core are cultures of curiosity and learning.

Therefore, in contrast to a culture of conviction that informs command-and-control organizations, a curious culture is not just about proving that we are as competent, better, or right, but about improving ourselves and the world by entering into the question, loving instead of loathing our ignorance as another opportunity to learn and cocreate.

It turns out that curiosity not only leads to our learning, but psychologists have found that when we listen carefully and reflect back the nuances in people's thinking they become more curious themselves and are open to different perspectives. In other words, curiosity breeds curiosity.

Are you feeling stale or stalled and incurious about others' points of view, especially as they differ from, even attack, your own, as is often the case in politics, and want to release yourself from judgment and self-righteousness? One way to recharge your curiosity is to interview other people. Interviewing is about two things: (1) asking questions that genuinely express your curiosity and (2) listening to the answers by mirroring what you hear and digging deeper with comments like, "Would you tell me more? Would you help me see how you came to that conclusion?" "I'm guessing that must be very frustrating or liberating. Is that the case? I'm wondering if you also feel this way about xyz?"

In fact, there's a defined process called motivational interviewing. Adam Grant describes the process this way:

> Instead of trying to force other people to change, you're better off helping them find their own intrinsic motivation to change. You do that by interviewing them—asking open-ended questions and listening carefully—and holding up a mirror so they can see their own thoughts more clearly. If they express a desire to change, you guide them toward a plan.[5]

From my perspective, the key factor in these interviews is suspending all judgment and attempts to convince or persuade and choosing to be continually curious.

While doing my original research on the purpose of business, I felt compelled to respond to some of the answers of the dean of a renowned business school to my questions, and instead of just listening, I countered his responses. So much so that he retorted, "I thought this was an interview!" Most recently, a very good friend and I had an extremely sensitive business misunderstanding. After a couple of weeks, I requested an opportunity to hear him out without rebuke or judgment. It was challenging, but armed with the BOSS practice for leading myself, I not only made it through, but we reconnected on an even deeper level. In fact, he now wanted to hear me out without rebuke or judgment.

You may recall that the three dimensions of Simultaneity are the inner, inter, and intra. These dimensions also apply to curiosity as a component of bringing a curious conviction in the process of Simultaneity.

Inner curiosity is about being curious about our own inner state of being or our own mental/emotional health. A key barrier to inner curiosity or self-awareness is self-judgment. If I judge my inner state—in other words, if I observe my inner state of thinking and feeling judgmentally and with self-condemnation—I am less likely to look inside myself. However, if on looking inside I choose to be patient, accepting, and compassionate rather than frustrated, angry, or shamed, I am more likely to look inside more often and increase my own self-awareness. In Chapter 7, I recommended journaling on a regular basis to address the Four Questions for Leading Yourself. This practice builds self-awareness and accelerates being aware more and more in the moment, which shortens or eliminates the gap between reactivity and the ability to respond in a calm, centered, and poised fashion.

Inter curiosity is all about being curious about the experiences, beliefs, questions, and convictions of others, particularly when they oppose and threaten our own. As we have explored, the guru of management gurus, Mary Parker Follett, sees the integration of our differences for the creation of something new as the highlight of human existence. There are many resources for deep listening, and I have outlined them in the section on inviting others to a curious conviction so will refer you there rather than repeating here.

Intra curiosity. The CEO of a Fortune 500 company wanted to engage her team in developing a 2020 Vision for their industrial manufacturing company. She knew something needed to shift but wasn't clear just what that something was. After introducing the We the Leader process, the team gathered for two days to dialogue by collectively practicing a curious conviction. Soon what appeared between the team and the center (designated as We the Leader in the WTL Flow Chart) was the realization that the "material flow was the boss" of the project. In fact, they named the center, The Boss. The curious conviction practice continued in order to understand what this meant and its implications for day-to-day operations. It soon became obvious that naming the in-the-moment operations "the boss" authorized those engaged to make decisions without waiting for one from the hierarchical decision-making tree.

On another level, this is an example of a panarchical structure of equal leaders on the front lines existing parallel to the top-down hierarchy and is similar to the hybrid hierarchy–panarchy structure, which we'll explore in Chapter 15. As some forty executives were gathered in a circle continuing the dialogue about the implications of the material flow as boss, I'll never forget when a woman twelve seats to my right inquired, "I wonder what 'The Boss' thinks of this idea." as she motioned to the center of the room.

That statement was the first of two examples of intra curiosity (meaning curiosity about what is emerging in the center of the WTL Flow Chart or between dialogue participants). The other was when the team recognized and named what emerged in the center as "the material flow is the boss."

Practicing all three dimensions of curiosity at once is possible and yet can be challenging at first. However, in this case, the team caught on quickly. Often, those like the woman twelve chairs to my right are able to step back and observe from this wider perspective because they are not in the mix challenging or supporting in the dialogue. Rather, they have a more detached yet acute perspective, and can naturally play this observer or third intra-curiosity role. Collective flow doesn't require that everyone play this role. But for collective flow inner curiosity or self-awareness that leads to the centered up-arrow benefits on the WTL Flow Chart, it is required by all most of the time. This inner curiosity, or listening to oneself, builds the foundation for listening to others with curiosity. We can only listen to others to the extent that we can listen to ourselves.

The Primacy of *Between*

A key assumption at play in the Simultaneity leadership methodology is the primacy of *between*. Prominent leadership theories and practices that support a leader–follower model often assumed that the key insight or inspiration for living lies within the individual. In that case, the leader's task is to instill their perspective in others. This model is consistent with their Western individual psychological model, which assumes the core of living is within the individual.

The Simultaneity model assumes the ultimate source of living exists between individuals, in the center of the collective. Individual insight and energy continue as vital contributors to the collective. Martin Buber, the renowned theologian and philosopher of dialogue, suggested that when two or more people are authentic with each other, an insight or energy appears between them.[6] Here, the leader's role is not to convince others of their point of view, but rather to offer their perspectives as a piece of the emerging collective puzzle and invite and teach others to do the same.

As a team consistently engages in open and authentic conversation, new ideas, insights, and energies appear in the center. This center then leads the team into the future. This image represents collective leadership not just from the top down and bottom up but also from the center out. (This activity is depicted in Rob Burch's diagrams in Chapter 11.)

Conversing with the Center

At its core, Simultaneity is a dialogue process, containing three dimensions of dialogue: inner, inter, and intra. Inner dialogue refers to the conversation within the individual, including the array of thinking and feeling of the reactive self and the centered self. Inter dialogue refers to the interaction from person to person. Intra dialogue depicts the insight and energy that begins to emerge between people. Learning to listen and speak to this center as well as to oneself and others goes a long way toward creating conditions for the exponential results that come from leadership from the center out. This can be seen in the emergence of "the material flow is the boss" and the woman's comment about it.

You can visualize the reality of leading from the center out by picturing a badminton birdy, thrust into the air like a satellite, the rubber tip leading the birdy forward in flight. The rubber tip represents the center and the material flow the boss that led that team to a new vision and strategy for 2020, what they called 2020 Vision.

Remember the Blackberry? It was all the rage at one point with business leaders and celebrities, who testified to how it changed their lives. What happened? Where did it go? Of course, you're familiar with the iPhone. Why is the iPhone thriving and the Blackberry gone? The iPhone almost didn't make it.

Back in 2004 when Apple engineers came to Steve Jobs with the idea of an iPhone (notice the engineer–followers came to lead the CEO–leader Steve Jobs), he allegedly shouted, "Why the fuck would I want to do that!" Jobs hated phones and was known to throw his cell phone on the ground when it was too slow or not working properly. He also didn't want to conform to the phone company's standards and demands. For six months Jobs was in a reactive vortex (as demonstrated by the down arrow in the WTL Flow Chart). It took him six months to become curious, receive the direction and leadership of his followers, and okay further research on the iPhone. For six months, Jobs clearly had a conviction but no curiosity. The creation of the iPhone was delayed.

In Twitter's Jack Dorsey, we had an example of a formal leader being curious yet withholding his convictions in order not to dominate. On the other hand, Steve Jobs brought a conviction but without a curiosity. Both spent months not making a decision, thereby losing time and sacrificing speed.

How to build and live as teams of equals despite the inherent inequality of hierarchies demands an adaptive and conscious way of making decisions and enables wise choices made quickly. Practicing a curious conviction with the high-octane Simultaneity decision-making process described in the next chapter accelerates decision-making and its subsequent execution.

CHAPTER 14

The Accelerator: Communication and Decision-Making

Decide how to decide.

—ANONYMOUS

Given the drive for the speed and agility that fuel innovation—96 percent of CEOs cited this as a top priority—many companies decided to create more equitable teams in order to creatively solve problems and realize possibilities. Some of these teams succeeded; others floundered. For example, George Wolfe, former vice-president of a leading corporate university, recognized that some of these teams never made any decisions, weren't very productive, and lacked accountability. To address this situation, both Steelcase and Apple assigned formal leaders to the teams. (Apple called these leaders Direct Responsible Individuals), who oversaw the work of the team, made crucial decisions, and were held accountable for results. As you might guess, the presence of a formal leader began to decrease or eliminate open and free dialogue, and consequently the creativity and effectiveness of the team. Instead of enhancing the flow, the additional structure prohibited it.

Clearly, they needed a method to ensure accountability and wise timely decisions that not only allowed for, but also enhanced, creativity.

In ideal circumstances, the team's real accelerator ought to be the trust built from the radical mutuality of everyone practicing curious conviction, which enables immediate decision-making rather than the slow process of extended deliberation. Some even claim that collective knowing eradicates any need for a decision, as there would come a moment when everybody just knows what to do. From this collective knowing comes the ownership, commitment, and zeal to execute seamlessly. Once the team and leaders shared in the experience of collective knowing, the team trusted the formal leader to make the wise choice. The lesson learned was that formal leaders needed the mindset and the skills to facilitate meaningful dialogue with curious convictions and a decision-making model.

I've found that a simple decision-making model, coupled with key dialogue skills, not only balances but harmonizes the seeming tension between individual authority and collective creativity. In other words, consilience—in this case, the jumping together of the seemingly opposite need for individual authority and collective freedom with a decision-making model that enhances the benefits of both simultaneously. The key is to exercise individual authority with the intent to enhance collective flow, which is exactly what the following decision-making model has accomplished for industry leaders across the globe.

Three Criteria for Successful Decision-Making

Balancing and harmonizing individual authority and equal creative participation requires a decision-making model that makes the right choice at the right time in the right way.

Right choice means choosing the correct option, making that wise decision that integrates all the factors and moves the project or the organization forward.

Right time means not too soon, not too late. There are windows of opportunity that open and close and the key is to make that "right choice" decision within the window of opportunity. Sometimes in teams of equals decisions are prolonged, often with the intention of getting everyone's input or collaboration; sometimes it is a way to avoid making a decision.

Right way means making a timely decision that includes everyone's input, accessing collective intelligence. This results in ownership, commitment, enthusiasm, engagement, and wiser choices.

I know of a renowned industry leader in the investment world that had a culture that integrated a hierarchy with a collaborative environment and therefore often made the right decisions the right way. However, the business failed to make those decisions at the right time. The problem was their collaborative approach required everybody to weigh in multiple times, which delayed important decisions. As a result, they missed windows of opportunity. This problem only expanded as the company doubled, then tripled, the number of its associates. Fortunately, as they grew, they brought on a number of top executives from other more hierarchical companies, which facilitated more timely decision-making. At the same time, tensions arose between a collaborative and more authoritarian model of decision-making.

Another client in the financial industry with a traditional hierarchy was, as you might guess, able to make decisions in a timely fashion, as typically one person made those decisions.

However, as the business became more complex, it required massive integration of technology. This advanced high-tech/high-touch process was too much for one person to handle, and issues of integrating high tech with high touch were so complex that the CEO at the time could not see all the pieces, let alone put them together. Therefore, the decision to move forward was thwarted—not because of an egalitarian group of people that couldn't make a decision, but because a single leader was overwhelmed by the massive amount of information necessary to make a decision. What was lacking was an infrastructure to access collective intelligence and an explicit shared decision-making model. What was lost was the opportunity to improve relationships across the company with stakeholders and customers.

In yet another case, when the new president of a well-respected tech company observed employees so overwhelmed that no one was making any decisions, she decided she just wanted people to decide, fail, and learn, then repeat. In this case, the problem wasn't about making the right choice at the right time the right way; it was about making a choice even if it was the wrong choice the wrong time the wrong way. The Simultaneity decision-making model empowered the company to avoid not only making wrong decisions, but to make the right choice at the right time in the right way.

What's Your Decision-Making Model?

Here are a few questions to clarify your thinking about your own process:

- What has been your experience with your company's or your team's decision-making model, and more specifically, your personal decision-making model? Do you have an explicit and repeatable model that consistently delivers the right choices, in the right time, done the right way?

- When have you made the right choice, the right time, the right way? Were you just lucky? Or did you have an intentional repeatable process that helped you hit that decision-making sweet spot over and over again?

- When it comes to making decisions, what is your primary mode of operation? Do you start from a more directive position, then maybe become more collaborative? Or are you more comfortable with a more collaborative approach and find it challenging to own a tough decision? In what ways does it depend upon the situation?

Gary Burnison, CEO of Korn Ferry, said this about work today: "Different work needs to get done, and work needs to get done differently. As such, roles are morphing, and responsibilities are broadening. Teams are coming together fluidly and in multiple combinations. Organizational charts need to be invisible, and hierarchy thrown out the window."[1]

While such talk of dismissing or dismantling hierarchy seems to be trendy, and I understand the negative reaction to overdone hierarchy attempting to control others, let's not throw everything out. Instead, let's utilize hierarchy to move creativity into action in a timely fashion. Temporary conformity, inequity, and exclusion is required when there is no time to access collective will. As Dave Kaufman reminds us (Chapter 15), "Ambiguity is the friend of creativity but the enemy of execution."

Consistent Collective Flow

Creativity thrives in groups of equals who figure out how to work together. Execution can require imposing some hierarchy, particularly for in-the-moment decision-making. In line with our working definition of innovation as *creativity with in-sync by execution,* I suggest that today's organizations prioritize innovation by starting with a fluid panarchical structure, where everyone is a leader and follower all the time, rather than a traditional hierarchical structure. They can then create a decision-making structure to serve that creativity, with in-sync execution. In my view, this harmonizes structure and creativity for more consistent collective flow.

How do we, as those involved in collective projects, teams, and organizations, make decisions? Our working definition of innovation is *creativity with in-sync execution.* Deciding how to apply decision-making is the link between creativity and execution. Given the fundamental egalitarian nature of our organizations as a community of leader–followers, how do we make decisions in a manner that supports collective flow? This is an important question! To impose decision-making without adequate input from the equal, different, and vital participants of an organization runs the risk of not tapping into the collective intelligence of the group and missing the necessary commitment and zeal needed to sustain collective flow. The lack of both of these stops innovation dead in its tracks. At the same time, to not make a decision, or to not do so within the window of opportunity, is to have creativity without execution, thus thwarting innovation.

I'm not sure timing is everything, but it's crucial. The questions then become:

- How do we make wise and timely decisions in a manner that ignites enthusiasm and feeds collective flow?
- How can leaders exercise their legitimate individual organizational authority in a way that activates, expands, and sustains collective flow or perpetual innovation while remaining engaging and enjoyable?
- How can we make these decisions in a way that explodes diversity, equity, and inclusion instead of undermining or putting them on hold?

Inevitably, unless the collective will is accessed, decision-making involves a necessary hierarchy or temporary moments of conformity, inequity, and exclusion. How can this be accomplished in a way that fuels the power of equality for collective flow? The call for a decision-making model that includes conformity, inequity, and exclusion within the context of diversity, equity, and inclusion is another example of the principle and practice of consilience applied to collective decision-making.

Components of Successful Decision-Making

Decision-making in this context is not leading another person, but leading a team or organization. This is an important distinction. Decision-making—the primary exercise of leading a team or organization—is not making decisions for other people but rather on behalf of the team, organization, or collective. We don't lead individuals; we lead only groups of people: teams and organizations. A main, if not *the* main, activity of leading is making decisions.

Making quality timely decisions while gaining the commitment of the team can be challenging. Making quick timely or responsive decisions risks missing the collective intelligence of the group. Moving forward without adequate input can diminish the quality of the decision, not to mention the needed buy-in necessary for aligned execution. On the other hand, spending time accessing the wisdom of the team and gaining buy-in can result in missing a window of opportunity. How do you make timely decisions in response to external demands and simultaneously assure quality choices?

There are three key components in the Simultaneity Decision-Making Process:

- Have a grasp of the five forms of communication.
- Utilize the three ways of making a decision:

    1. Directive or giving a directive
    2. A directive with dialogue or giving a directive after accessing the collective intelligence of the team
    3. Dialogue that accesses the collective will when everyone comes to a common understanding

- Follow the three simple steps of deciding:

    1. Deciding how to decide from the three types of decisions
    2. Communicating the decision-making process to the team or organization
    3. Following through with the decided process

Five Communication Strategies and How to Use Them

All leaders have five forms of communication at their disposal. Part of being a conscious leader is being aware of them and knowing when to use which one. I argue that dialogue, when used properly and in the right situation, is by far the most productive form of communication because it offers the possibility of creating from our differences. Yet it's not always the most productive or even appropriate. For instance, if our house were burning down, it would be irresponsible to invite my daughters to a dialogue around the kitchen table. That's the time for directives. Yet, if I primarily give my children directives, I'll raise good followers, but not the leaders they truly are. However, the quality of the outcome depends on the quality and extent of the dialogue as well as whether or not the participants bring a curious conviction to it.

Before we go further, let's examine the five strategies:

1. **Dialogue,** from *dia-logos*, which means, among other things, a flow of meaning. As a communication strategy, its purpose is to discover, to innovate, but not to make a decision per se (although sometimes a new third way from differences emerges). One CEO of a major pharmaceutical company noted, "We don't really make decisions. Often, they just exude from our conversations. Everyone has a knowing of what to do." The goal of dialogue is to access the collective intelligence of the group, which includes the collective will.

2. **Discussion** means to break down. Its purpose in this context is to inform decisions by investigating the pros and cons, or explaining a decision to others by giving the rationale for the choice and facilitating a Q&A to get input and buy-in.

3. **Debate** means, in this context, to win the conversation or to convince others of your point of view. Although seldom used in the context of decision-making, a debate between two members of a team who hold opposing views can help clarify those differences and initiate a dialogue. Providing clarity of opposing perspectives up front can speed up the process of creating from these differences through dialogue. If a dialogue starts and the differences lie under the surface, the dialogue may linger longer than necessary.

4. **Discourse** means to lecture through a one-to-many presentation. The purpose is to instruct or inform. Information is always changing. If the sales leaders withhold information the operations leaders don't have, and vice versa, it will not only slow the process but also further confuse it.

5. **Directive** is a demand, and its purpose is to control or lead (think of the role of a board of directors). In a time of crisis, conducting a dialogue, discussion, debate, or discourse would be irresponsible. At such times, it is crucial that the "formal," hierarchical leader give directives. That directive might be to shut the business down, or reallocate resources. If the hierarchical leader has built up trust with their team through ongoing dialogue, the exercise of authority with an appropriate directive can build upon that collective trust. Although few want their leader to lead with command and control, most team members understand the need in those few moments of crisis.

Good leaders discern when to lead with directives and when to lead with dialogue. Exceptional leaders create conditions that allow the collective will to emerge. Like a soulful jazz maestro, they artfully blend the sounds of dialogue, discussion, debate, directives, and discourse, orchestrating a melody of quality timely choices.

Here is an example of what I mean by how a soulful maestro works. I had been working with Luisa's executive team at an industry-leading global logistics company for months. So she and her team were prepared when she received a lunchtime call from the CEO, who needed a decision about a crucial logistics matter by 5 p.m. that day.

To arrive at a decision, Luisa applied the Simultaneity decision-making process. We reviewed the three steps for making a decision: (1) decide how to decide, (2) communicate how the decision will be made, and (3) follow through. Of the three ways to make a decision—(1) directive, (2) directive with dialogue, and (3) dialogue to collective will—Luisa decided on the third method. Now it was time to communicate how the decision would be made and follow through with her team.

Luisa gathered her team immediately after lunch:

During the lunch break, I received an urgent call from Dana [the company's CEO] needing a decision relating to the interrelationship between shipping in Europe and Asia by 5 p.m. today. This is how we are going to proceed [a directive]. First, starting at 1 p.m., we will hear from Karl, head of Europe, then Meng, head of Asia, to get us all up to speed on the latest developments in each of their areas [fifteen-minute discourse]. Next, to sharpen all of our understanding about the different issues at stake, we will have Emily, who is experienced with option A, debate Sanjay, who believes in option Z, for fifteen minutes. Then at 1:30, we'll move into a dialogue about this matter, in which we will practice the three actions of a curious conviction, which are (1) believing in consilience by airing our differences, (2) bringing our convictions as pieces of the conversational puzzle, and (3) being constantly curious, that we've learned and have been practicing. Remember, the purpose of our dialogue is not to make a decision; rather it is to listen for what collective will might emerge from our deliberation. If after two hours, we haven't come to a creative common understanding, we'll move toward making a decision. After a break at around 3:30, we'll begin to identify the various options, weighing the pros and cons of each [discussion], interspersed with dialogue until 4:30. If we have not come to a common understanding, I will draw upon the collective intelligence we've created and shared, and then make a decision [directive].

By 3:15, just fifteen minutes before the end of the designated time for dialogue, it was apparent that the team was close to accessing the collective will. Therefore, Luisa said, "It seems that we are close to creating something from our differences. How about extending the dialogue by thirty minutes?" Sure enough, just after 4 p.m., a third new way arose from their differences and became obvious to all. Emily named it. There was a moment of silence when the fourteen people in attendance looked at one another and, with a subtle nod, expressed their inner and collective knowing and confidence.

Often, a team does not discover a collective will so quickly. When that happens, the formal leader would take what she learned and make the call. (In these situations, the *Harvard Business Review* article "The Elements of Good Judgment" provides very helpful guidance. One finding reported in the article is that leaders with good judgment gather their convictions via a perpetual curiosity.)[2]

As the soulful decision-making maestro that she is, Luisa consistently orchestrates making the right decision in the right time and the right way. She has the skills to open, hold, and close a dialogue. In times of crisis, she'll give the necessary immediate directives. When the dialogue lingers as the window of opportunity begins to close, she will gather the insights from her diverse team and make informed choices.

After several months of practicing curious conviction, this global logistics team accessed a third way from their differences 25 percent of the time, up from 10 percent. Still, 65 percent of the time decisions were made by directives with dialogue, and in 10 percent with directives only. As might be predicted, given the decision-making structure, the team thrives because they know in advance how the decision will be made, thereby eliminating past nightmares of wandering rudderless in the dark.

Also, the practice of curious conviction, making room for and listening to everyone's pieces of the puzzle, ensured that people felt heard in their differences and engaged as equal, different, and vital members of the team. They were contributors to the decision, whether it reflected their opinion or not. As a result, increasingly, their team's decision-making process produced the right choice, in the right time, done the right way. Conducting this intentional and explicit decision-making process, Luisa not only experienced her own confidence as a decision-making maestro rising, but also experienced a marked rise in her own individual authority as reflected in 360 feedback.

Are you more comfortable with being in a more authoritative role and making a decision yourself, or are you more comfortable with facilitating the team to make a decision? There is no right or wrong answer; it's just helpful to know this about yourself, and it may depend on the situation. With one team, building around strategy, you might be more comfortable with a more collaborative approach (dialogue). With another team, or in another situation or project, you might be more comfortable with a more directive approach. Again, there is no right or wrong, but being aware of how you operate is going to help you when you move into the three criteria of decision-making.

How Not to Make a Decision: Compromise

I have not included compromise, or even majority rule, as options for ways to make a decision because, in many ways, compromise isn't really a decision. Or if it *is* a decision, it's primarily a choice to agree on what we already agree on, rather than creating from our differences. Identifying what we already agree on can be a helpful place to start, yet to stop there has nothing to do with innovation. Access to wisdom feeds creativity. In-sync execution thrives on making the right choices at the right time; it is the goal of decision-making and vital to the practice of innovation.

As Mary Parker Follett wrote, "A collective thought is one evolved by a collective process. The essential feature of a common thought is not that it is held in common, but that it has been produced in common."[3] A thought held in common represents the herd mentality or groupthink. The common thought produced in common is the collective will. From our differences comes the collective innovation of new insights, connections, and perspectives—and that leads to new procedures, systems, products, and services. In contrast to herd mentality, group spirit is the energy of a team that is aroused when everyone shows up as equal, different, and vital pieces of the project puzzle. This spirit inspires collective intelligence and action.

The notion of the group spirit becoming the "master" or leader of the collective corresponds to the notion of leading from the center of the group out. (Rob Burch's diagrams in Chapter 11 illustrate this.)

If we get only compromise, the conflict will come up again and again in some other form, for in compromise we give up part of our desire, and because we shall not be content to rest there, sometime we shall try to get the whole of our desire.[4]

—MARY PARKER FOLLETT
Prophet of Management

Today, in the United States and other democracies, we're experiencing the division that comes from the limits of compromise. As with compromise, when the majority rules, the minority gives up their desire only to have the conflict come up repeatedly. A prime example of this is the long-term rule of the majority, which leads to increased partisan divide, eliminates access to the collective will, and rarely allows for compromise. Ironically, perpetual compromise creates cynicism and distrust, which yields less compromise. Politically, we get caught in the downward spiral of anger/avoidance, distrust, weak decisions, and eventual societal demise.

I understand that there is a place for compromise, and that assessing a collective will from our differences in a timely fashion isn't always possible. Yet it's crucial that all points of view be heard and included as equal, different, and vital—not to "split the difference," but to create anew from our differences. Identifying what we hold in common can be a helpful place to start, yet stopping there is like composing a piece of music with only one common note: dull, boring, unimaginative, and the opposite of innovative. With every endeavor or project, we owe it to ourselves and future generations to go beyond our commonalities, to venture into the unknown and scary parts of our differences, not so we succumb to fighting and war, but to communicate and create from our differences, *because* of our differences.

It's true that collective deliberation takes time and appears at times to slow innovation, decisions, and execution. Yet, if done effectively, it is an example of the value of slowing down to speed up. There's nothing slower than a decision that just doesn't work. The founder and CEO of a major construction company in Ohio was bashed with delays and cost runovers time and time again until he gathered all parties involved in the construction projects, including unions and suppliers, for two days of dialogue. The only reason he continues these two-day dialogues is that it works, by lowering costs and finishing projects on schedule. How might you slow down to speed up?

Now that we've traveled our way through the WTL Flow Chart into the realm of consistent collective flow, where speed and diversity are harmonized, it's time to learn about other perspectives. In the interviews that follow, you'll hear from a pair of clients deeply engaged in the working operations of We the Leader and an expert in DEI who has traveled to over 50 countries to build bridges. Last, you will gain the perspectives of a scholar from Oxford, an attorney from the world's largest law firm, and the CEO of a Global Fortune Top 50 company.

PART V

We the Leader

Conversations with Real-World Leaders

CHAPTER 15

A Hierarchy–
Panarchy Hybrid

David Kaufman and John Kessler

With too much organizational structure, you find
yourself in a ditch: it's all command and control, with
no innovation. If you don't have any structure, though,
you're facing a flood. Everything's open, transparent,
collaborative—but you're not getting anything done.
What I want is the optimal flow of a river. You've got just
enough structure for decision-making and execution, but
not so much that you're stifling dialogue or innovation.

—DAVID KAUFMAN
former CEO, Motorists Insurance Group / Current Director,
Encova Mutual Insurance Group and President, Capital University

Dave Kaufman (DK) and I started working together soon after he became CEO at Motorists Insurance Group. Dave was intent on reinventing Motorists by recalibrating the organizational structure by building the required trust and responsiveness through integrated, cross-functional teams overlaying the traditional hierarchy. The challenge was to unite sixteen companies around a common mission with shared values. The ultimate goal was to integrate the organization as a super-regional financial institution recognized as the most trusted and responsive provider of innovative risk management solutions. Dave assumed the CEO role with broad executive experience that included stints as a chief financial officer, chief information officer, and chief operating officer. He also had deep experience serving on corporate boards and leading industry and community organizations. Dave had demonstrated the innate capacity—both intellectually and emotionally—to initiate, motivate, and activate multiple initiatives at the same time. This was exactly what was required to reinvent an eighty-five-year-old organization in a rapidly changing world.

When Dave invited me to work with their executive team, I met John Kessler (JK). As an IT executive John had a big heart, strong self-awareness, and keen insight into human dynamics. With his active listening, questions, and insights John constantly reminded the team of the tyranny of "or" and the genius of "and."

DK: When I entered the CEO role at what was then Motorists Insurance Group, there were sixteen companies in the group, eight boards of directors, across twenty-six states. All the business units were pretty much autonomous. Although there were operational challenges with the affiliation business model, it was an effective strategy to expand our geographic reach, build a strong financial foundation, and upgrade the talent and diversity of the board. Although I needed to address the high expense structure and antiquated systems, the foundation was in place to pave the way for the next evolution of change.

When I became CEO, I developed a one-company vision designed to unite the organization and implement a culture based on trust, responsiveness, and high performance. The intent was to create one company, leaving the customer-facing capabilities distributed across the headquarters for each of the sixteen companies but centralizing everything else. In the early days, the autonomous operations had created silos across the organization. There was no way to prioritize the different companies' needs and allocate resources efficiently because there was no collaboration. Leadership was focused on the needs of the silo they were accountable for and knew best as opposed to the good and priorities of the group overall.

JK: When Dave came in I'd already spent twenty-five-plus years in this industry and in corporate America, and I viewed it only through one lens. I wouldn't say I was jaded, but my sense of what was possible was limited.

What we had was a culture of command and control, a culture driven by fear as opposed to one inspired by love. I've since become comfortable using the word "love" in reference to my corporate experience. But when we first went there, it was so awkward to use the word when talking about work, the company you work for, work–life integration—all those things.

Now the old culture wasn't bad or wrong; it's just the culture that was. We'd grown through this affiliation model, the sixteen companies across twenty-six states, but across all these entities, everyone was allowed to maintain their own autonomy, their identity, their brand. We brought to the table a financial note and propped them up, and we took over some key leadership positions, but, for the most part, we left these companies alone.

When Dave became CEO in 2011, one of the first things he said was that the model wasn't working. He went off to his proverbial mountaintop and wrote a thirty-one-page vision statement, which was all about using soft concepts to drive hard results. It was all about culture first—culture trumps strategy.

DK: I started with a pretty detailed vision and wrote a comprehensive document that laid out what all these companies would look like together as one: *Here's what will differentiate us. Here are the capabilities we need. And here's the culture that will get us there.*

But what had to be answered first was *How do you get 1,500 people to own that vision?* I knew for a team to own any assignment, they had to understand it, and to understand it, they had to participate in it. I also knew that at times you have to slow down to speed up. We introduced the vision to every person in the organization through two-day Leadership Vision Summits for 250 people at a time. Holding these summits and taking the time for everyone to participate and understand the vision meant slowing down; ultimately, getting that kind of understanding and commitment enabled us to go faster.

JS: This leadership summit wasn't just to hear the formal leader share his vision. It was a gathering of all 1,500 leaders/associates across Motorists. Yes, they heard "the leader" pontificate, yet the purpose wasn't just to inform or inspire, but also to initiate a genuine dialogue. The attendees came in as equal, different, and vital participants to restart this company with a fresh purpose. Each table dialogued about a particular aspect of the vision and values among themselves, then reported their key points and takeaways. This was repeated by each of the twenty to twenty-five tables during the two-day summit. The buzz was electrifying. Something was happening! Critically, that "something" didn't stop after the two days. These integrated table teams continued and became a permanent part of the company's structure.

JK: The whole experience was an unbelievable investment, an unbelievable journey to make the pivot from a culture of command and control to a culture of engagement. It required a tremendous amount of patience, leadership, and courage on Dave's part. He was deliberate and methodical and put a lot of due diligence into it. He had to! Motorists, at the time, was the youngest company of the group—an eighty-five-year-old that we were approaching as a startup. It was an important mindset. We had the innovation and flexibility of a startup, but unlike a startup, we had the stability and financial strength, which enabled us to take some risks, to be even more innovative. Imagine all these small companies that had been around for 100 and 125 years, deep-rooted in their communities, deep-rooted in the way they'd always done things, then picture trying to get them to embrace a one-company mindset or one-company culture.

JS: This combination—of decades old difference versus a single new culture—reflects the individual and collective give and take of consilience.

DK: The summits had to be inclusive and engaging. We orchestrated them so that each person would start the morning at a table of eight to ten—but they were sitting with people from different companies, from different levels of the organization, with different functional responsibilities. We were building *integrated teams* at those tables.

JS: See how Dave's language—his use of the words "engaging," "building," and even "orchestration"—shows how he perceives these differences not as something to be smoothed over but rather as diversity to be leveraged. This is what the concept of consilience is all about!

DK: As CEO, during the summits, I was on stage presenting the components of the vision, the beliefs we should all be championing, the behaviors that would be expected of each of us. And what it was really about—getting to a trusted culture. I wanted all of us to trust one another and work effectively as one team to achieve superior results.

That trust had to start by getting to know each other, understanding our capabilities, and making sure we were all comfortable with our values. As I presented the vision and values, the teams would dialogue them for shared understanding. Crucially, we adhered initially to a circular dialogue structure: teams would go clockwise around the table, taking turns sharing insights and listening to each person's input. Everyone had a voice. Everyone was heard. At the end, we came to see that through the dialogue of diverse perspectives came the most innovative takeaways.

JS: Here's an example of initiating dialogue. It's a move made by the formal leader, but the intention is to generate dialogue, mutual learning, and leading. Because everyone had a voice at these summits, the assumption was that all could be leaders. Critically, the outcome was not predetermined. Dave and the rest of the formal leadership were open to mutual learning.

DK: Everyone left with a vision-related assignment so they had to continue to connect and work together across functions and companies. When you have 1,500 people talking and connecting like that—when they are back in their home company performing their individual functions—you see those silos start to crumble. We all started gaining an appreciation for what others were doing across the organization and building the trust necessary to work effectively as integrated teams.

JK: I was the CIO when Dave commenced the vision journey in May of 2012, and I saw the effects of those summits across the enterprise. With the executive team, Dave used a similar structure in terms of dialogue, but it was even more in-depth. The executive team went through this incredible change process involving four stages: vision, diagnosis, design, and integration.

JS: John isn't mentioning it here, but the form of dialogue evolved from circular, where people contributed one by one in a highly ordered way, to more of a "flow" dialogue, which might include circular dialogue as part of the discussion, but which also makes room for more spontaneous give-and-take.

JK: In the vision stage, we were identifying the ideal state, the aspirational state, if you will, and our desired business outcomes along with desired human outcomes. That's all got to be leader-led, leader-driven, so that started with Dave's vision.

JS: Here we see authoritative leadership, but in the service of mutual leadership. Everything Dave did was with the intention of enhancing leadership across the team.

DK: When you jump from the current state to the vision state, there's a gap between the two. We initially called that gap "chaos," and our goal was to move through chaos and achieve clarity as quickly as possible. We spent a lot of time in dialogue reinforcing the drivers of change so everyone understood that there was no going back. We modified our approach after a leadership team visit to Google. While there, I asked what they looked for when interviewing a perspective employee. Their answer? "Googliness." We were told that people who work at Google need to be comfortable with ambiguity because that fosters the innovation needed in their business model.

After that trip, chaos was no longer chaos to us. It was ambiguity. The goal was no longer to sprint through chaos to realize the vision, but to use that ambiguity, that lack of clarity, as an opportunity to innovate. After we got through that period, we realized that ambiguity is the friend of innovation, but the enemy of execution. We embraced the ambiguity while we pursued the clarity needed to execute and perform.

We made sure that we didn't get to the structure, where the clarity comes from, until we completely exhausted what innovations—the strategies and strategic choices—could come out of the ambiguity. Then, the structure that enabled those strategies and choices started to come into place. And with that structure, we gained the clarity, accountability, and support needed to achieve the vision. The final step was putting people in that structure, getting the skill sets aligned to shift to execution. Not only did we need the right people on the bus, but they had to be in the right seat. And that's the model we followed going forward.

JK: Next, Dave took the executive team into a diagnosis phase, where we went through an environmental assessment, which is a SWOT [strengths, weaknesses, opportunities, and threats] analysis. We went through a stakeholder assessment, where we assessed more than forty stakeholders, how they viewed us, how we viewed them, how they could help us, and how they could hurt us. We went through an organizational assessment and compiled a gap analysis between our target state and our current state. And then we identified the sixteen critical success factors that we had to do to achieve that target vision.

After the diagnosis stage, we transitioned into the design phase. We took the outputs from our diagnoses, and came up with a new mission, which was to answer the four questions: the who, the what, the how, and the why. The mission is the bullseye for the organization. The design identifies the body of work necessary to get there.

JS: It's important to note that this new mission was a shared mission. The initial vision was Dave's, but the process allowed that vision to be integrated and adjusted, so that the mission belonged to everyone.

DK: If you look at John's level, the executive team, we really positioned them as having this once-in-a-lifetime opportunity. Despite our eighty-five-year history, we challenged our strategic choices, distribution channel, and portfolio of products and services. More than WHAT we do, we focused on WHY we do it. The team responded to this broader purpose—not to sell insurance policies, or to make a return on an asset, but to create risk management solutions so that when bad things happen to good people, we're there for them. What motivated us was the bigger why, the significant impact we could make in society.

John and others had to own and stand by this elevated mission. The entire senior team had to engage their organizations in the startup mentality. I told them, "Dialogue the trends and strategic choices. Explore what we should stop doing and how to build on the things that are working. Encourage your teams to identify new concepts that we need to consider. We have to challenge everything we're doing to move from where we are to where the vision calls us to be."

JS: "Challenge everything" is a vital move for dialogue and reflects the importance of bringing convictions to the table, especially when they differ. A key to Dave's success is that he initiated with vigor and energy and also insisted on being challenged. Dave sees being challenged as a relief rather than an agitation or a threat, because it proves that people trust each other. Trust increases as we continue to create from our differences. Challenging in this context comes from an innate curiosity and belief in creating from our differences—the crucial elements of a curious conviction.

While some recognized this fact about Dave earlier than others, everybody eventually acted on their challenges or differences with Dave. And that's not because he conducted some faux collaboration by attempting to make room for others' opinions by holding back or silencing his own. Instead, he came straight out with his convictions and demanded—he didn't suggest, he insisted—that everyone challenge everything. In other words, he demanded that everyone show up as a leader, expressing what they thought and felt in the moment, especially when it contradicted the prevailing point of view.

JK: After we'd gone through vision, diagnosis, and design, we entered the fourth stage, where things really ignited. "Integration" was around establishing and building those core capabilities to bring the vision to light. For the executive team, those core capabilities were integrated teaming, responsive communications, knowledge management, and aligned infrastructure. And I'll never forget it—everybody in that room just assumed that infrastructure was my area: "Oh that's Kessler's thing because he's IT." But, to me, that capability felt like something bigger.

So, we had a dialogue. At first, we came up with wording for the "infrastructure" capability and it read like this: *Reinvent and integrate our infrastructure to ensure consistent delivery of customer value and grow profitably as one company.* And we all liked it, but the executive team still seemed to think, "Well that one belongs to Kessler," and I'd respond, "No, it's all of ours."

This is where we got through circular dialogue: we changed the wording of our infrastructure capability to

*Reinvent and integrate our **business** infrastructure to ensure consistent delivery of customer value and grow profitably as one company.* By inserting that one word, *business*, well that flipped the thinking of everybody in the room. Now they realized, "Man, we all want in on that," because business infrastructure is operational, it's organizational, it's financial, it's technological, and it's administrative. It's all those things.

JS: These challenges aren't for the sake of argument. They're not attempts to convince others or to win the debate. It's about putting a puzzle together, respecting each other's unique and vital contributions, especially when those contributions differ. This happens on a bedrock of respect—a suspension of judgment about the person in favor of a deep and constant curiosity.

JK: During this whole transformation, we made the boldest investment we had ever made in the history of our company: we purchased and implemented a fully integrated suite to serve as our new technology platform. We had been working with about twenty different core systems. And when I say core systems, I'm talking about everything—policy, billing, claims. And not one of these systems fulfilled our target state aspirations because each one was proprietary, built on legacy technology. But the legacy wasn't just in the technology, it was in the mindset of the executives themselves.

As with the vision summits, the first thing we did with the new suite was to bring together the company presidents to get their input about what that target state looked like: "What should the ideal core platform do for you?" To a person, they kept trying to insert changes to the core platform that emulated the way they'd always done business. And my team started buying into that, which is a mistake a lot of companies make. We were heading down a slippery slope when we finally realized—through field trips and time spent with other thought leaders—*Oh my God, we're spending millions of dollars on this new core system and we're making it into our old one.* We were trying to pave the core path!

At our leadership summit, Dave had said, "You will change the way you do business to take advantage of the software out of the box as much as possible. We're not going to customize this. And we're going to stand up an entire infrastructure to support the launching of a new commercial lines company in the market."

JS: This is another example of an authoritative directive helping to steer and ignite a wider, deeper dialogue. From my observation, this dynamic started with and was strongest in Dave and John, but it didn't stop there. There were many moments when I had the opportunity to catch, name, recognize, and celebrate other executives bringing a challenge, especially in opposition to the sway of the team's or Dave's opinion.

JK: So we pivoted. We purchased and implemented a fully integrated suite for policy, billing, and claims, to maximize the Motorists brand presence and dominate the commercial lines marketplace.

We created an entirely new commercial product portfolio—and we stood up an entire business infrastructure to support the launch of that new commercial lines company in the marketplace.

DK: One thing I learned through the whole process was that you always want a learning organization. The collaboration processes and integrated teaming principles help do that—we're all learning from each other.

JS: I love what Dave said there. It highlights a working definition of flow dialogue as a process of mutual learning, where each participant teaches and learns in the same action. This mutual learning is also a mutual *leading*—each person leads and follows in the same action, and all of this invites others to bring their own curious conviction.

DK: Another principle was something Jeff helped with in real time: promoting a coaching culture both within the executive team and across the organization. Jeff brought in a simple framework where no matter who you're interacting with, you're asking, "Well, what's working?" Then you explore, "How could you do more of it?" And then you step in: "But, what kind of blind spots are potentially out there?" And then, "How can you uncover and address those blind spots?"

The team could see that this process was live and real time. It wasn't orchestrated. When they all saw Jeff coaching me in this manner—observing a meeting and then interjecting for clarity or shaping things a little bit differently—the team was prepared to promote a coaching culture across the organization and coach their teams that way. One thing we celebrated was catching teammates doing something good and using that as a positive coaching session. Recognizing the specific good behavior or contribution, and being timely with that recognition, creates the trust needed to have more difficult conversations in the future.

DK: Jeff also helped me name and communicate three distinct decision-making models. The first level is to inform others of your independent decisions: "It's within my authority to do this and I'm confident it's the right thing to do, but you all need to be aware of the decision I made."

213

The second level is consultative decisions which are centered on dialogue. I'd say, "Hey, I want everyone to have a voice in this. It's my call to make but I value your perspectives and thoughts on it." I bet that around a third of the time the decision I went into the meeting with actually changed because of what I heard. It also made it easier for the team to support the decisions I made.

The third level is also a form of consultation, but it's more formal. I would tell them, "Okay, this decision impacts many areas and requires the support of everyone around the table. We need to get consensus on this. I expect you to recommend an alternative or support the decision on the table. " At the end of those meetings, I'd have each person say, "I support it." Nobody could leave the room unless he or she felt comfortable expressing that support. That way, no one could later say, "Hey, I wanted to do this, but they wanted to do that." The idea was, *We're a team. And we're moving forward together.* If the group couldn't arrive at a decision, the formal leader would change the decision-making model from consensus to independent or consultative.

JK: The biggest takeaway for me was that he gave me the reason and permission to pause and ask, *How am I thinking? How am I communicating? How am I collaborating? Am I truly listening, or am I too busy thinking of what I want to say next?*

We had a circular dialogue that we were practicing when we brought Jeff into the organization, and I think Jeff's approach helped lift that dialog even more. And then, after practicing the process for a while, Jeff helped tweak it to make it even more efficient and effective. But I think maybe one of my biggest takeaways from Jeff was how to effectively communicate. How to collaborate. And how to determine when the communication should be a dialogue versus when it should be a directive.

JS: By referencing directives and dialogue, John is pointing to the five dominant forms of communication: assertive, directive, passive-aggressive, submissive, and manipulative. As he's suggesting here, it's critical for formal leaders to understand when to employ which form and in what context.

JK: As I reflect on all the things Jeff taught me, I like to summarize it this way: I learned when to lead, when to follow, how to communicate upward, how to communicate downward, how to communicate laterally, how to deal with success, how to deal with failure, and how to deal with adversity. I liken Jeff's work to teaching the tango: It's a dance, and leaders do need to learn how to lead and how to follow, sometimes simultaneously. And they need to learn when it's the right time to lead and when it's the right time to follow.

JS: For me, this dance is about how to lead and follow *at the same time.*

DK: When BrickStreet Mutual Insurance Company joined us, we had two similar-sized organizations coming together. We called it an affiliation of equals and it was very close to a merger. We combined boards—six directors from each company. We also combined executive teams—six leaders from each organization. The cultures were different but complemented each other. BrickStreet was low in collaboration and very decisive. Motorists, because of what we'd gone through, was high in collaboration and not as decisive. It was an opportunity to create a collaborative environment with a bias toward decision-making.

JK: There's something called a Sigmoid curve. It looks like an arc upward to a plateau—and then it starts downward. I bring up this concept because a few years after the big transformation, Motorists was traveling that curve to where we had hit that plateau and were starting down. Fortunately, at the time we started down, we hit a new curve upward—the affiliation with BrickStreet. This was our opportunity to reinvent ourselves proactively and avoid the trap of complacency.

JS: This story demonstrates how John was able to pause, step back, and take a macro view of where the organization was from a developmental context.

JK: Once an organization becomes complacent and that curve starts downward, you can't always turn it around. But if you have the creativity, the foresight, and the ability to innovate to start a new upward curve before the original one starts downward, you can build something sustainable for the future. The key to sustaining a healthy business is to transform to a new curve before the current one is in decline. Likewise, the key to sustaining a healthy career is to be self-aware of where you are on life's curve. Much like business, it's important to fight complacency and be willing to transform, to reinvent yourself. The key to transforming a company is to have vision. The key to implementing vision is collective collaboration across the company. The key to collective change is personal change. I realized I had to make a significant change in myself to effectively lead. It is personal!

JS: A core assumption of Simultaneity and its coaching process is that we can't really change another person. We can externally (extrinsically) coerce them with fear and the threat of no raise or losing their job, but we can't fundamentally make them commit from the inside (intrinsically). However, we can change, or lead our own lives, and invite, or even inspire, others to do the same. This invitation applies equally to leading.

DK: I often speak of a ditch/flood analogy, where the ditch is a command-and-control structure—strict hierarchy, decision-making at the top, accountability is clear—but you stifle the creativity of the company to move forward. Then there's the flood—tons of great ideas, open collaboration, but no clear accountability for execution. For us, by overlaying the integrated teams on top of a traditional functional organization, we thought we had the right mix. The organization structure provided the accountability for decision-making, while the integrated teams provided the underlying collaboration and innovation. And with that, we struck the right balance of flow.

Jeff Spahn, On Further Reflection

Balance is key. In an understandable reaction to the "ditching" of too much hierarchy, many organizations may be overreacting by attempting to eliminate all hierarchy. This trend is popular now, in part because it's our basic human tendency to overreact and negate what came before instead of evolving by including and transcending what was previously in place. Of course, it depends on the context. Consulting agencies like McKinsey and Korn Ferry can probably use less structure and more flow. But startups experience more of a crisis mode, as do my restaurant clients. For them, if the ideal of shared collaboration has no direction, or unchanneled energy, it can easily result in floods of inefficiencies. It's all about balance, or as I prefer, the harmony of structure and energy for optimal flow depending upon the context. When I say "harmony," I mean not just balance, but the integration of structure and energy in a mutually enhancing way such that the energy enhances the structure and the structure enhances the energy.

What Dave experienced, and this book offers, is a radical mutual leadership that includes and transcends the needed hierarchy—depending upon what the situation requires. For example, when a crisis hits, it's usually time to exercise hierarchical authority through directives. Instead of no hierarchy, a radical mutual leadership model—leading and following in the same action—results in the proverbial power pie getting larger and increasing the size of the power pieces of that pie for everyone.

What Dave did not mention is that he made those integrated teams permanent, and, by doing so, he fully authorized leadership by all, or panarchical leadership. Because teams are cross-functional, with participants from across, not down, the organization, they lead each other *within* the hierarchical, structured leadership. Keeping the hierarchy ensured that there was the necessary structure to avoid a flood, while the integrated teams practicing dialogue kept the optimal flow.

Crucial to consistently harmonizing structure and energy for optimal flow is a very simple and potent decision-making process. By simultaneously allowing for free flow of energy through dialogue, and the necessary authority and discipline for timely decisions, the Simultaneity decision-making model concurrently enhances energy and the channel or structure for that energy to flow. The free flow dialogue ensures access to collective wisdom and team buy-in. At the same time, a shared decision-making process provides the agility to be responsive to customers' needs or marketplace volatility.

There are a number of ways to describe the decision-making options. Dave chose the three options of independent, consultative, and consensus decision-making. For any of these options, it's helpful that the decision maker decides *how to decide*, then communicates that decision-making process to the team so that everyone knows the process ahead of time.

Although decisions may grow out of dialogue, its purpose is to access collective intelligence and creativity. I've heard many leaders say that, as the dialogue deepens, a collective knowing emerges that includes everyone recognizing a course of action with the commitment and readiness to execute. When this happens, it doesn't feel as though a decision has been made, but rather that this collective knowing has occurred. This is one way a deep collective flow shows up.

CHAPTER 16

Creating Bridges: Diversity, Equity, Inclusion

Roslyn Taylor O'Neale

And that's what's true in organizations. The more different I am, the more time I spend explaining myself. The more time I spend doing that, the less time I have to provide the intelligence and the ideas and the creativity and the work that I am hired to do.

—ROSALYN TAYLOR O'NEALE
Principal Consultant, Cook Ross

'll never forget Jim Evan's thrill at the thought of introducing me to Rosalyn Taylor O'Neale. It's her magnitude! I mean wow! There is just an ever-expanding insight, passion, wisdom, understanding, directness, and love that is Rosalyn. The problem I found editing Rosalyn's interview is that it provided way too many great options for the epigraph.

JS: Could you say a few words about yourself and what you do.

RTO: I'm Rosalyn Taylor O'Neale, an African American woman born in the segregated South, who embarked on a journey of forty-plus years across fifty countries and five continents to help leaders and individuals in organizations create and transform their cultures so that they work for more people, not fewer. I'm also a wife, mother, and grandmother. I'm also someone who, in the mid-1970s, was asked: Why do members of some groups—and at this time, we were talking about white men—stay in organizations for, on average, seven to ten years, and people of color—at that time, we were talking about black and African Americans—and white women have a tenure fewer than three years? What is it about an organization that makes it welcoming to some and not as welcoming to others? Answering that question has been my quest. That's the question that's driven me.

JS: What was some of the thinking at that time around why that was the case?

RTO: The groups I found that thrive and the groups that seem to stumble have changed based on the country I'm in and the kind of organization. Interestingly, the thinking has remained consistent throughout the last forty-plus years. When members of the dominant group perform and succeed, and are rewarded for their work, they ask "Why was I successful?" "What was it about me?" And, when offered an opportunity, they bring in people who are like them, based on the notion that they've identified the characteristics of success.

Success brings success. Whether it's race, similar ideas about education, social norms, how people present in meetings—meaning how they give a presentation, walk into meetings, they look, they sound—leaders in organizations, without recognizing their inherent biases and assumptions, start with a group of people who are like-minded, with whom they have connections through education or social networks, because it's easier to quickly establish trust and relationships.

And when these leaders begin to expand the organization, they bring in more like-minded people. So, it makes sense that the first six to ten years of an organization's development is based on the idea that the more similar we are, the quicker we can make decisions, the easier it is for us to agree on and expand the brand. After ten, fifteen, forty, one hundred years, you still have organizations led by a small group of people, who are similar to each other.

It's the same if you're a group of people who are either more risk-adverse or risk-takers, white men, or individuals with Spanish as the dominant language. Organizations develop a root system based on being comfortable with one another as they struggle with the normal challenges of growing the business.

Human beings are similar in this respect. We are easily guided by the idea that *If I feel comfortable with Jim because Jim and I share a racial similarity, I'm more likely to engage in higher risk-taking behavior with Jim, give him greater latitude to make decisions, and forgive performance misses because I believe that we see the world in the same way.* Forty years ago and it is still true this afternoon, that it is easier to view and treat white men as either successful or having high potential. Because the rules of engagement were created by groups who were and are similar, while the rules of engagement for people who are different, and often seem foreign, the bar for their success is much higher.

For instance, the way a black woman might wear her hair seems foreign in an organization of white men who all wear their hair the same way. A black woman who wears her hair in a style that is culturally natural—for example, braids—may trigger in the mind of a white manager the question, "Are you trying to tell me something?" I submit that few managers have ever said to a white man, "Bob, when I look at the way you wear your hair, I want to know if you're trying to tell me something?" That's the dilemma. If I have to spend time explaining how I wear my hair, why I wear my hair this way, and what hair means to me, I don't have as much emotional and intellectual energy to focus on what the organization is asking me to do. As a result, I now have one and a quarter jobs. I have the job that my colleagues have, which is making the organization successful, and I have another job, that of making people comfortable with characteristics that don't have anything to do with making the organization successful.

If I'm going to work two jobs, I either need to be paid 25 percent more money, or I'm going to find an organization where I don't have to work two jobs.

JS: What I'm hearing you describe is homogeneity, and, for that reason, organizations are set up to attract and work with people like those already there.

RTO: Yes. As human beings, we are more comfortable with people like us, people who strike us as like us, although it's possible they may or may not actually *be* like us. We're more comfortable when we are familiar with the norms, the customs. It's only when I started traveling internationally that I spent time learning and developing an understanding of other cultures—their customs, norms, and behaviors. I read about the history and culture, reached out to individuals who were either raised in or had a deep understanding of the culture. I also *intentionally* listened and watched for cultural cues–how people greeted each other, what they said and what they asked about personal matters, and what were acceptable business practices.

We like people who are like us. We find similarities quickly when we meet new people, whether that is, "So you know Jim? I know Jim." Or "You have grandchildren? I have grandchildren." "You play golf? I play golf." That connection happens quickly. It's important for us to acknowledge that the more different I am from the dominant group, especially if that group is not aware of their comfort with similarities, the more time I spend explaining myself. The more time I spend doing that, the less time I have to provide the intelligence, ideas, creativity, and work I'm hired to do.

The challenge is when we find either fewer similarities or we find distinct differences that are less comfortable for us, we have to choose to either understand the value of those differences or move on to more similarity.

JS: I'm guessing that this dynamic you're describing is across all cultures. I mean, that every culture has the same natural inclination to be with people like themselves.

RTO: Yes. Based on all the literature I've reviewed, that's, in part, the way human beings evolve, and we've evolved that way for safety. For instance, when I see someone who looks like me, I have a belief system that says, "I'm safer with them" than when I see someone who looks very different from me. Now, different may mean our outer appearance, how we dress. It may mean different in terms of our first language. I used to tell people, "Go to any cafeteria, in any organization, around the world, and, where people have a choice of tables, you'll find significant segregation by similarity." Because while I need to be comfortable with diversity when I'm working at my cubicle or my desk, lunchtime is choice time, and I can find people similar to me.

If I'm working in a medical facility, hospital, or university, I'll find executives at one table, nurses at another, even nurses from similar backgrounds—Chinese, Japanese, Korean, African American, Latino, Latina—seated together. I maintain that if I walk into a room of one hundred people, and there's a group of five African American women, a total of six of us in this room of one hundred people, I'm more likely to walk over to the group of African-American women and introduce myself before I introduce myself to a group of white men or white women.

It's true for all people. When I attend recruiting events at historically black colleges and 90 percent of the people in the room are African American, it's interesting to watch white men who don't know anyone enter the room. They walk right up to another white man or group of men. Now, there are people who'll say, "Not me. I don't." And I say to them, "It's a bell curve. There are people on both ends." But it's natural.

I worked for a large organization and all the lawyers—a small team—ate lunch together every day. My team, the DEI team, most often went to lunch together, too. We knew one another. We sat together. Seldom, even in the DEI space, did we say, "Let's go to lunch, and let's separate." It's how human beings operate. And it's the challenge, specifically, to diversity, equity, and leadership.

JS: So am I hearing that the tendency toward being with people like ourselves is the natural way we evolved as a species to protect ourselves, to be safe, and only after we are comfortable can we then move forward?

RTO: Right. A lot of the time we're not even aware that it feels safer. People say to me, "Well, little kids don't do that." And that's true. It's not true that children don't recognize differences in one another; they absolutely do and from a very young age, even six to nine months. Infants recognize race. But when we get to the age of about twelve, thirteen, fourteen, we begin to become very group aware—we're geeks, techies, jocks—and that awareness extends to people who look like one another.

JS: It sounds to me that that question posed to you in the mid-70s was a foundational question, one that moved you and helped you understand your own passion or interest in that dynamic that one might name diversity, equity, inclusion. Is that a fair statement?

RTO: It was very much around diversity and inclusion. Equity is fairly new in the lexicon—it is what we do, relative to diversity, how we create inclusion. And yes, the work forty years ago was the beginning of how I define the work. It was the start of my understanding the need to create bridges for people to cross and come together—to walk toward each other recognizing that we are both different and similar. That has been the foundation of my inclusion, diversity, and equity work. It has absolutely been my path.

JS: What's strikes me, as I hear you describe this, is this isn't just a different race issue or different gender issue or a different class issue. It's a human issue. And that, at least for me, is an intriguing starting point. I noticed the shift in myself, like, "Oh, it's really about how we relate to each other as human beings, and how that works for us, and how that works against us." Is that fair?

RTO: Yes. It is about race, gender, sexual orientation, class, and religion, and any other ways in which you and I are different and similar. The important thing is that no human being has just one characteristic. So, when I hear that diversity is about race, I say, "That won't work, because I'm not just an African American. I'm not merely one characteristic."

Power exacerbates the divide between differences and similarities. We're taught early on, especially in our educational system in the United States, that holding power is positive. When you look at US organizations, and their top

227

10 percent in terms of power and leadership, you notice that, overwhelmingly— disproportionately if you think about the population—somewhere between 65–70 to 90 percent are white, heterosexual, cisgender identifying, able-bodied men. When you recognize the power that group holds, the notion of inclusion becomes challenging. People who have power desire to hold onto it.

Having power, gaining power, and holding power is rewarded, so being at the top of your class, being the highest paid is a sign of success. And you can't separate race, gender, class, and abilities from what constitutes success and achievement, otherwise the leaders in organizations would more closely mirror the available talent. And that's the real challenge around inclusion. You're saying to people that power isn't equitably distributed. And that power is held based on characteristics that we know do *not* define intellect, do not define creativity, do not in fact lead to the best solution. They lead to solutions, just not the best. But power, the ability to reward, punish, decide who gets to speak in meetings and who gets heard, to determine where people are in the hierarchy, acquire project funding, get your child into the organization as an intern is held in the hands of a small group of people. The outcome is that the 90 percent that are not at the top of the organization are much more diverse than the 10 percent who are.

That's when inclusion and equity must become conscious outcomes, especially because leaders have the greatest amount of power. Now, we use the term leaders, and we say anybody can be a leader. If we lived in an egalitarian society, that would be true. But let's cut the BS. For that to be true, the majority of people who function as leaders and have the most power in an organization, need to make a conscious decision to behave differently.

JS: So what we are talking about right now is primarily about human beings organizing and becoming a part of an organization. Until now, we were talking more generally about human behavior in any situation. When people have power over others in the traditional hierarchy, the leaders need to be aware of that power dynamic, and make conscious choices to act or to create opportunities or to lead by, for example, having meetings, conversations, relationships that are equitable. Doing that seems to be the initial pathway to experiencing diversity, equity, and inclusion in the context of an organization typically based on conformity, inequity, and exclusion.

RTO: Absolutely. In the 1970s, activist Peggy McIntosh coined the phrase "white privilege." Since then, the notion of white privilege frightens and angers people. Those who seem ready to jump out of their skin challenge the term, "I didn't get here, to the top, because of some characteristic. I got here because I put in more effort and worked harder." Yes, hard work gets us a lot. However, the analogy that I use is a 400-meter race, the starting line is staggered to equalize the distance for all runners; otherwise it's farther to run from the outside lane than the inside lane.

The race appears to be "fair" since everyone is running the same distance—400 meters; however, off the racetrack—in life's race—it's anything but. The truth is white men and other "majority runners" start 100 meters ahead of the start line (staggered in lanes 1–8). They have a 100-meter starting position advantage. White women and other secondary majority runners start 40 meters ahead of the starting line (in lanes 1–8), giving them a 40-meter starting position advantage. The other marginalized and underrepresented individuals are not only not advantaged (by either 100 or 40 meters), they're locked outside the arena.

The groups who have a 40- to 100-meter advantage at the beginning aren't even aware they're advantaged. (The race is fair; it's staggered, and if "they" don't win, it's their fault.)

Leaders have to say to themselves, "I'm starting on the 100-meter line in a 400-meter race, and there are people locked outside. I know they are because they've told me they're locked outside, I've seen that they're locked outside, and I know they must be locked outside because there aren't enough people in here." If they say to themselves, "The people who are locked outside know something I don't know that could really make my organization extraordinary," then they've got to agree to give up their advantage and risk not being first across the line. Because if they open the doors, there may be people who can in fact run faster. So those at the 100-meter line need to be able to say to themselves, *I'm standing at the hundred meter, and you're now asking me to A: know that I'm in the most desirable spot; and B: know that I was born at the 100-meter line; and C: if I make this race equitable, I run the risk of losing something.* Human beings will do anything to avoid loss. We'll do more to avoid loss than we will to seek gain. Now you're asking someone to risk power, prestige, and all of the trappings of success.

When we start to talk about the word "privilege," people immediately say, "I don't have privilege." And I say, "Of course you do. I do, all of us do. It may show up differently. I have able-bodied privilege, or at least temporary able-bodied privilege. I have English-as-a-first-language privilege. I grew up upper-middle class. I have socioeconomic privilege. Now you can say, "But I've worked hard." Nobody's saying you haven't worked hard.

Leaders have to say to themselves, "I don't even know how hard some people have worked. They're locked outside. I also don't know if they can help me, not only to win the race as an organization, but to win the race as an individual."

230

That's the challenge for the notion of leader–followers, follower–leaders. We're taught that it's important to be the first person who crosses the line. Yet to be truly inclusive and equitable, we have to ask ourselves, *Is it more important for one hundred of us to cross the line than it is for me to cross first?* We may say, "I've been raised to believe that my crossing first is the best, that there's first place, and maybe second place, and then there's last, or loser, place." We in the inclusion, diversity, and equity space are trying to help people understand that one hundred of us crossing first, as an organization, makes us far more powerful than *me* crossing first. So that's a mind shift for me, you, and everyone else.

JS: The equalizer.

RTO: The challenge is not that leaders in organizations don't believe in the value of diversity, that they don't say to themselves, *We should be equitable. Everybody should have an opportunity to win, to participate.* The challenge is for them to say: *For me to ensure an equitable opportunity, I have to behave in ways that may not come naturally. I have to behave in ways that come to me thoughtfully.* It's the notion that if we're all going to be on Zoom, Skype, Teams, or another video-conferencing platform, as a leader I might have a separate part of my house from which to make these calls. I may have someone who's taking care of the people or animals that need to be cared for during that call. But, as a leader, I have to ask myself, *"How do I ensure that the person who is in their kitchen, because their spouse is in the living room, their kids are in the bedrooms, everybody is on the internet, everybody is talking, and they've got two dogs— how do I help that person contribute to the conversation, knowing their ability to answer questions is more challenging than mine?"*

And if I want to be inclusive, I may have to say to the person I'm speaking with, "You know what? Let's find a time where you and I can just chat." Because I know that person has knowledge, ideas, and solutions that I don't have. I also know they are distracted by things that I'm not distracted by, not because I'm a better human being, but because I have more resources. Leaders have to ask themselves, *Do the people who are on Skype, Zoom, or Teams, with me, have the same possibility of contributing as I do and as others on the call do?* That's where inclusion and equity become part of the equation.

If I'm a leader and I'm on the East Coast, and I hold a 9 a.m. meeting, am I aware of the fact that my West Coast people may not be as engaged at six in the morning as I am at 9? Do I create a way in which we share the pain? Do I say, "Okay, this morning, you're going to be up at 6 a.m. Tell you what, we'll run the next one at 7 p.m., Eastern Standard Time, so that it's 4 p.m. for you. And we'll run next month's meeting at 1 a.m., because that's fair for *our* colleagues who are in Asia. We'll all share the pain." That's what inclusion is. That's what creates equity.

It's not about whom you bring into the room. It's about what you do when you've brought them in the room.

JS: How does that principle apply to a conversation, in terms of what people think and feel? And, bringing that forward, in terms of the equity of time and space and also the freedom to say what they think and feel?

RTO: When I think about inclusive leaders, I say your job is to engage, empower, and energize the people who work with you and for you. That means being aware of the processes, practices, and actions that, in reality, make inclusion easier or create roadblocks to it. If you ask me what most angers me, it is that leaders who don't work at learning about their blind spots, increasing their understanding of people and groups who have different identities and experiences, and do not intentionally create inclusive, diverse, and equitable teams and organizations, receive and accept money from the organization.

Now, they may say, "Oh, no, I am paid because I've got to balance the books, and talk with board members." I tell them, 90 percent of what you are paid to do is to empower, engage, and energize the people who work with you and for you. That's 90 percent of your job. If you want to see only 10 percent of your paycheck, I'm okay with you not doing the rest. But if you want to receive 100 percent of your paycheck, 90 percent of your energy has to be put into what that job really is.

I like analogies, and so I say a leader's job is to clear the area and turn the soil, so the seeds that are planted have the greatest probability of growing, flowering, and becoming what they're supposed to be. The leader's job is to clear the field, get rid of the weeds, and understand that weeds have deep roots, which require digging deeper and maybe pulling harder to unearth them. Their job is to turn the soil, plant, water, and nourish the seeds. And as the seeds grow, to celebrate that growth. A leader's job is not just to meet with other leaders and decide the direction of the organization. That's 10 percent of their job. Ninety percent of their job is figuring out what does Larry know that Michael doesn't know? What does Michael know that Rosalyn, Cara, Larry, and Joe don't know? And how do I get each one of them to bring forth the fruit?

That's the job of leaders—to listen, to investigate, to be diligently, consciously, and passionately inclusive. I've known some great leaders, and what seems to be a thread running through incredible leaders is the understanding and belief that human beings want to be successful. Human beings strive to achieve. We come in wanting to be successful, and the leader can feed that by asking, "Tell me what you know that I don't know." They can feed it by saying, "What are the things that are in the way of your ability to really shine?" The great leaders think about "What can *I* do so that *you* can do better?" Because their fundamental belief is if you're successful, we're successful. If we're successful, I'm going to be doing really well.

JS: Right. I am successful; a mutuality there.

RTO: My challenge around words like mutuality is that we *both* have a mutual obligation. And if you're the leader, you have *more* than a mutual obligation. You have a disproportionate obligation, and it is disproportionate because you receive disproportionately more money, prestige, and freedom.

JS: That gets back to the analogy of the different starting points in the 400-meter race.

RTO: Yes. You're on the 100-meter line and you can't tell me, "If we just open the doors, I'll run a little slower for the first 10 meters," or "If we open the doors, I know there's more than one LeBron James or Serena Williams out there who can catch up with me." That's not what leadership is. Leadership is not *There are probably three exceptions that, no matter what we do, will succeed.* Leadership is *We are in this together.* And if 97 percent of us don't succeed, that's not success.

JS: It seems you're expanding the metaphor beyond where we all finish together to we're all in first place. It's also about everybody showing up.

RTO: It's always about everybody. My notion is that organizations are a network of promises and commitments. We are in it together. I'm doing work with an automobile manufacturer. It occurred to me that someone must have said, "You know what? We should put a mirror on the inside of the visor." I would bet that that someone was not a CEO but someone who needed to rush out of the house and halfway to work thought, *I need to make sure that I've got my lipstick on,* or *I need to make sure I don't have anything in my teeth.* That's the challenge of being a leader. I have to understand that somewhere out there somebody has the idea of putting a mirror on the visor. If I've made it difficult for that person to bring their ideas to the table, or, even more important, if I haven't made it *easy* for that person to bring their ideas to the table, shame on me. It's my loss, because that's how innovation happens.

It's rare that you have a leader who can make an organization of people who are high performing without people feeling that they matter. The majority of people who read your books and my books cannot make an organization successful without, as a foundation, taking on the challenge of listening, being empathetic, and inclusive—without being someone who enables and energizes others.

They can't be successful unless that's what they do. You'll lose the people who had the idea about the mirror on the visor, because if I can't bring my ideas, if it becomes clear that I'm not going to be able to get into the stadium, I may go to the stadium down the street where not only are the doors unlocked but people are waiting for me. And, after I do, I'm going to bring three of my friends. That's when we see significant turnover among marginalized people in organizations.

CHAPTER 17

Provocation

Steven Mostyn

I was speaking to a conductor today who talked about a chamber orchestra having to perform and listen at the same time. So the idea of simultaneous listening and performing is there in the chamber orchestra. I thought that was quite a nice metaphor for your work.

—STEVEN MOSTYN

Steve and I co-led a workshop. When my portion was complete, Steve was leading the workshop to a close when he turned to me and asked, "Jeff what story do you have to add?" *Steve,* I thought. *What are you doing to me?* I'd told all my stories. Then, I paused, listened within, and a story came to me. *Maybe this story will work.* Halfway into the story I found myself thinking the story was perfect for closing the session. And it was! This type of challenge is what Steve does for his friends, clients, colleagues, and students. It's not always comfortable, but he brings the best out of us.

JS: I'm curious, Steve, with all your experience, what has leadership development been like, at least in your lifetime? What was the cutting edge back when you were at Motorola? How did that evolve and shift at the Royal Bank of Scotland? How is it for you now? And where do you see it going?

SM: My only interest is what's relevant and what works. Your historical question is a little bit of a red herring. When I am asked, "What's new?" I always say, "What works?" And the number one contributor to what works, in an organizational setting, is a sponsor who's absolutely active and really wants to do whatever it is to drive things forward. Unless you have that, in the most real sense, nothing's going to happen.

So let's start with that, going back to the 1980s, where, historically, Jack Welch and his leadership advisor, Neil Tischler, personified that type of leadership. I think what they had was probably one of the most successful leadership development programs. GE had a huge link to Motorola in the '80s as well, and talent moved between GE and Motorola quite easily. So if you think about Six Sigma [a methodology/tool for continuous improvement], Motorola invented it. GE implemented it big time, arguably in a more direct way than Motorola did, but it was Motorola execs who did that. The two overlapped, but the two were clear, and they both had huge sponsors. I don't mean sponsors in the wonderful CEO who comes to the launch dinner and says great things; I mean a sponsor for whom this is a real issue. For Motorola, it was Bob Galvin. And at GE, it was Jack Welch and, later, various people helping architect the solution.

I think that still stands today. I don't think it's moved on, particularly. The '70s were a time when people like David Burnham and David McClelland developed the competency movement, which became a huge influence on leadership development. I would argue that it's less influential today, but, again, that's up for discussion. And then it's what you do, what works—and what works is strong self-awareness. The lessons of reflective practice, journaling, reflective groups, they're all part of it, and that leads of course into dialogue.

The competency movement and self-awareness probably allow dialogue to take place better than others' do; that would be my historic setting of it. But I wouldn't say I think those evolutions of strong sponsors inform everything we do today, and that then you just follow the leaders. Everyone, even today, talks about "making it business relevant." And I say, "Well, GE in the 1980s was business relevant. They were applying Six Sigma and turning around businesses. They were making leadership development business relevant." I even challenge this whole assumption that there's a modernity to it. I don't really buy it, to be honest.

JS: Part of the significance of a sponsor (in other words, an advocate), I assume, is that sponsorship fits within the business strategy. It's about accomplishing the goals of the organization, not checking something off that we should do or want to do. Would you elaborate a little bit more on what a sponsor means for you?

SM: I think a sponsor optimally is the chief exec, but it can be the unit or functional head as well, whoever has talent development and business development as two equal goals—simultaneously, to use your language. I would argue it started with Motorola. Motorola University probably inspired GE in the early '80s. I remember how Motorola University described itself as being the first ever corporate university. I think corporate universities are very good vehicles. You just have to make sure that they don't become bureaucracies in their own right or that, instead of playing their necessary part in leadership development, CEOs don't cast that work off to the corporate university.

Leadership development needs to be a constant leadership responsibility, not something delegated to the corporate university. Think of building an extension to your house. If you are a sponsor who is really interested in the roof design and the garage design, you're speaking to the builders every day. Whereas if you go to the launch meeting and say, "I trust it will be fine," it's a different relationship. That's a metaphor of sponsorship I quite like—building something. As a sponsor, you're pretty involved. Not in the direct management of it or physically building it, but you are absolutely involved in the constant design parameter discussion.

JS: When we talk about leadership development, I'd like to just break it into two words. What from your perspective is leadership? And then, what from your perspective is development? And, last, how do you see the two coming together?

SM: Leadership for me is an activity; it's a verb, not a noun. It's about organizing success, whatever that success might be. But it's twofold. There's individual leader development, which I'm not very interested in, and then there's leadership, which has capacity and capability building. The leadership capability of an organization or a team is where my real interest is, what I spend my time doing. Leader development is a very nice side effect, but it is not what I'm focused on, although it happens to many people I work with.

JS: You focus on the activity of leading, rather than the development of a person or a role. How do those two interact? I know you're not a coach. You've said leader development lends itself to coaches very well. So not being a coach, how do you describe the work you do? How do you know that team and organization has built or is building leadership capability?

SM: A theoretical answer is Brinkerhoff's Success Case Method.

JS: You're talking about studying the performance of the most successful and least successful participants rather than the average performance to determine what to change to make the training more successful.

SM: Yes. I think that's always very useful. It's in the communities of the groups we work with. For example, we're running one program now called Preparing for CEO. We have a 25 percent hit rate of people being appointed CEO after having gone through that one-year program. That's quite an interesting stat. Of course, we are not solely responsible, but it is quite a statistic.

JS: Yes, it is. What activities of leading indicate to you that capacity is being built? That's one indicator—getting a CEO position. What's another, and what does that activity look like? What would you be seeing, hearing, and feeling from a leader?

SM: Ultimately, the business performance of the unit or organization has to be the measure for assessing organization performance. And that would mean accomplishing the goals they've set for themselves.

JS: Then, leadership is an activity intended to accomplish the goals that the organization has set out for itself?

SM: Well, it's more than that, isn't it? It's about sensemaking. What those goals are . . . the whole link to purpose is so important. The achievement of the goals, I think is management. I see leadership as something much more exciting. It's entrepreneurial potentially. Again, everything around leadership is about context, isn't it?

JS: Would you talk a bit about the difference between management and leadership, from your perspective? Does that relate at all to Heifetz's distinction between technical and adaptive, or taking the same action even though the context has changed or needs to change? Heifetz argues that technical problems have been solved before in some shape or form. Adaptive problems need adaptation and are focused on social, behavioral, and attitudinal change.

SM: Well, yes. Technical tends to be a managerial responsibility, I think. I don't want to get into a huge debate about management versus leadership. It's a bit dull. But Stephen Covey's woodcutter versus the person who says, "wrong jungle," that's the definition for me, that's what I would use.

SM: Six Sigma is something that worked back in the '80s. And it's still working. It was developed by, I guess, a bunch of leaders at some stage, but it's a continuous improvement tool. I think it's a huge question, Jeff. There's definitely a focus on purpose right now. But that's not a tool; it's more like a discussion linking into an individual's purpose. Then there is the whole agile movement. I don't even know where to start with that, but there are so many tools and processes.

JS: Something that comes to mind is design thinking, which, from my perspective, is a way of taking the scientific method and bringing that same rigor of exploration—including experimentation—into business problem solving, so you invite questions, participation, and taking intelligent, calculated risks. I'm wondering what your perspective is on something like a design thinking as an activity for leading.

You mentioned purpose. And it is amazing how prominent purpose is right now compared to fifteen or twenty years ago. It was something that was there back then, and I'm curious what you think about Mary Parker Follett's work. It fascinates me, and I feel like she was totally ahead of her time. She described purpose as the invisible leader of an organization, whether you are in governance, on the board, or have just started this morning. An overriding sense of purpose . . . Now, I'm not exactly sure what that means, but I think, for her, it would also mean process. Does anything resonate for you around that?

SM: I think purpose is an evolution from where organizations are, at any given moment. Around fifteen or twenty years ago, the focus would probably be CSR, corporate social responsibility, and purpose was ultimately the strategic intent. But purpose today has, I think, a much stronger human engagement. I think Gen X and the millennials joining the workforce drove some of it; they are people who have a much stronger sense of individual purpose. Let's think about two very dominant movements, environmental action and Black Lives Matter, which are now important to many people. If an organization reaches out and says, "Let's share some of those ideas," other people in and outside the organization become more engaged. It all comes down to the discretionary effort of employees, I think. It's a very big topic right now.

JS: Yes, it's huge. One of the things that developed in the context of this book is the notion that everyone is a leader of their own life, that everyone has the capacity to be a leader in the full sense of the word, and that to get a project done requires a group of leaders at the table. That's the trend moving forward. At the same time that everyone is emerging as a leader, we have the great equalizer, the leader known as "the common purpose," which, really, if we take it seriously, makes everyone a follower. That means we have organizations where, by definition, everyone is a leader and a follower, by identity. To me, the questions then are, okay, how does that happen? How does that occur? What is leadership development if you accept that context, or, at least in part, accept that context?

SM: Well, I'm not sure I agree with that. One thing we forget is that an organization is not a democracy. It's almost as if everyone has a point of view, but only a few people have a vote, if you take it in the purest sense. Regarding the recent interest in governance, unless you understand governance of an organization, are some of these wonderful things simply "greenwashing" organizations to make them seem more attractive? The reality is, in Tesla, for example, not everyone has a vote, yet everyone says Elon Musk is a leader, big time. And the people who are around him are obsessed with his leadership, but many people don't stick it out there. So let's be critical of this "everyone's a leader and a follower." I'm not sure I buy that, really. Yes, of course everyone's a leader when it comes to leading their life or their team, but not everyone's a leader of the corporation or the firm or the Health Authority.

JS: Therefore, leaders don't lead people, they lead teams, projects, and organizations.

SM: Everyone is a leader. It's a nice illusion to get people to bow down to the organization ultimately. I get the philosophy around "everyone's a leader" and all that good stuff, but it's not how it really is in an organization. We differentiate in salaries, bonuses, and so on. Everyone talks about earning trust and then everyone gets into this wonderful debate about transparency, which is another wonderful illusion because the real things around power aren't transparent. Salaries and benefits, share options, rewards, they are always super-secret, unless you're in a very open governmental organization.

JS: Okay, let's move on to another model. I see a series of models in this notion of the necessity for hierarchy, but I would also say the necessity for an egalitarian approach.

SM: Who's saying an egalitarian approach? I don't know one organization that really means that.

JS: Well, back around 1968, there was an organizational behavior journal article on the emergence of the egalitarian organization, and the case study was the Cleveland Clinic; those were the same people behind the Appreciative Inquiry movement. Employee-owned businesses are movements in this direction. And now you have the call for diversity, equity, and inclusion.

If you have a hierarchy, as you are saying, built on conformity, inequity, and exclusion, how can you sincerely be calling for diversity, equity, and inclusion? To me it's like taking an ice cube and putting it in the oven and wondering why it melts.

SM: Well, I think Frederic Laloux [author of *Reinventing Organizations*] has looked at this, hasn't he? Laloux's description of an organization without hierarchy is a model that has been around since the '50s. I think that's fine, but I see very few organizations really doing, or wanting to do, that. The shift is too much; there's too much to lose. They'd much prefer to create the illusion of being diverse and inclusive.

Wasn't it interesting that a couple of months ago, *Harvard Business Review* decided to dispense with their top one hundred CEOs report. They said the reason they did so was, "It just creates another stereotype." It was all white guys in their fifties and sixties. By doing away with the report, they think they're going to energize a different debate. My reading of doing away with the report is there's a system keeping that stereotype in place. It serves itself. It doesn't really serve these more enlightened views that you have. I've got to get real with that. And as a leader, you need to understand how the system keeps serving itself, and then develop leaders within the context you are in.

JS: I want to make sure I understand you correctly. *Harvard Business Review* did away with this top one hundred CEO list because they were all white males over fifty?

SM: Well, I think you should read what *they* say about their reason for doing it. I think it was to start a debate.

JS: Basically, they did it in an attempt to be more diverse, equitable, and inclusive.

SM: And said, "We'll take exemplars from a much broader variety of organizations."

JS: That's an interesting step for something like *Harvard Business Review* to make. I'm getting that you are pointing out the illusion of an egalitarian organization or egalitarian model in today's world. In your view, it's hierarchical, and we just need to accept that, because that's the way it is.

SM: Who's saying we have to accept it? I'm not saying that. I'm just trying to describe reality as it is.

JS: Here's a thought. In the context of leaders, who have to learn how to lead each other, when you lead leaders, you create leaders.

SM: Good. I agree with that.

JS: And then when you lead followers, you create followers.

SM: Do you? I'm not sure. What does that mean, Jeff? I'm not really sure what it means.

JS: I think that one of the things about the given structure—and maybe this is part of what's behind that *Harvard Business Review* piece—is that there's a whole infrastructure around leadership development and executive leadership development, but what if you had a context where leaders were leading each other, and everyone was a leader? I've seen it in small pockets where, as groups start to lead each other and view each other as leaders, they increasingly show up as a group of leaders. They figure out how to leverage the problem of too many chefs in the kitchen, and that creates a team culture, or a broader culture, in which everyone is a leader.

SM: Nice.

JS: However, in order to avoid chaos, if everyone isn't also a follower, it's going to be a mess. In order to make leading leaders work, they need to show up as leaders and followers.

SM: Yep.

JS: So, it seems to me that most leadership development is set up to create leaders, but they actually create followers most of the time. The structures do, the organizational structures. Any thoughts on that?

SM: My advice is always that your number one responsibility as a leader is to grow more leaders, so I reject the idea that they just create more followers. They create a process to organize success, and that's about organizing work. I don't see it as so black and white as you do.

JS: This is a little bit of an aside. Another observation that's come up in my research that I would love to hear your take on is how neuroscience supports the notion of everyone showing up as a leader, or, at least, that everyone has that capacity. I've attended seminars where they talk about the left brain being about knowing and the right brain being about not knowing. But that's not true. One of the things they've discovered from brain scans is that it's not just the right brain controlling one thing, and the left brain controlling another, but that the right brain and left brain intermingle all the time. They always work together.

I am curious about how this plays out for you, if it does at all, in terms of the knowing of leading and the unknowing of following; the idea that leading and following at the same time mirror the way the brain functions. This also applies to the notion of a curious conviction. I remember the CFO of Capital Group saying, "I know how to be curious in one moment, and bring a conviction in another, but how do I bring a curious conviction at the same time?" Doing both at the same time is at the heart of Simultaneity, and it seems to reflect the way the brain functions. Is this making sense at all? What comes up for you around this?

SM: I think it's a nice link. Dr. Tara Swart has a lot to say about that. And all this left brain, right brain thing, if you speak to Tara, it's neuroscientists making a huge, huge, huge oversimplification, so we can understand it. I want to put it in that caution red box. On the other hand, I was speaking to a conductor today who talked about a chamber orchestra having to perform and listen at the same time. So the idea of simultaneous listening and performing is there in the chamber orchestra. I thought that was quite a nice metaphor for your work.

JS: And that also relates to improvisational music. Where you don't have a predetermined score. Your score is the sound in the moment, which informs the playing. That's beautiful. In terms of leading, it shows up as speaking being a piece of the conversational puzzle, where the speaker, simultaneously, is curious about the other pieces. This is different from speaking to convince others that one's piece is the whole puzzle, or better. That framework quickly leads to either/or thinking rather than both/and thinking.

CHAPTER 18

Leading without Leading

Elke Rehbock

*Empowering members of your team allows you
to grow. Because you allow the project to be no
longer entirely your own, the team can contribute
and their input can improve the work processes
and, ultimately, the project as a whole.*

—ELKE REHBOCK
Dentons US LLP

Elke Rehbock is a partner in the world's largest law firm, Dentons, where she is the cohead of the US Banking and Finance practice. She focuses on cross-border and finance transactions. I wondered how she was able to practice the dialogue language of partnership in a business typically structured hierarchically, with associates reporting to partners and partners reporting to a management. To gain some insight into this question, Elke and I discussed her work in two different contexts: (1) her role within Dentons and (2) her role within a much smaller egalitarian network she cofounded during the pandemic called Network 2025. Our discussion provided a fascinating opportunity to compare and contrast the two and their approaches to leadership.

ER: Thank you for the opportunity to contribute to *We the Leader*. I am honored and thrilled to be part of the team. As a partner at Dentons, I wear several hats. First and foremost, I'm a lending lawyer advising lenders about financial transactions. Second, I manage several global client engagements for the firm. In this context, one of my traditional lending clients has entrusted me with their global compliance program. Managing this program means I work with a number of our local offices around the globe to monitor regulatory change—how all the laws that apply to this highly regulated company change over time.

In addition to my day job at Dentons, in the early days of the pandemic, I worked with the American Council on Germany (where I serve on the board) to create a working group called Network 2025. It's not a think tank, but an interested group of Europeans and Americans who met to talk—and think—about the impact of the pandemic on society, business, and politics. But first, let us talk about my work at Dentons.

Dentons is the largest law firm in the world, with more than 20,000 people, 12,000 lawyers, and 200 locations all over the globe. In the United States alone, we are about 1,300 attorneys strong and growing. We look back on a long and proud history in each of our regions. Our Chicago office, where I am resident, was the founding office of Sonnenschein Nath & Rosenthal (Sonnenschein). Sonnenschein went through a number of combinations with law firms built around similar philosophies and longevity. Our offices in the United Kingdom, for example, date back to the eighteenth century—all our constituent firms are very well established in their own culture and market. This reflects the reality that the law is by nature a profession with local roots: from our admission to practice to how to best negotiate, local rules and practices matter. So while a law firm can have global reach, the local lawyers need to master local customs and behaviors. Consequently, our strategy has been to grow by adding firms with offices that are very well established and connected in their market.

JS: What brought you to Dentons and your own particular practice?

ER: Already at my prior law firm, I enjoyed great working relationships. Right around the time my current firm set out to become truly global, a former colleague asked me to rejoin forces and team up again, this time at Dentons. Given my background—a JD from Cornell Law School, a business degree from Sciences-Po in Paris,[1] a *Maîtrise en Droit* from *Panthéon-Assas*,[2] and my initial two years at *Universität des Saarlande*[3] in Germany—this newly created international platform allowed me to reincorporate my French and German relationships into my professional life. It made perfect sense.

I knew it was going to be a lot of fun to grow my practice at Dentons. Having lived the majority of my adult life outside my country of origin, I'm comfortable being continuously exposed to something new, cross-border, or other complex issues. That's why my legal practice looks as it does today—that is how I thrive. I'm certainly not trained in the legal systems of my colleagues abroad, let alone in the cultural intricacies of each of their countries. Consequently, each new engagement—global or not—affords me the opportunity to expand my horizons and knowledge. That is how I define fun—constant learning along the way that adds to my expertise. Clients call, because they need help navigating a situation that is unfamiliar, complex, or, in the truest sense of the word, foreign to them.

JS: Could you tell me a bit about your global team? Have you developed particular approaches to working with your other offices? Have you found some approaches work better than others?

ER: I already mentioned the global regulatory project I lead for a financial institution client. The project was born out of a conversation where the client voiced frustration with how the project was run by another firm. The open conversation about existing pain points (reoccurring turnover in the in-house position managing this project, among other things) allowed me to rethink the project as a whole and design an innovative framework. Ultimately, we were able to incorporate three legal technologies and create a team in the United States to work with and oversee the regulatory requirements in about forty offices around the world.

Today, our work allows the client to maximize new business generation while managing its compliance risk around the world. As you can imagine, our collective success depends heavily on my ability to manage cross-border projects in terms of cultural differences and multiple, complex, maybe even contradictory regulations—all with an eye toward delivering an excellent work product and related communication to all client stakeholders.

Back to your question about the best approaches to take. You and I talked about framing different forms of communication depending on the situation at a time when I was wondering how to structure the project to enroll the whole team. If you recall, we discussed how many times legal assignments are handed out using a directive tone; in other words, a neatly defined piece of work needs to be handled by a colleague, so that colleague is told what to do. That works for certain assignments, but it's an insufficient approach when it comes to coordinating larger scale projects across the globe. Simply giving a directive does not leave room for everyone's specific concerns or requirements, ranging from varying legal systems to cultural differences. If any of those concerns remain unaddressed, the team members won't be fully on board. These concerns will linger and find a way to disrupt and potentially threaten the success of the project down the road.

As a result of our discussion, every one of my local experts had the opportunity to truly take ownership of their part of the project. I also invited them to give me feedback about past projects and concerns we should address going forward. As a result of the very open discussion, we efficiently (1) adapted the client deliverable to ensure it works for all regions, (2) adjusted the frequency and top of quality controls, and (3) aligned with the most recent billing guidelines of the client.

The feedback was phenomenal and provided the foundation for the timely and consistent work product we are proud to deliver to the client today.

JS: What do you think made that work? Typically, it takes a while for the leader to earn that openness, but it seems as if openness happened pretty quickly. Any sense of why that happened? Maybe some of your relationships, or your attitude, or your openness, or your listening helped create the environment where people were straightforward, at least to some extent.

ER: My reputation for being collaborative yet getting things done reflects on my ability to be open, to listen, to tackle issues without blame, and to take ownership of my decisions. Let me elaborate. The universe of partners working on this particular type of cross-border project is rather small. We respect and trust each other. In addition, we all strive to deliver the best work product to our clients, so opening the floor allowed everyone to speak freely about the project at hand. It also helped that I expressed my desire to go above and beyond for the client, articulated challenges I saw, and let everyone feel how important it was for me to ensure the success of the whole team.

Opening the discussion allowed two other partners to describe and ask for input on their similar international projects. This means that my honesty about challenges I saw gave others permission to turn this into a much larger conversation.

The global team raised structural questions ranging from currency fluctuation to project-specific comments. We all laughed when one colleague bemoaned the proposed means of delivery, so we agreed we would ask the client if another format would be acceptable. Ultimately, the client agreed to a much improved revised format.

Inviting more open and engaging communication in meetings and putting active listening into practice allowed me to treat my partners significantly more like *partners*. The traditional law firm partner may have been directive, laying out the project without taking the pulse of the team. This technique of dialogue allowed me to enroll all partners into the project and create enthusiasm about it as a whole.

As mentioned above, our conversations enabled us to deliver not only an assessment of multiple and complex regulations across about 40 jurisdictions allowing my client to navigate regulatory frameworks to better manage their regulatory risks on a global basis but also a road map for their business teams to go out in the world and generate new business.

JS: You were intentional about opening the conversation to your partners. And in that opening, you revealed a couple layers of understanding. The thing I would like to emphasize is the idea that you actually treated partners as partners. Rather than just giving a directive, which is more of a boss move, you opened up a conversation. Each of them had something to contribute to help build understanding and to resolve the challenge.

What does it mean to treat a partner as a partner? It sounds rather basic and yet can easily be overlooked. Often, and particularly in hierarchical partnerships like law firms, partners act more like bosses or leaders. Can what you just described—this philosophy and practice—be applied to all teams within law firms or would it only succeed at the partner level?

ER: As in any big structure, certain rules and organizational hierarchies will always have to exist to make sure the engine runs smoothly. Although, apart from what is required to keep the engine running, the approach of giving everyone a voice can and should apply across all functions of professional service firms.

In the best teams, everyone has a voice. For example, my wonderful assistant, Terry Scott, knows the billing procedures of my firm as well as those of my clients best. Naturally, she guides me quite a bit. When we discussed which billing frequency made sense for the cross-border project we touched on before, her opinion was paramount. She simply is the most knowledgeable, and I would not want to decide how to coordinate bills from close to forty offices without her input.

With our associates, it's also a back and forth. Logically, when we teach our craft, we have to be directive to some extent. However, the new generation of attorneys coming up through the ranks has new skills that we can weave into our practice more easily by leaning on them. The younger the lawyer, the greater the ease and the desire to incorporate new legal technologies. For example, my summer associate, now first-year associate, Jaisel Patel, helped think through some of the processes we used on a global project relying heavily on legal technologies.

The traditional law firm training does not ingrain the type of collaboration we're talking about here. You can only deliver on complex global projects if you actually collaborate well with your colleagues. As my example shows, the space we created for all voices to be heard created efficiencies and spared all otherwise inevitable aggravation.

JS: Okay. So, instead of using a directive like, "I have to have this," you asked a question. At the same time, I'm guessing that you were genuine in your questioning. It wasn't a ploy to get people to buy into what you wanted. You were genuinely curious. I want to emphasize that, because sometimes people can feel whether your question is genuine or manipulative or some kind of technique to get what you want.

It seems your new way of billing just evolved, which often happens in using a dialogue approach as opposed to a directive one. And then, people own it or are more likely to execute it.

ER: Definitely. I'm repeatedly struck by the importance of bringing openness to a meeting. For this project, as with future projects, it seems paramount to open the floor to the whole team after laying out the background and the client's goal. Everyone feels valued and can contribute so that we can discuss each step in a project. It does away with the assumption that the way we have always done something is best.

That is very different from the more old-fashioned approach where the senior person sets the tone and leads the project, often with little input from the whole team.

JS: Law firms by training are more of a debate culture than a dialogue culture. Lawyers need their debate skills when in court, yet they also need dialogue skills working with one another. So, they have kind of a culture of debate on one level, in terms of a skill, but then there is a directive component as well because someone's usually the leader, the person who brought the business in, so it's theirs and people expect that. That works to some extent, but with matters that are a little more complex, particularly global issues, a dialogue approach, such as you used by leading with your questions or your own sense of frustration, seems to work better.

ER: That's right. A little dose of humility and vulnerability gives others a tremendous amount of space to open up. Giving team members the feeling that *this isn't someone who will disregard my experience, and my opinions matter.* While you still own the project, by the way you are leading it, you are inviting others at any level of the organization to own and lead it with you.

JS: You mentioned Network 2025. What's interesting to me is that it is different from the hierarchical structure of any professional service firm. As the initiator, you are the leader of this group, but I recall you reached a point with this group where you just did not know where to take it next. Could you talk more about that?

ER: At the beginning of the pandemic, Network 2025 was called into life based on a common desire to do something as the simultaneous public health, economic, and social justice crises were converging. I thought that regularly convening with a number of engaged and motivated and intelligent people with diverse personal and professional backgrounds would be a good start.

At the very outset, we organized a series of conversations to take place every six weeks. I did not have a specific plan or agenda regarding where the conversations would lead us after our planned series of talks would run out in December 2020. For each discussion we were joined by an outside expert on the topic we were discussing (which ranged from healthcare, education, social inequities, mis- and disinformation, ESG, to the changing world order). A number of participants in the working group said that they truly enjoyed our conversations, and took a lot away from them, and we decided to continue, but I was not sure what we would do. More of the same didn't feel like enough action to move the needle.

And so, I spoke to a few of the participants and asked for their input in thinking through where we should go next. My request for input made room for a very creative set of suggestions. One of them was to conduct a series of interviews with thought leaders, distill trends regarding where the world might be going by 2025, and possibly discuss those in writing. That is what we are working on now.

JS: You clearly didn't lead the way people would traditionally expect. You led by not leading. You didn't know where to go, for people to follow you, so you invited them to lead with you.

ER: That's nicely said. And I was very happy to follow along this time around. Our first meeting was influenced by the fact that I brought the group together. So, it was remarkable that the group grew together so that a shift could happen. It's turning into a new wheel, to use your analogy.

JS: In the global project, with partners throughout the world, or throughout Europe at least, you applied a different method of leading within a more hierarchical structure. And, in Network 2025, you also provided leadership. Then your leadership moved from suggesting or giving directives to "What's next?" and that opened up a whole realm of opportunities and creativity. You were really accessing the collective intelligence of the group. The question that comes to mind is if and how that approach could be utilized more within a hierarchical structure. Are there opportunities to have those kinds of conversations, where you can leverage what you don't know? Maybe you're already doing this; for example, calling and asking another partner for help. Do you see other opportunities within a professional services firm based on hierarchical job titles where you may apply a more networked way of leading? I'm not looking for specifics; I just want to hear whatever comes to you.

ER: By initiating Network 2025, I was a catalyst, but the work of the group then and now was carried on many shoulders. It's amazing to see how being the catalyst and instigator can push you into a leadership position. Yet there are also opportunities for others to lead. That's happening now with Network 2025. But we're also seeing how important it is for people to feel they have ownership.

There certainly are opportunities for this in any hierarchy. The key is to distinguish the functions in any company that require direction in order to organize a large group of people from those that allow for more room. One tremendous opportunity a more collaborative way of working holds is that this practice creates a very inclusive work environment. It just happens automatically since all voices are invited and welcomed. In a space where all opinions are valued, a sense of self-worth can emerge and blossom for any employee, no matter their background, leaving employees engaged. As a result, a sense of belonging can grow and lead to both employee happiness and retention.

JS: As a legal expert, you're paid to know. When does it help to not know?

ER: Structuring projects as a collaborative effort is a shift from the expert mentality. The more global the project, though, the more it requires a collaborative effort. Only through this type of collaboration can the collective give input and overcome cultural differences. Note that the project grows beyond yourself as others are empowered to make it better, to add a puzzle piece—as you would say—to their expertise.

It is as if a lawyer's career goes full circle. To make partner you have to demonstrate expertise. But then, that approach, in the legal profession, only gets you so far. The best projects come from the client calling about a project that no one really knows how to structure. The client team and our team face a novel situation that takes multiple puzzle pieces to solve—that is lawyering at its best.

One common pitfall is that we tend to misinterpret not knowing as weakness and asking for input as giving up control. Of course, if misinterpreted, either one makes many people (not just lawyers) feel uncomfortable. On the contrary, I find "I don't know" to be really powerful. Inviting feedback is an opportunity for all to contribute and for the collective to grow. Note that the collective includes the one who invited the feedback. So it is a win–win for all.

CHAPTER 19

A Career of Leading Leaders

Mike Kaufmann

This country is diverse and becoming more diverse every day. If you don't have a team that's diverse, you won't be asking or answering all the right questions. Diverse perspectives are critical to remain relevant, drive innovation and meet the needs of your customers.

—MIKE KAUFMANN
CEO, Cardinal Health

I met Mike Kaufmann while working with the board of his alma mater, Ohio Northern University. I immediately noticed he had that "leader" presence: confident in himself and open to others, willing to listen first, and very capable of articulating his point of view—not so much to convince or win, but to engage in an exploration. No wonder he has risen to the top of Cardinal Health after serving as president of various business segments and CFO. Perhaps, most important, in 2014 the California-based Institute for Women's Leadership gave him their first "Guy Who Gets It" award.

JS: So you sit at top of a very large organization and you've come up through various iterations in your career. How have you seen leadership evolve?

MK: I would say I've seen several big changes. One that stands out is the shift from the more command-and-control style of management, in which direction was set from the top down. When Cardinal Health was smaller, we definitely reflected this, and as the trend shifted and we got bigger, we came to rely on a larger group of leaders to collaborate and align as they make decisions to move the business and our culture forward.

My management style is to seek feedback from truth tellers and subject matter experts in order to quickly make decisions. This context helps me create the right kind of alignment, assess risk, and make decisions that are in the best interest of our customers and shareholders.

Another change I've seen is a shift in the balance between the *what* and *how*. These days the *how* matters as much as the *what*; that wasn't always the case. For example, focusing on culture and how you build a diverse, inclusive organization is as important as other decisions you make. As a leader, you have to spend a lot of your time finding ways to drive change so that your work environment encourages and promotes diversity, and employees feel comfortable bringing 100 percent of themselves to work every single day. Diversity and inclusion are crucial to attract new talent, retain the talent you have and deliver results. It's all connected.

JS: So true and interesting. Of course, since every employee is a follower of the company's common purpose, there is a level playing field in principle, structure, and goals, but not in actual practice.

MK: Diversity and inclusion are both the *right* thing to do and the *smart* thing to do. Given the changing demographics of the country, if you're not able to attract and retain diverse talent, you're just not going to be able to compete. When I started thirty years ago, you gained influence and power as a leader from your title. Now, more often, you have to earn it, particularly with younger people. I still think older employees generally will do whatever the CEO says, almost just *because* you are the CEO. Younger employees generally want to understand *why* you're doing it, and they want to know that, in your decision-making process, you've considered the environment and diversity. So when you communicate with them, you have to think about how to get their buy-in.

JS: What are your leadership imperatives today? What do you feel you have to do to motivate, to understand, to be understood, to provide vision, things like that? What are some of the really key leadership skills that people have to have today, and why?

MK: Probably not in any particular order, but one of the things that comes to mind is speed or sense of urgency. Today's environment is changing rapidly. A customer can become a competitor, or a new competitor can emerge quickly and disrupt the industry. So, as a leader, trying to make sure folks have a sense of urgency—speed—and can get things done is important. That is very difficult to do in larger, more established organizations.

I think building teams is super important because an all-knowing leader that can figure out everything is just not possible. You can't be good at everything. If you think you are, then you are more dangerous than you are helpful. As a leader, it's critical to understand your weaknesses and your strengths. You have to build teams that balance your skills to help you navigate rapidly changing environments. It's so important to be surrounded by a team that can come together, collaborate, move fast, and can pivot as they learn from mistakes or if the environment changes. It might be equally important that your team can challenge you along the way.

As a leader, I believe you have to listen more and communicate with your employees—hear what they say and sometimes what they don't. We heard our teammates say very clearly that they didn't understand our mission—something that to me is critical—so we undertook a project to fix that. Today we have a very simple answer to the question of "why do we exist?"; it is to deliver products and solutions to improve the lives of people every day. Simple, authentic, and everyone can remember it. That's our simple why or mission statement and it really describes how we want to show up for our employees, customers, and communities. One of the things that is important to us is building trusting relationships in healthcare; therefore, we talk about this with employees as well. We value trust internally and externally.

JS: What helps you do that? What makes you successful at that?

MK: I think honesty and transparency have always been the way I've built strong relationships with customers and employees. When I sit with customers, I listen carefully; I'm friendly, direct, and honest. Customers come to know that if I say I will do something, I do it. And if I can't do it, I'll tell them that too. I think follow-up and honesty are two huge things that you have to get right.

JS: That's a good example of conviction. Now, going back to the original idea of things changing over time. I mean, we have generational changes, right? You have millennials and Gen-Xers and others who are famous for having certain behaviors. What are you finding that they want from their leaders? These are the people coming up; they are the people who are going to formally assume leadership roles. But informally they also want to be leaders in their own right and listened to by senior people who, as you said, have to earn their title, in a way now, with the younger crowd. So what is it that these millennials and Gen-Xers and so forth want from their leaders? What do they want from you, Mike?

MK: More and more I believe that people want to know that they have a purpose. They want to believe there's a purpose in what they're doing and that they're contributing to the betterment of society. And they want the company they work for to align with this sense of purpose. We're in healthcare, so we naturally benefit from having a positive purpose. At Cardinal Health, many people, literally, can save lives on a daily basis because of what we do. That helps people connect, and I think that makes establishing purpose easier for us.

JS: This emphasis on a meaningful purpose plays right into everyone being a follower of a common purpose. This not only makes work meaningful, but structurally levels the playing field, allowing for a genuine relationship among equal, different, and vital partners as demonstrated in the Aviary—why don't you tell us about that.

MK: People want to connect with others in the company and we've learned that this type of less formal connection is often where good ideas are born. So when we evaluated our space and noticed that a product demonstration area off our lobby was rarely used, we decided to use the space differently. After visiting a pharmaceutical company known for how they were building culture, I had an idea about how we could repurpose that space to help build connections in a relaxed, more social setting. This company had built a gathering place where people came together every afternoon to enjoy drinks and snacks, but what they were really doing was connecting. And so we did it, and called it the Aviary.

We opened the Aviary in November 2019. What surprised me was how often the space was used for meetings and connecting, even when no food or drinks were served. Other times, people congregate there, and perhaps try the wine, and just sit there, talk, and stay late. They would exchange ideas and network. They'd have meetings. They saw people they wouldn't normally see, and they'd connect. This ability to socialize, communicate, and work in a more open environment is very important.

JS: When you talk about career development, do you mean in part leadership development? Does this generation want to be led and lead? Is that part of their cultural makeup?

MK: Generally, I'd say the answer to that is yes. If you're really attracting the top students, they love to hear about your lessons learned and what you've done well and not well, and how you got there, and what they need to do. They want to be successful, and they want to contribute even as interns or younger leaders.

Other employees might prefer to be led, but they want to be led by someone whom they can call on, and they want to be communicated with, and they want to have a chance to make a difference and work in a safe environment. Both groups want to understand about leadership—how it comes with time, how you have to live it.

JS: A lot of it sounds like the leaders are leading and adjusting and reacting to cultural events. Do you think of yourself possibly as not just the CEO, but the chief culture officer—somebody who's responsible for leading your company's culture?

MK: Yes, as CEO I definitely own the culture. It's my job. It's why, when I took over, I reevaluated our mission, vision, and values. Now you can walk through the halls and get on an elevator, and say, "Hey why does Cardinal Health exist?" And people will say, "It's to deliver product solutions every day to improve the lives of people." They know that. Then you say, "What are our values?" and they know. They know the five values: integrity, inclusive, innovative, accountable, and mission driven. They not only know what they are, they know what they mean, and they *want* to know.

All employees know that I want everyone to feel like they can bring 100 percent of themselves to work every single day. I talk about it a lot. And they know that embracing diversity, equity, and inclusion are important to our culture—just as respect, dignity, and kindness are. We all have to demonstrate these characteristics every day, and it starts with me and our leaders.

I talk with our leaders a lot about what it means to lead their teams and to grow as leaders. Leaders who can lead and influence other leaders, and their teams, have to ensure that their words and actions align and that their communication has the right balance of vulnerability, confidence, and authenticity.

JS: Bigger picture here: Obviously, health is a huge multi-faceted Hydra. It's providers, it's suppliers, it's consultants, etcetera—all kinds of leaders, all kinds of roles, all kinds of very intelligent people doing complicated things. What if you were to describe how healthcare leaders in general can be more effective; how can they adapt to, for example, being more retail-oriented providers, more consumer focused, etcetera, and innovating a little bit more? How can healthcare leaders become more effective and adopt some innovations coming from other industries and what would those things be?

MK: As I said before, without a diverse team you risk not asking or answering the right questions. You risk not understanding your customers or suppliers. Diverse perspectives are critical to meet the needs of your customers and to innovate.

JS: So you are very focused on diversity and bringing many perspectives in.

MK: I think you have to be. I mean, the demographics are changing, over 50 percent of college graduates are women, not men. African American, Hispanic, and Asian populations are growing. Every leader's job is to build the best team, but you can't build the best team if you are only attracting people from one demographic. Diversity is critical to attracting the best talent, and inclusion is critical to then retaining the best talent so you can build the best team.

PLAYBOOK

How to Apply We the Leader to Organizations, Movements, Teams, and Projects

Read the book as a team or an organization. Dialogue about the three steps of a curious conviction by practicing the three steps (found in Chapter 13):

1. Believe in consilience or the innovative process of creating from opposites.
2. Bring a conviction as a piece of the conversation or project puzzle.
3. Be constantly curious.

- Put these three playbook steps into the language and context of your culture as it is today.
- Agree to practice and be held accountable to these three steps.
- Review. Take a moment, a short pause during and after your meetings, to reflect on how you're doing with the three steps.
- Pair up with a coaching buddy. Meet for stand up— meaning 3 to 5 minutes—once a week for mutual

coaching sessions, asking and actively listening to each other around the following three questions:

- How are you practicing a curious conviction? Give specific examples of practicing one or all three steps.
- How might you expand your practice of a curious conviction?
- What are the barriers or challenges in doing so?

- Once a month, engage in a 15–20 minute sit-down session with your buddy, asking and listening to the same three questions.
- As the formal leader of the team incorporates this coaching process within your current accountability structure, engaging in both the stand-up and sit-down segments, utilize the same process, except as a one-way coaching practice, unless you welcome a two-way engagement.
- Initiate a broader dialogue practicing a curious conviction. Review the river analogy in Chapter 15 as you observe and contemplate the interrelationship of energy flow and structural channeling of that energy in your current team and/or organization. Exploring questions could include:

  - Where do we have too much structure that inhibits flow?
  - Where do we have too much flow that is starting to or has been flooding, that is, that's not decisive or holding each other accountable?
  - Given our unique context, how might we integrate a panarchical structure with our hierarchical structure?

- Review Chapter 15 to see in what ways David Kaufman and John Kessler's hybrid model of integrated teams alongside the hierarchy may work for your particular context. What models of organizational or team structure might be emerging for you, from traditional hierarchy, to hierarchy with more cross-functional or integrated teams, to more egalitarian structures?

- For the CEO and executive team, engage in a dialogue practicing the Three Steps of a Curious Conviction about an appropriate and enhancing way to define and actualize your organization as an egalitarian community of leader–followers. This could also be the place to start.

NOTES

Introduction

1. "2021 CEO Study—Find Your Essential: How to Thrive in a Post-Pandemic Reality," *IBM Institute for Business Value,* accessed May 30, 2021, https://ibm.co/3uypKFT.
2. Marko Valk, "Starling murmuration 2020 #Geldermalsen," YouTube video, 5:02, February 8, 2020. Accessed August 20, 2021, https://www.youtube.com/watch?v=uV54oa0SyMc.
3. Vincent Firth, Managing Director, Chief Executive Program, "CEO Priorities in 2020," *Deloitte*, October 20, 2020. Accessed May 30, 2021, https://www2.deloitte.com/us/en/pages/chief-executive-officer/articles/ceo-survey-gauging-priorities.html?id=us:2em:3cc:4dcom_share:5awa:6dcom:other.
4. Vincent Firth, "CEO Priorities in 2020."
5. Behnam Tabrizi, "75% of Cross-Functional Teams Are Dysfunctional." *Harvard Business Review*. (2015, November 13). https://hbr.org/2015/06/75-of-cross-functional-teams-are-dysfunctional.

Chapter 1

1. "2021 CEO Study—Find Your Essential: How to Thrive in a Post-Pandemic Reality," *IBM Institute for Business Value*. Accessed May 30, 2021, https://ibm.co/3uypKFT.
2. Frederick Taylor Winslow, *The Principles of Scientific Management* (Eastford, CT: Martino Fine Books 2014 [1911]).
3. Robert K. Greenleaf, *The Servant as Leader* (The Greenleaf Center for Servant Leadership, 2008).

Chapter 2

1. "We're All CEOs Here Series Part One," *Gravity Payments*, December 14, 2020, https://gravitypayments.com/blog/ceos -series-part-one/.
2. Definition of "organization" by Oxford Dictionary on Lexico .com, English. Accessed May 30, 2021, https://www.lexico.com /en/definition/organization.
3. E. O. Wilson, *Consilience: the Unity of Knowledge* (New York: Vintage, 2014).

Chapter 3

1. Gary Burnison, "What Really Makes Teams Click Today," *Korn Ferry*, April 15, 2021. Accessed August 20, 2021, https://www .kornferry.com/insights/articles/what-really-makes-teams-click -today?utm_campaign=8-27-20-twil&utm_source=marketo& utm_medium=email&mkt_tok=eyJpIjoiTm1VM01EWTFaalE 1T0RNMyIsInQiOiI2bko0NDZmQ3VkOVFQZHdlU2ZX UGlLcnNnRVBuNFg1R2VKeCtFVjJ4U0o2VGs0ZlwvS0FH Qnd3N2ppbkxzUTFFEa0ZrK0QxMFduS0dWc0EwOEJiaGGJ RN3FZS3RJYW9YR1U0aytFWTI3NEZSZ2FKNklXQ0xP bjdYRnYyS1hQY3c4UnoifQ%3D%3D.
2. See "Starling Murmuration: Starling Flocks and Roosting," *The RSPB* (website). Accessed May 30, 2021, https://www.rspb .org.uk/birds-and-wildlife/wildlife-guides/bird-a-z/starling /starling-murmurations/.
3. Darrell Etherington, "Open-Source Project Spins up 3D-Printed Ventilator Validation Prototype in Just One Week," *TechCrunch*, March 19, 2020. Accessed August 20, 2021, https://tcrn.ch /3fXN76B.
4. Hannah Beech, Richard C. Paddock, and Muktita Suhartono, "'Still Can't Believe It Worked': The Story of the Thailand Cave Rescue," *New York Times*, July 13, 2018. Accessed August 20, 2021, https://nyti.ms/3i81Gafhttps://timreview.ca/article/915.
5. Laurent Simon, "Setting the Stage for Collaborative Creative Leadership at Cirque Du Soleil," *Technology Innovation Management Review*, January 1, 1970. Accessed August 20, 2021, https://timreview.ca/article/915.

6. Patrick Lencioni and Kensuke Okabayashi, *The Five Dysfunctions of a Team: An Illustrated Leadership Fable* (Singapore: John Wiley & Sons (Asia), 2008).

7. "Rewriting the Rules for the Digital Age: 2017 Deloitte Global Human Capital Trends," Deloitte University Press Accessed May 30, 2021, https://www2.deloitte.com/content/dam/Deloitte /global/Documents/About-Deloitte/central-europe/ce-global -human-capital-trends.pdf.

Chapter 4

1. Kenneth Chang, "NASA's Mars Helicopter Completes First Flight on Another Planet," *New York Times,* April 19, 2021. Accessed August 20, 2021, https://nyti.ms/3wMkzDX.

2. Kenneth Chang, "A Helicopter Flies on Mars," *New York Times,* April 19, 2021. Accessed August 20, 2021, https://nyti.ms /3wGFQi8.

3. "Analog vs. Digital," *sparkfun.* Accessed May 30, 2021, https:// learn.sparkfun.com/tutorials/analog-vs-digital/all.

4. Julie E. Maybee, "Hegel's Dialectics." *Stanford Encyclopedia of Philosophy*, Stanford University. Accessed October 2, 2020, https://stanford.io/3wOjCLw.

5. "Hegelian Dialectic Definition and Meaning," *Collins English Dictionary*, HarperCollins Publishers Ltd. Accessed May 30, 2021, https://www.collinsdictionary.com/us/dictionary /english/hegelian-dialectic#:~:text=Hegelian%20dialectic %20in%20British%20English,higher%20level%20of%20truth %20(synthesis).

6. Mary Parker Follett, *The New State: Group Organization the Solution of Popular Government*, (Martin Fine Books, 2016), pp. 29–40.

7. Follett, *The New State*, p. 40.

8. Dan Barry, *"A Vote That Flew in the Face of Fear Itself,"* *New York Times*, November 4, 2020. Accessed August 20, 2021, https:// www.nytimes.com/2020/11/04/us/presidential-election-trump -biden.html.

9. J. Baldwin, "The Blind Men and the Elephant" (n.d.), Americanliterature.com. Accessed August 20, 2021, https:// americanliterature.com/author/james-baldwin/short-story/the -blind-men-and-the-elephant.

10. Follett, *The New State*, p. 40.
11. T. L. Friedman, T. L. (2020, October 20). "After the Pandemic, a Revolution in Education and Work Awaits," *New York Times*, October 20, 2020. Accessed August 20, 2021, https://www.nytimes.com/2020/10/20/opinion/covid-education-work.html.

Chapter 5

1. Tara Swart, Kitty Chisholm, and Paul Brown, *Neuroscience for Leadership: Harnessing the Brain Gain Advantage* (London: Palgrave Macmillan, 2015).
2. Tara Swart, *The Source: The Secrets of the Universe, the Science of the Brain*, (HarperOne, an imprint of HarperCollins Publishers), p. 7.
3. Michael E. Porter and Nitin Nohria, "How CEOs Manage Time," *Harvard Business Review*, February 12, 2021. Accessed August 20, 2021, https://hbr.org/2018/07/how-ceos-manage-time.
4. Carol Dweck, *Mindset: The New Psychology of Success*, updated edition (New York: Random House, 2006).
5. Swart, *The Source*, 73.
6. Swart, *The Source*, 93.
7. Kalyan B. Bhattacharyya, "Godfrey Newbold Hounsfield (1919-2004): The Man Who Revolutionized Neuroimaging," *Annals of Indian Academy of Neurology* (Medknow Publications & Media Pvt Ltd, 2016. Accessed August 20, 2021 https://www.ncbi.nlm.nih.gov/pmc/articles/PMC5144463/.
8. American Psychological Association, "Scanning the Brain," American Psychological Association (website), August 1, 2014. Accessed May 31, 2021, https://www.apa.org/action/resources/research-in-action/scan.
9. Helen Shen, "Does the Adult Brain Really Grow New Neurons?" *Scientific American*, March 7, 2018. Accessed August 20, 2021, https://www.scientificamerican.com/article/does-the-adult-brain-really-grow-new-neurons/.
10. Swart, *The Source*, 5.
11. Larry Alton, "Millennials Are Ready to Be Leaders: Here's How They're Doing It," *Forbes Magazine*, January 17, 2018. Accessed August 20, 2021, https://www.forbes.com/sites/larryalton/2018/01/17/millennials-are-ready-to-be-leaders-heres-how-theyre-doing-it/?sh=11bfa58436f9.
12. Swart, Chisholm, and Brown. *Neuroscience for Leadership*, 52.

Chapter 6

1. Tara Swart, *The Source: The Secrets of the Universe, the Science of the Brain*, (HarperOne, an imprint of HarperCollins Publishers, 2020), p. 73.
2. Tara Swart, Kitty Chisholm, and Paul Brown, *Neuroscience for Leadership: Harnessing the Brain Gain Advantage* (London: Palgrave Macmillan, 2015), p. xv.
3. Peter M. Senge, *The Fifth Discipline: The Art and Practice of the Learning Organization* (New York, Currency/Doubleday, 2006, p. 3.
4. Behnam Tabrizi, "75% Of Cross-Functional Teams Are Dysfunctional," *Harvard Business Review*, June 23, 2015. Accessed September 13, 2021, https://hbr.org/2015/06/75-of-cross -functional-teams-are-dysfunctional.

Chapter 7

1. O'Brien, Paul J. Silvia and Maureen E., Paul J. Silvia, "Self-Awareness and Constructive Functioning: Revisiting 'the Human Dilemma." *Journal of Social and Clinical Psychology,* June 1, 2005. Accessed August 20, 2021, https://guilfordjournals .com/doi/abs/10.1521/jscp.23.4.475.40307.
2. D. Scott Ridley, Paul A. Schutz, Robert S. Glanz and Claire E. Weinstein, "Self-Regulated Learning: The Interactive Influence of Metacognitive Awareness and Goal-Setting," JSTOR, *The Journal for Experimental Education*, Vol. 6, No. 4, Summer 1992. Accessed August 20, 2021, https://www.jstor.org/stable /20152338?seq=1.
3. Clive Fletcher and Caroline Bailey, "Assessing Self-Awareness: Some Issues and Methods," *Journal of Managerial Psychology*, MCB UP Ltd, August 1, 2003. Accessed August 20, 2021, https://www.emerald.com/insight/content/doi/10.1108 /02683940310484008/full/html.
4. Kenneth N. Wexley, Ralph A. Alexander, James P. Greenawalt, and Michael A. Couch, "Attitudinal Congruence and Similarity as Related to Interpersonal Evaluations in Manager-Subordinate Dyads," *Academy of Management Journal*, Vol. 23, No. 2, November 30, 2017. Accessed August 20, 2021, https:// journals.aom.org/doi/abs/10.5465/255434.

5. "A Better Return on Self-Awareness," *Korn Ferry Institute*, March 30, 2020. Accessed August 20, 2021, https://www .kornferry.com/insights/articles/647-a-better-return-on-self -awareness#:~:text=The%20analysis%20revealed%20companies %20with,employees%20consistently%20outperformed%20the %20rest.

6. "What Self-Awareness Really Is (and How to Cultivate It)," *Harvard Business Review*, April 14, 2021. Accessed August 20, 2021, https://hbr.org/2018/01/what-self-awareness-really-is-and-how -to-cultivate-it.

7. Eckhart Tolle, *A New Earth: Awakening to Your Life's Purpose* (New York: Penguin Life, 2018), p.140.

8. Jalāl al-Dīn Rūmī, "The Guest House," in *The Essential Rumi: New Expanded Edition*, translated by Coleman Barks (San Francisco: HarperOne, 2004). p. 108.

9. Neville Goddard, *The Power of Awareness,* Kindle edition (General Press, 2018 [1952]).

10. Tara Swart, *The Source: The Secrets of the Universe, the Science of the Brain*, (HarperOne, an imprint of HarperCollins Publishers, 2020), p. 75.

11. Jorina Elbers and Rollin McCraty, "HeartMath approach to self-regulation and psychosocial well-being," *Journal of Psychology in Africa*, 30:1 (2020), pp. 69–79.

12. Tara Swart, *The Source,* p. 170.

Chapter 8

1. "Why Breathing Is So Effective at Reducing Stress," *Harvard Business Review*, September 29, 2020. Accessed August 20, 2021, https://hbr.org/2020/09/research-why-breathing-is-so -effective-at-reducing-stress.

2. Jorina Elbers and Rollin McCraty (2020) "HeartMath approach to self-regulation and psychosocial well-being," *Journal of Psychology in Africa,* 30:1, p. 69–79.

3. Tara Swart, *The Source: The Secrets of the Universe, the Science of the Brain*, (HarperOne, an imprint of HarperCollins Publishers, 2020), p. 75.

Chapter 10

1. Behnam Tabrizi, "75% of Cross-Functional Teams Are Dysfunctional." *Harvard Business Review*, November 13, 2015. Accessed August 20, 2021, https://hbr.org/2015/06/75-of-cross-functional-teams-are-dysfunctional.
2. Justin Bariso, "Why Intelligent Minds Like Elon Musk and Steve Jobs Embrace the 'No Silo Rule,'" Inc.com. Inc., October 28, 2020. Accessed August 20, 2021, https://www.inc.com/justin-bariso/why-intelligent-minds-like-elon-musk-steve-jobs-embrace-no-silo-rule.html.
3. Rollo May, *The Courage to Create* (New York: W. W. Norton, 1975), p. 20.
4. May, *The Courage to Create*, 21.
5. May, *The Courage to Create*, 20.
6. Thomas L Friedman, "After the Pandemic, a Revolution in Education and Work Awaits," *New York Times*, October 20, 2020. Accessed August 20, 2021, https://nyti.ms/2SF8K3E.
7. "After the Pandemic," *New York Times*.
8. "After the Pandemic," *New York Times*.
9. "After the Pandemic," *New York Times*.
10. "After the Pandemic," *New York Times*.
11. Tara Swart, *The Source: The Secrets of the Universe, the Science of the Brain*, (HarperOne, an imprint of HarperCollins Publishers, November 17, 2020). p. 171.
12. Swart, *The Source*, p. 172.
13. Martin Buber, *I and Thou*, translated by Walter Kaufmann (New York: Scribner's, 1972).

Chapter 11

1. Martin Buber, *Between Man and Man*, New York: Routledge, 2003), pp. 203–205.
2. Alden M. Hayashi, "When to Trust Your Gut," *Harvard Business Review*, August 1, 2014. Accessed August 20, 2021, https://hbr.org/2001/02/when-to-trust-your-gut.
3. Barbara Kellerman, *The End of Leadership* (New York: Harper Business, 2012).
4. Tara Swart, *The Source: The Secrets of the Universe, the Science of the Brain*, (HarperOne, an imprint of HarperCollins Publishers, 2020), p. 73.

5. Tara Swart, Kitty Chisholm, and Paul Brown, *Neuroscience for Leadership: Harnessing the Brain Gain Advantage*, electronic edition (London: Palgrave Macmillan, 2015), location 3609.

6. Swart, Chisolm, and Brown, *Neuroscience for Leadership*, location 3604.

7. Swart, *The Source*, 119.

Chapter 12

1. "We're All CEOs Here Series Part One," *Gravity Payments*, December 14, 2020. Accessed August 20, 2021, https://gravitypayments.com/blog/ceos-series-part-one/.

2. "We're All CEOs," Gravity Payments.

3. Behnam Tabrizi, "75% of Cross-Functional Teams Are Dysfunctional," *Harvard Business Review*, November 13, 2015. Accessed August 20, 2021, https://hbr.org/2015/06/75-of-cross-functional-teams-are-dysfunctional.

4. Stephanie Schomer, "7 Ways Teams Can Problem Solve Better Than Individuals," *Entrepreneur*, December 2, 2020. Accessed September 15, 2021, https://www.entrepreneur.com/article/359946.

5. "7 Ways Teams Can Problem Solve Better Than Individuals," *Entrepreneur*.

6. "7 Ways Teams Can Problem Solve Better Than Individuals," *Entrepreneur*.

7. "7 Ways Teams Can Problem Solve Better Than Individuals," *Entrepreneur*.

8. M. Shapiro, "Debriefing: A Simple Tool to Help Your Team Tackle Tough Problems," *Harvard Business Review*, July 2, 2015. Accessed August 20, 2021, https://hbr.org/2015/07/debriefing-a-simple-tool-to-help-your-team-tackle-tough-problems.

Chapter 13

1. Tara Swart, *The Source: The Secrets of the Universe, the Science of the Brain* (HarperOne, an imprint of HarperCollins Publishers, 2020), p. 74.

2. Mary Parker Follett, *Creative Experience* (Ravenio Books, 2016 [1924]), loc. 795.

3. Rollo May, *The Courage to Create*, (New York: W. W. Norton, 1975), p. 20.

4. Kate Conger, "Twitter Had Been Drawing a Line for Months When Trump Crossed It," *New York Times*, May 30, 2020. Accessed August 20, 2021, https://www.nytimes.com/2020/05/30/technology/twitter-trump-dorsey.html.

5. Adam Grant, "The Science of Reasoning with Unreasonable People," *New York Times*, January 31, 2021. Accessed August 20, 2021, https://www.nytimes.com/2021/01/31/opinion/change-someones-mind.html?smid=em-share.

6. Martin Buber, *Between Man and Man* (Eastford, CT: Martino Fine Books, 2014), pp. 203–205.

Chapter 14

1. Gary Burnison, "What Really Makes Teams Click Today," *Korn Ferry*, April 15, 2021. Accessed August 290, 2021, https://www.kornferry.com/insights/articles/what-really-makes-teams-click-today?utm_campaign=8-27-20-twil&utm_source=marketo&utm_medium=email&mkt_tok=eyJpIjoiTm1VM01EWTFaaIE1T0RNMyIsInQiOiI2bko0NDZmQ3VkOVFQZHdlU2ZXUGlLcnNnRVBuNFg1R2VKeCtFVjJ4U0o2VGs0ZlwvS0FHQnd3N2ppbkxzUTFFEa0ZrK0QxMFduS0dWc0EwOEJiaGJRN3FZS3RRJYW9YR1U0aytFWTI3NEZSZ2FKNklXQ0xPbjdYRnYyS1hQY3c4UnoifQ%3D%3D.

2. "The Elements of Good Judgment," *Harvard Business Review*, November 24, 2020. Accessed August 20, 2021, https://hbr.org/2020/01/the-elements-of-good-judgment.

3. Mary Parker Follett, *The New State: Group Organization the Solution of Popular Government* (Mansfield Centre, CT: Martino Publishing, 2016 [1918]), p. 34.

4. Pauline Graham, Ed., *Mary Parker Follett: The Prophet of Management* (Washington, D.C.: Beard Books, 2003), p. 201.

Chapter 18

1. L'Institut d'Études Politiques de Paris—Ecofi (France, 2001).

2. Université Panthéon-Assas, Maîtrise en Droit (Paris, France 2000).

3. Universität des Saarlandes—DEUG, Mention Droit (Germany, 1998).

INDEX

ABOUT THE AUTHOR

D r. Jeffrey Spahn, founder and president of Leading Leaders Inc. and creator of Simultaneity® and the We the Leader™ operating system, is a researcher, executive educator, entrepreneur, executive coach, storyteller, and speaker. With more than twenty years of experience, Jeff continues to design a unique and powerful leadership practice for leaders, executives, teams, organizations, and networks. As an organic diversity, equity, and inclusion operating system, We the Leader includes a seismic shift in the evolution of leadership theory and practice that ignites the transforming of complexity and ambiguity into accelerated innovation, wise decisions, and in-sync execution

Disciplines and insights from business and philosophy, arts and athletics, science and spirituality enliven this practice. A degree in business from the University of Michigan and a doctorate from the University of Chicago ground Jeff's practice in sound scholarship. After more than twelve years of executive leadership, he taught business graduate students and conducted research on the purpose of business. During this investigation, he engaged many of the top executives in the United States. Clients include industry leaders such as Capital Group Companies and Steelcase. Board membership includes goProdigii, a multisided technology and business services company that serves purpose-driven entrepreneurs;

OMNIA Institute for Contextual Leadership; and The Chicago Moving Company, a modern dance enterprise.

Jeff relishes experiencing live improvisational jazz. He also enjoys reading flash fiction, swimming in natural waters, practicing yoga, and playing tennis.

To learn more about Jeff and Leading Leaders Inc., visit www.leadingleadersinc.com.